Joseph Gerard Brennan

THREE PHILOSOPHICAL NOVELISTS

≈§ James Joyce
≈§ André Gide
≈§ Thomas Mann

The Macmillan Company, New York
Collier-Macmillan Limited, London

First Printing

Printed in the United States of America

THE MACMILLAN COMPANY, NEW YORK

COLLIER-MACMILLAN CANADA, LTD., TORONTO, ONTARIO

Library of Congress Catalog Card Number: 63-15676

Acknowledgments for permissions to quote from copyrighted material appear in the Notes at the back of the book.

To Barnard College
for her 75th year

Preface

THE TITLE of this book occurred to me as I was rereading George Santayana's *Three Philosophical Poets*.* Originally a series of lectures given at Columbia University in 1910, Santayana's graceful study draws attention to three figures of world literature: Lucretius, Dante, and Goethe. Each poet, says Santayana, presupposes a world view— a cosmology and a moral philosophy. Lucretius celebrates the naturalism of his master Epicurus who identified the real with atoms and found the good in pleasure. *The Divine Comedy* assumes the dialectic and symbolism of the Christian high Middle Ages, whose greatest theologian was Thomas Aquinas. Goethe's Faust implies an essentially modern world perspective, romanticism, which raised up will and feeling from their ancient status subordinate to reason. Now it struck me that I, without inviting comparison to the finished perfection of Santayana's treatment, might at least playfully guide my three men around the same turn. By reason of his naturalism and exaltation of desire, André Gide, the moralist of the *troika* is an obvious candidate for the post of Epicurean. My logician and dialectician, James Joyce, has often reminded critics of "Denti Alligator." Finally Thomas Mann, the metaphysician of the trio, is the obvious analogue to Goethe, the poet to whom the author of *The Magic Mountain* traces his cultural and literary ancestry.

I have made something of a survey of each man's work, freely and intermittently commenting on matters of philosophical interest. But it will be clear that what drew me to the writing of these essays

* For bibliographical references see Notes starting on p. 173.

🙠 iii

was not the philosophy of the novels concerned, but their poetry. Partly for this reason, I have allowed myself to play the critic, saying what I think is better and what worse. Professional literary critics may not find my comments interesting, since there is little in them that they do not know already. Good critics are usually quite able to handle philosophical matters when they come up in connection with works of literature. For example, James Joyce's "concept of time" has been compared on occasion to Bergson's. The fact that Joyce's time-machinery has nothing whatever in common with Bergson's duration or with Einstein's or Whitehead's time either, but is on the contrary a throwback to a most unprogressive Greek and medieval time notion, might encourage us to believe in the need to create a job for a philosopher trained to spot such misreadings. But it was, after all, a critic and scholar of literature who picked it up. Harry Levin spotted the misinterpretation (or one very much like it) and gave it a line or two in his book on Joyce. Which may be all it deserves.

For what audience, then, is this book intended? It is written for anyone whose taste runs to the European novel. I also had my undergraduate classes in mind, thinking they would like to read something like this and might even be interested in a sequel dealing with novelists of a following generation. That is not to say, had I wanted to, I could have written the book differently or aimed at some presumably higher level or category of readers. No, I wrote as well as I could, and that, as Dorothy Parker would say, is what kills me.

I must express my thanks to my Barnard colleagues who read and criticized sections of the book in manuscript—Professors Leroy Breunig, Ursula Jarvis, and Joann Morse. I am grateful to Dr. Robert De Maria of the New School, to Mr. Henry Meisel of the Bethpage Public Library, and to Miss Elizabeth Seanor of the Hofstra University Library. I owe particular remembrance to the members of the old Modern Prose Coffee Club (Hofstra '58) and especially to its (then) president, Miss Mary Pangalos.

J. G. B.

Contents

Introduction

JAMES JOYCE, André Gide, and Thomas Mann belong to an older, now classical, generation of twentieth century novelists whose work, springing from roots in the culture of the last century, still considered man in some sense as a being reacting against a social environment of importance and bulk. It is a group of writers considerably junior to them who are now currently classified as philosophical. Today the term "philosophical novelist" is most often applied to a line of French writers from Malraux to Sartre and the "Mandarins"—a series sometimes extended to include Robbe-Grillet and Butor, even though these two do not like being called metaphysical. Recent studies like Victor Brombert's *The Intellectual Hero* and John Cruickshank's anthology *The Novelist as Philosopher* make the point that, since Malraux, the French novelist has tended to define himself in terms of an attitude toward the problem of human existence. For such a novelist the question is not what it means to be a human in this or that social context, but what it means to exist as a human at all. "In my view," says the author of *La Condition humaine,* "the modern novel is a privileged means of expressing the tragic element in man."

French intellectuals take a special interest in the novel because of the peculiar relation of that literary form to phenomenology, the philosophical technique of careful and patient accounting for things and events as they are actually experienced in human consciousness. They point out that certain novels, say of Proust or Mauriac, set forth a virtual phenomenology of love or jealousy, a task to which scientific psychology is totally incapable of addressing itself. Moreover, the philosophical novel has classical precedent in France, where the "novel of ideas" dates from Voltaire. But little corresponding attraction to this type exists in the case of English or American novelists. According to certain critics, the novel in America early took the form of a *romance;* hence its lack of interest in "ideas." Others say that American novelists after Henry James simply have not been men of high intellectual gifts or largeness of mind. Those to whom the novel par excellence is a peculiarly British organism hold that it is characteristic of the English novel to draw its seriocomic material from the contemplation of social manners, a procedure which allows satire free play. By way of contrast they point to the fact that Existentialism, at least in the manner of Sartre and Simone de Beauvoir, has the regrettable effect of striking humor dead the moment it is put to work in a novel, adding (as Gide might) that phenomenology may be the beginning of wisdom, but it is the end of wit.

Why then the growing interest in England and the United States in the philosophical novel and in the relation of philosophy to literature generally? It would be very easy to say that such interest is the result of the almost total alienation of the public from academic philosophy, that the discipline once known as Queen of the Sciences has today shrunk, like Balzac's *peau de chagrin,* to a hard little bag of linguistic tricks. (*What does it mean to say "I like oysters, but I don't believe it"?*) People who are anxious about the isolation of the educated classes of the Anglo-American world from technical philosophy often do say this, pointing by way of contrast to the easy relation in which Continental philosophy, particularly of the French Existentialist sort, stands to poetry, drama, and the novel. "When philosophers abandon the metaphysical threshold," says Saint-John Perse, "it falls to the poet to take upon himself the role of metaphysician; at such times it is poetry not philosophy that is revealed as the true daughter of Wonder." Iris Murdoch, philosopher-novelist and admirer of Sartre, cites the success of novels and plays in showing the uniqueness and opacity of the human person as well as the complexities that may enter a situation of moral choice. "We need more concepts in terms of which to picture the substance of our being," she says. "It is here that literature is so important since it has taken over some of the tasks formerly performed by philosophy. Through literature we can discover a sense of the density of our lives." She notes the existence of common elements in the man of Stuart Hampshire's *Thought and Action* and the heroes of Sartre's novels. In each, man is a being isolated from his environment, totally free; his virtue is sincerity. She finds the analysis of choice much the same in both cases, although in another place she smiles at the contrast between the dangerous thoughts of Sartre and the harmless ruminations of the British empiricists: "The 'world' of *The Concept of Mind*," says Miss Murdoch, "is the world in which people play cricket, cook cakes, make simple decisions, remember their childhood and go to the circus; not the world in which they commit sins, fall in love, say prayers, or join the Communist Party."

Everybody knows that in French Existentialism, philosophy and the drama are on excellent terms. Gabriel Marcel composes his own plays and untiringly recites their plots to prove ontological points—at what length and with what energy those patient inquirers can testify who have done justice to *The Mystery of Being* or sat through its author's lecture on philosophy and the theatre. Sartre's plays are better than his novels, and his large book on the criminal playwright Genet serves him as a frame in which to set out some of his post-*l'Être et le néant* philosophy. Plays are fine instruments for staging moral conflicts without clutter; freedom of the will has been on the boards from Calderón to the United States Steel Hour. But it is harder for a novelist to do away with social background. Those who have been successful have produced novels that translate rather easily into plays—Kafka's *The Trial* is a classical instance. Generally, the novel as a literary vehicle seems to run at its easiest, to show least nervousness and strain, when it deals with the interplay of characters and their social environments. Typical are the nineteenth century classics, including the "true" novel built to the tastes of the older and more insular British critics to whom James Joyce is but a spoiled priest, Gide a talented pederast, and Mann a disappointed symphony orchestra conductor. Sir Harold Nicolson holds that the novel as an art form is moribund, since the novel can flourish only when there exists in society a stability of social class, a certain tranquil convention. In their turn, Communist critics point to the Existentialist theme of the solitary man, tortured and blocked, free, but unable to do anything with his freedom, as the final product of a bourgeois rake's progress which ends in the illusion, stark but consoling, that social facts do not really have very much to do with the human predicament. Marxists deny that a social dynamic can be derived from: *pues el major delito del hombre es haber naçido.*

The popularity of the late Albert Camus, now anthologized in the United States as a *philosopher,* is frequently offered as evidence of growing concern for the need of connection between philosophy and literature. Camus, like Sartre, is a French phenomenon. Traditionally, the Frenchman looks to his poets for moral guidance and to his philosophers for fine style. Camus's glowing-ember prose and Protestant moral earnestness appeal not only to a worldwide literary public, but also to many people who do not normally read much literary work—bankers, industrial executives, college presidents, preachers, and the like. In addition, Camus's isolated hero Meursault, with his couldn't-care-less attitude, carries a powerful appeal for the high school set to whom he stands as a rebel without a cause, a sort of literary James Dean. It is interesting to note that, for a writer so often cited as representative of the twentieth century, Camus has not the slightest interest in science. (Sartre resembles him in this.) As far as philosophy is concerned, what absorbed Camus were questions like those that engaged the attention of an earlier and more able philosophical amateur, William James. In *The Myth of Sisyphus,* we read:

There is but one only truly serious philosophical problem, and that is suicide. Judging whether life is or is not worth living amounts to answering the fundamental question of philosophy. All the rest —whether the mind has nine or twelve categories—comes afterwards. These are games. One must first answer. . . . I have never seen anyone die for the ontological argument.

Now this is just what people who do not know much about the subject expect philosophy to be like. No more than Camus do they care for technical philosophy which to them is hairsplitting and logic-chopping. In their opinion, philosophy should deal with the larger questions, and for discussion of such problems no particular training other than an earnest moral concern is necessary. One response to this attitude is to raise the question whether there has ever been in fact any philosophy which was *not* technical. (God knows, French phenomenology is technical enough.) Today it is often said that philosophy should get back into the marketplace. But there is no evidence that philosophy ever was in the marketplace to begin with, unless one takes literally the Platonic legend of Socrates as pedagogue. It is true that from time to time philosophy has needed correction, that it has been improved and refreshed by change of pace and aim. Such change of direction has often (but by no means always) been the effect of pressure from brilliant outsiders like Pascal and Nietzsche. Those who seek philosophical satisfaction in plays and novels are often people who are simply unable to make or to sustain the level of abstraction philosophy demands. The slogan "philosophy through literature" may encourage amateurishness and dilettantism—one can indulge in semiphilosophical generalizations about "the loneliness of modern man." At the same time, there is some weight to the other side of the argument. Mounting evidence of public interest in the relation between philosophy and literature may be a symptom of a real deficiency in certain main lines of professional philosophy in the West. If humanism has dried out of philosophy to the point of dangerous aridity, and if there is no way to reverse the process, then it may well turn out that for future generations, poetry, not philosophy, will be the true child of Surprise.

"Every major literary work," says Erich Heller, "has a *syntax of ideas* upon which it may ultimately depend for its rank and status." Would a corollary be that every major novel has a philosophical structure? Most critics start nervously when the question of philosophical implications of a master novel is raised, for they are afraid that someone is trying to "superimpose a philosophy" on what is, after all, a work of art. Some of the skittishness where philosophy is concerned has understandable grounds. It is surprising how many of the first-generation critics of the moderns eked out their appreciations or polemics by slapdash appeals to metaphysics. The Kafka situation, of course, is still a scandal. Many of the older Joyce critics lost their heads in the the excitement of myth-hunting and symbol-sticking (in themselves perfectly legitimate sports where Joyce is concerned) and helped turn *symbolism* into an "out" word. Generally speaking, there *is* something irritating about most attempts to decode ideas from the work of an artist. Plato would say that our annoyance has metaphysical grounds; such ideas are *four* times removed from reality. Besides, we know that in those cases where the poet or novelist has a genuine interest in philosophical concepts, his obsession with the work at hand will inevitably lead him to exploit these ideas for his own purposes, to bend them all out of shape if need be to suit his book. It was Gide who said that ideas were all right so long as they remained in the service of beauty. (He also said that a work of art is the exaggeration of an idea.) But if philosophy can therefore be only a handmaid to poetry, as it is to theology, the fact remains that a handmaid is (or, alas, was) a useful creature. In any case, she is not a nothing.

Assuming that it may be in some sense useful to speak of philosophy in connection with Joyce, Gide, and Mann, it does not follow that these novelists are "philosophical" in the same way. For they are not novelists in the same way. Of the three, only Joyce and Mann are thoroughbred novelists. Gide is a first-rank man of letters who has written some beautiful small novels (*Immoralist; Strait Is the Gate*), a clever one of moderate size (*Lafcadio*), and one big "real" novel (*Counterfeiters*)—a doubtful masterpiece. To assess the greatness of Joyce and Mann, yet to tell why they are so different as novelists, would require not only a longish essay on culture-psychology but one on the theory of the novel as well. Who is right: Henry James, who holds that the novel copies reality ("represents experience"), or T. S. Eliot who maintains that reality has no form but that the novelist can impose one on it, should society fail to do so. Could we hazard the proposition that Joyce represents the novelist as *creator*, and Mann the novelist as *imitator*—and that Mann is the greater novelist thereby? Joyce thought of the artist as a God of creation and wrote his big novels accordingly, like Plato's Demiurge, throwing everything into certain preconceived intellectual matrices. Joyce enthusiasts tend to think of the master as a maker of immortal "characters" and of his highest success in this respect as Leopold Bloom of *Ulysses*. But there is a peculiar quirk in Joyce's character drawing, perhaps a fault of excess rather than of defect. In his recent book *Surface and Symbol*, Mr. Robert Martin Adams has claimed that in his ambition to make *Ulysses* a large-scale design or collage, Joyce pumped so many incompatible elements into Bloom as to impair his internal consistency as a character. One might even dare to say (*audemus dicere*) that Joyce created only one fully achieved character, Stephen Dedalus, and that even he is to a certain extent a stage rather than a novelistic figure. With Thomas Mann, it is another matter. Although the German novelist had a very lofty theory of art and the artist—in the tradition of Flaubert, Mann made the literary man an "artist"—he never thought of the artist as God the creator. True, he compared him to Hermes, mediator between the divine and the mortal; but Hermes is the god of thieves, and Mann refused to abandon his belief that the artist is, at base, a rascal, a clown, an entertaining mimic. Mann's career begins with *Buddenbrooks* which grew out of a caricature of his own family; it ends with *Doctor Faustus* and the theory of art as parody. All this may amount to no more than saying that Mann is a conservative, moving in the grand tradition of the nineteenth century novel, while Joyce was an early twentieth century experimentalist, like Picasso and Stravinsky, assuming styles, then shedding them like snakeskins. Is the fact that critics and commentators have found a hundred James Joyces, but only one Thomas Mann, evidence of Joyce's *superiority* as a writer of novels? Although as man and artist he is the more heroic figure of the two, Joyce as novelist remains something of a crank, a queer fellow.

Differences between the three men as novelists carry over into the philosophical resonances of their works. To borrow a metaphor from the Marxists, there is little philosophy in the base of Joyce's work, but a lot of it in his superstructure. Joyce's rational-Catholic mind shows up in his dialectical method (his characters make distinctions, syllogize, detect undistributed middles, construct epicheiremes) and in his increasing need for elaborate metaphysical apparatus as his work goes on. Gide's mind is the opposite of Scholastic temperament; he has no interest in abstractions. German and Irishman devoured metaphysical treatises with gusto, but such things usually bored Gide. The philosopher who most attracted him was Nietzsche, a philosophical poet. It is evidence of Gide's shrewdness that he saw that Nietzsche's specifically *metaphysical* notions—like the Eternal Return—were superfluous. Gide has the directness of any moralist. He does not use ethical problems as apparatus or stage sets, or even as brushstrokes in a painting, despite his own words in the second-thought preface to *L'Immoraliste*. He creates his novels directly out of his moral experience, without the aid of much analogical invention.

Critics may object that a better case can be made for Marcel Proust as philosophical novelist, that the author of *A la recherche du temps perdu* outranks Gide both as writer of novels and as metaphysician. It is true that Gide can offer nothing to compare with Proust's poetic-ontological distinction between the world of time and that other world transcending it, hidden, yet so close at hand—that paradise called by Santayana the Realm of Essence, "where all things are crystallized into the images of themselves, and have lost their urgency and their venom." No, Gide cannot oblige with marvels such as these. But, just as Settembrini, whose nose was out of joint when a more formidable personality in the shape of Pieter Peeperkorn loomed on the scene of his fantastic *Lungensanatorium* yet remained a faithful tutor to Hans Castorp, so Gide is one to whom we can still go to school, although we may be lost in admiration for Proust. Less metaphysically talented than Proust, Gide is the more interesting if not the more edifying moralist of the two.

It is Thomas Mann whom everybody cites when philosophical novelists are mentioned, and the citation is well earned. While a good deal of Mann's metaphysics is in his superstructure, there is no small amount of it in his base. For Mann's novels, the

Schopenhauerian dualism of Will and Idea is not just theoretical window dressing; it enters the substance of his stories and their characters. Every major Mann performance is a high tale of how Will gets the better of Idea. Not that his philosophical quality as a novelist is simply a question of Schopenhauer's "influence." Mann found himself *confirmed* by Schopenhauer. The novelist's speculative and critical mind was quite at home with intellectual concepts which, Kant-fashion, he needed to give vision, order, and direction to his artistic perceptions. At the same time, it would be well to remember that Mann believed himself to be at heart a *Künstlerkind*. He wrote to Gerhart Hauptmann, "I have much more of the child artist in me than is suspected by those who babble about my 'intellectualism.' " Mann admired Hermann Hesse's book *Das Glasperlenspiel* to the point of feeling he should have written it himself. This is the novel about Castalia, a community of the future whose highest aesthetic and intellectual activity is based on a child's sport, a bead game. Yet every active bead-player dreams of a perpetual enlargement of the content of the Game until it should embrace the whole world.

❧ 1 ❧

James Joyce

James Joyce

˥ *There are no appearances in Joyce; it is all syllogism.*

GEORGE MOORE

˥ *He affirmed his significance as a conscious rational animal proceeding syllogistically from the known to the unknown and a conscious rational reagent between a micro- and a macrocosm ineluctably constructed upon the incertitude of the void.*

STEPHEN DEDALUS in Ulysses

˥ *. . . all the talk about the artist's vocation and the artist's mission, and so forth, began to strike me as being very empty, and hollow, and meaningless at bottom.*

PROFESSOR RUBEK in When We Dead Awaken

IN HIS ADMIRABLE BOOK *The Classical Temper,* Mr. S. L. Goldberg states that Joyce's work has neither Gide's restless exploration of ethics nor Mann's massive deployment of abstract knowledge. Joyce's art, he says, turns upon certain focal themes inseparable from their dramatic matrix, and in no sense do these themes compose a "philosophy" or doctrine. It is quite true that Joyce is not a philosophical novelist in the sense that philosophy as "doctrine" can be abstracted from his works. True as well that the peculiar nature of Joyce's art has attracted a good deal of commentary of a sort that critics (when it is not a question of their own opinion) call solemn and intellectually pretentious. Joyce is the professor's darling—in the United States anyway. "When we consider that America is the original home of smoke signals," said Gogarty in Texas, "the popularity of Joyce here can be explained." So the younger critics—Mr. Goldberg is a young Australian professor—are suspicious of anything that seems like more importation of fancy intellectualism to the Joycean excavation from without, when there is so much already there *in situ.* Respectful toward Stuart Gilbert as an elder Joycean, they regard his philological pedantries as dated and tiresome. They are weary of Mr. Tindall's ardent ways with sacramental cocoa; they want no more of his ubiquitous and symbolical chamberpots. The market for "symbolism" is bearish at present, and philosophy is associated with archetypes. Joyce, says Mr. Goldberg, "paid more attention to the dramatic necessities of his art than to such abstract 'metaphysical' and—for an artist—ultimately frivolous profundities." *Ulysses,* he reminds his readers, is not a spiritual guide, but a novel. Yet what he finds most interesting in *Ulysses* in particular and in the novel in general is "Its imaginative illumination of the moral—and ultimately spiritual—experience of representative human beings." Surely that formula is wide enough to accommodate a philosophical element, with a bit of room left over for spiritual guidance. Moreover, Gide's fables of Michel and Alissa, and Thomas Mann's of Castorp and Joseph—different as they may be from Joyce's stories and from each other—are unmistakably tales which illuminate the moral and spiritual experience of "representative human beings."

Philosophy is still occasionally defined as that science which treats of general concepts presupposed in all the particular sciences, although studied by none of them. Now Joyce is a master of the particular, a sort of novelistic William of Ockham. With him, the literal and the specific always precede the symbolic and the general both in the ontological and the aesthetic order. It is not any city, it is Dublin; and it is not Dublin-in-General, it is this Dublin, Joyce's Dublin— Mrs. Dedalus's kitchen; the fireless Committee Room; Kiernan's bar; Bella Cohen's bawdyhouse; this man, Lenehan; this song, "The Croppy Boy," this cheese, Gorgonzola with its feety smell. But Joyce's love of the specific, his appalling gift for the particular is attended by a passion for the universal. Those critics are probably right who claim that Joyce's typology has less to do with his success as a novelist than was formerly supposed, that our delight in his work springs more from its literal than from its symbolic sense. But Joyce's compulsion to relate species to genera, singular to exemplar, fact to myth, is an integral part of his art and refuses to be detached from it. His insistence on linking facts to their types increased at a geometrical rate as his art developed and matured. *Dubliners* began simply enough, but soon called up Peer Gynt, then Odysseus to Joyce's mind; even one of its small stories evoked the tripartite division of *The Divine Comedy*. In *A Portrait of the Artist as a Young Man,* Stephen consciously identifies himself French-romantic-fashion with Icarus, son of Daedalus. In *Ulysses,* the same young man unconsciously re-creates himself as Telemachus of Homer's *Odyssey* and this time finds a spiritual father for an hour or two in Leopold Bloom, a resourceful Odysseus to be sure, but also a Wandering Jew, a crucified Christ, an Everyman, a Noman, an "allaroundman." *Ulysses* took Joyce seven years to write; its sequel needed seventeen. Hard by Phoenix Park at Chapelizod, types proliferate in the sleeping consciousness of H. C. Earwicker to the point where they nearly strangle him. Oppressed in his nightmare by the load of all the history human and divine his poor soul has been stretched to accommodate, Earwicker-Finn-Tristan-Adam-Everyman can put his all-consuming question no more clearly than in a drunken mutter, *"What was thaas? Fog was whaas?"* In *Finnegans Wake* the particular is almost totally obscured by the flickering of universals on the wall of the world.

Joyce's work as a whole shows a queer correspondence to the parts of the medieval trivium—logic, rhetoric, and grammar. There are the dialectical and Scholastic formulas of the last forty pages of the *Portrait*. *Ulysses* is as full of speeches as Hibernian Hall. *Finnegans Wake* is a grammarian's nightmare. Joyce's more explicit bent for dialectic and syllogism date from his earlier career. Of Stephen Dedalus, Joyce's youthful alter ego, Lynch says, "He likes dialectic, the universal language." With Stephen we associate the Scholastic vocabulary, the Catholic rationalism, the self-conscious theories of art and artist that ring so misleadingly Thomistical. Leopold Bloom has a more modest talent for dialectic, but it is there:

From inexistence to existence he came to many and was as one received; existence with existence he was as any with any; from existence to non-existence gone he would be by all as none perceived.

If you object that it is Joyce himself here who gives explicit rational order to Bloom's confused meditations on his last end, that point in itself is enough to prove that dialectic is more than a stage prop for Stephen Dedalus; it is a method Joyce uses to order his material. In *Finnegans Wake,* the dialectic implicit in the Bloom-Stephen "Ithaca" catechism is taken up by a hundred querulous voices: Berkeley disputes with St. Patrick, Mutt with Jeff, washerwoman with neighbor, hero with eponymous hero, while at the same time Mass, Rosary, sermon, and Benediction are carried on as usual at the side altars. Recalling his Aristotle in the library scene of *Ulysses,* Stephen defined "horseness" as "the whatness of allhorse." But this is topped in the *Wake* by the splendid hypothetical:

if a negative of a horse happens to melt enough while drying, well, what you do get is, well, a positively grotesquely distorted macromass of all sorts of horse-happy values and masses of meltwhile horse.

II

Joyce makes his youthful ruminations on theory of art an integral part of the subject matter of his novels; his theory of the artist he treated as a rule of life for Stephen. The classical locus of these doctrines is the *Portrait,* although much spills over into the earlier sections of *Ulysses.* As expounded by Stephen Dedalus in the "University" chapter, the formal philosophy of art of the *Portrait* is an odd mixture in which float two main sorts of ingredients. One consists of ideas or at least of vocabulary taken from Aristotle and Aquinas, some of it apparently secondhand for all Stephen's boast later in *Ulysses* about Thomas Aquinas, "whose gorbellied works I enjoyed reading in the original." The other is made of cuttings from doctrines of the high estate and autonomous character of art, a mixture that can be run back from Walter Pater and the French romantics to Kant's *Critique of Judgment.* Stephen blurs the distinction between the two source lines by compounding a theory of aesthetic experience with a metaphysics of beauty. Aristotle's remarks on the emotions aroused in the spectator by tragic drama belong to the first category. Stephen knows that the Philosopher had laid it down that tragedy should produce the feelings of pity and fear in the beholder. Aristotle was well aware that nonpoetic experiences, such as the sight of a battlefield, may also produce these emotions; but he pointed out the difference in the condition of feelings in each case. The emotions of those who attend the tragic play are processed in the special manner Aristotle labels *catharsis* or purgation. Exactly what this term means the Stagirite conveniently left unspecified. Stephen Dedalus interprets it as *stasis* or "arrest" of the emotions. That is, in the aesthetic state, our feelings are aroused, but in such a way that we are neither impelled toward the object (as to a savory dish) nor repelled by it (as we would be by the sight of a street accident). Pornography attracts the lout, while didactic art causes us to back away as from a schoolmaster. The aesthetic emotion, says Stephen, is static:

The feelings excited by improper art are kinetic, desire or loathing. Desire urges us to possess, to go to something. The arts which excite them, pornographical or didactic are therefore improper arts. The esthetic emotion . . . is therefore static. The mind is arrested and raised above desire and loathing.

But how can an emotion be static or nonmotion? Stephen might have got around the contradiction by admitting that in aesthetic experience our emotions are aroused, but emphasizing that they are put into a state of balance or equilibrium. The state of feelings under such conditions might be compared to a gyroscope, the motion of which tends to bring the machine to a state of stability. The emotional state proper to art then, in Stephen's view, would not be far from I. A. Richards's *synaesthesia* or harmony of the feelings.

The notion of the psychological state proper to aesthetic experience as one unmoved by anything outside itself derives not from Aristotle but from Kant—although Stephen Dedalus got it from the general stock of late nineteenth century ideas rather than directly from *The Critique of Judgment*. The German philosopher's treatment of the autonomy of *aesthetic* value in his third Critique corresponds exactly to his claim of absolute independence of the *moral* realm in *The Critique of Practical Reason*. Stephen cites Aquinas on beauty to the Dean of Studies, *pulcra sunt quae visa placent*—those things are beautiful which, when beheld, please. But to be properly associated with art, Kant would say, the pleasure must be "disinterested" (*interesseloses Wohlgefallen*). Thus Kant's denial of "interest" (self-benefit; utility) to the aesthetic state is matched by Stephen's interdiction of *kinetic* quality where the aesthetic experience is concerned. Stephen's irreverent college mate Lynch would explain the beauty of the marble Venus in terms of the promise of heroes yet unborn in those splendid flanks—at least Stephen attributes the notion to him. But in Stephen's eyes, this is to confuse art with eugenics.

Kant's antifunctional doctrine of "disinterested pleasure" was pushed to an extreme by Schopenhauer who proclaimed the total separation of the aesthetic state from sexual desire. The gloomy metaphysician claimed that the proper effect of art was to put out of action the cravings of the World Will within us. This segregation of art from sex struck Schopenhauer's student Nietzsche as puritanism, as metaphysical old-maidishness. With heavy irony the author of *The Genealogy of Morals* called attention to the remarkable unanimity with which artists, ancient and modern, have concerned themselves "disinterestedly" with the nude female body. As a fillip, he threw in the example of Pygmalion. By the time the doctrine of "disinterest" had filtered down from the Germans through the enthusiasms of the French romantics (*l'art pour l'art!*) and English aesthetes, it had taken on the form of a proclamation of the independence of art from the moral realm. New York Mayor James Walker's single contribution to the philosophy of art, "No girl was ever seduced by a book," is simply a vulgarization of Oscar Wilde's dictum that a book is either well or badly written, that it cannot be moral or immoral. But Stephen Dedalus's concern for the independence of art is loftier than mere anxiety about the problem of art and sex. He defends the autonomy of art as a monk of the Middle Ages might champion the privileges and exalted status of the Virgin. Even for the French romantics, who did not have the benefit of Stephen's Scholastic philosophy, the doctrine of the independence of poetry was a dogma of the religion of art.

The psychological condition of *stasis*—that composed or balanced state of the emotions proper to aesthetic experience—is matched in the ontological order by the property of *consonantia* or harmony. At least so Stephen interprets Aquinas on beauty to the disrespectful Lynch. *"Ad pulcritudinem tria requiruntur: integritas, consonantia, claritas.* I translate it so: *Three things are needed for beauty, wholeness, harmony and radiance."* Stephen takes *integritas* to refer to the oneness of the beautiful object, and *consonantia* to the balance or harmony of its parts. This is classical doctrine, not at all original. *Claritas* gives him a little trouble. At first he had interpreted it Platonically: *claritas* might be the effect of the transcendent universal Form or Essence shining through the humble object in the visible world reflecting it. But distrusting the Platonic tendency to locate

reality *apart* from the particular experience, Stephen dismisses this
as "literary talk," preferring instead to believe that the radiance of
which Aquinas speaks is the Scholastic *quidditas,* the whatness dis-
tinct yet inseparable from the particularity of the thing. Thus the
discussion is brought around to a more Aristotelian tack—*claritas*
refers to our apprehension of the *form* of the object, a form not
separate from but integrally united with its *matter.* More than one
commentator on Stephen's aesthetic has thought that the "supreme
quality felt by the artist when the esthetic image is first conceived
by the imagination" would be better rendered by the Scotist *haec-
ceitas* or *this-ness* than by the Thomist *quidditas* or whatness. If so,
then Stephen's *claritas* would be cousin to the Scotus-loving Gerard
Manley Hopkins's *inscape,* that quality of an object which reveals
to our intuition its individual nature. Young Dedalus compares the
effect of *claritas* to "that mysterious instant Shelley likened beauti-
fully to a fading coal," although he is wary of the poet's Platonic con-
ception of art as a regression, a stage removed from the divine source
of light.

   In the early draft of the *Portrait* we now call *Stephen Hero,*
Dedalus springs the word 'epiphany' on his college-mate Cranly. As
the name of a feast in the liturgical calendar, 'epiphany' means the
manifestation or showing-forth of the infant Jesus to the visitor
kings who come in the name of all the peoples of the earth. Stephen's
more personal meaning for the word retains this element of showing-
forth—"By an epiphany he meant a sudden spiritual manifestation,
whether in the vulgarity of speech or of gesture or in a memorable
phrase of the mind itself." He goes on to link "epiphany" with
claritas: at such moments, "The soul of the commonest object . . .
seems to us radiant. The object achieves its epiphany." There is a
doubleness in the way Stephen plays with the word *claritas* here that
raises a question. Is radiance an *ontological* property of the beautiful,
an attribute possessed by the aesthetic object in its own right apart
from the perceiving self? Or is it a subjective phenomenon, a quality
of aesthetic experience, an event primarily in the *psychological* order?

At any rate, when Stephen tells us that it is the task of the man of letters to "record these epiphanies with extreme care, seeing that they are the most delicate and evanescent of moments," adding that even the clock of the nearby Ballast Office is capable of an epiphany, we think of Symbolism rather than Scholasticism—Proust or Yeats perhaps but not Aquinas. The hero of Proust's *A la recherche du temps perdu* experiences intense though passing moments with trees and church spires, moments in which the sight of these objects builds up to a luminosity bringing joy, resolving conflicts, giving meaning to life gone dry. Yeats recorded a similar experience in a London tea shop:

> While on the shop and street I gazed
> My body of a sudden blazed;
> And twenty minutes more or less
> It seemed, so great my happiness
> That I was blessèd and could bless.

This motif of objects which suddenly glow and reveal themselves charged with meaning is a peculiar mark of Symbolist literature. Nothing could have been further from St. Thomas's mind when he distinguished his three properties of the Beautiful than such exalted "creative" moments as Stephen describes. The Angelic Doctor was thinking of the Trinity, not of fading coals or of girls with their feet in the water.

We may take it then that in fusing the meaning of *claritas* with "epiphany" Stephen tried to reconcile the dialectic of Aquinas with his own theory of aesthetic experience, and that this theory is one showing Symbolist inclinations. Now Symbolism always carries with it a temptation to Platonize; the Symbolist poet tends to locate the source of the reality of an object, or of the significance of an experience, in some transcendent realm of Forms or Essences, a better, "realer" kingdom than this world of brute natural fact. In extreme cases the Symbolist may go over to the occult. It is to Stephen's credit that he resists the temptation to Platonize Aquinas. His dictum in the *Portrait* runs:

The connotation of the word [*claritas*] is rather vague. Aquinas uses a term which seems to be inexact. It baffled me for a long time. It would lead you to believe that he had in mind symbolism or idealism, the supreme quality of beauty being a light from some other world, the idea of which the matter was but the shadow, the reality of which it was the symbol. I thought he might mean that *claritas* was the artistic discovery and representation of divine purpose in anything or a force of generalization which would make the esthetic image a universal one, make it outshine its proper conditions. But that is literary talk.

Later in the library scene of *Ulysses,* George Russell, poet and seer, declares oracularly that the business of art is to reveal— "ideas, formless spiritual essences." The poetry of Shakespeare and Shelley, says the occultist, "bring our minds into contact with eternal wisdom, Plato's world of ideas." Responding, Stephen—who once acknowledged the occult Thoth as his symbol—silently mocks the hermetic pantheism that would claim ultimate reality for the "formless" (how could the Forms be formless?) spiritual essences, the glib formula of *tat twam asi* that would annihilate the reality of the individual: "Hiesos Kristos, magician of the beautiful, the Logos who suffers in us at every moment. This verily is that. I am the fire upon the altar. I am the sacrificial butter." Declining Blake's vision of eternity of which this vegetable world is but a shadow, Stephen heroically adjures himself, *"Hold to the now, the here, through which all future plunges into the past."* Yet this very self-admonition—ranking the particular above the universal, fact before symbol—stings itself with its own tail. For if all the future plunges into the past, *time,* as Plato said, can only be "the moving image of eternity." And if time is unreal, so is history, and nothing really new can happen. Thus in resolving that his novel-to-come *Ulysses* shall deal with "the now, the here" Stephen touches the gong of the Eternal Return.

III

The figure of the artist casts a long shadow in Joyce's writings. To the young Dubliner, the poet is a hero-type, a perfect man.

The pursuit of art is a vocation, a life ideal and complete in itself, a destiny analogous to but transcending that of the priest. In the *Portrait,* Stephen considers the dignity of the priestly office he had once thought to be his vocation, but rejects it in favor of the higher calling of the artist, whose symbol is Icarus the hawk-like man flying sunward over the sea. The religion of art is a portion of Stephen's inheritance from his French masters of the nineteenth century. "In art," said Théophile Gautier, "we have no religion but the religion of art itself." Identification of the artist with *Icarus,* says Mr. Maurice Shroder in his study of that title, is peculiar to romanticism; Joyce stands at the end of a tradition which glorified the artist's personality and assimilated it to the image of the brave youth with wings. Gautier recorded the voices of the younger poets:

The fate of Icarus frightened no one. Wing! Wings! Wings! they cried from all sides, even if we should fall into the sea. To fall from the sky, one must climb there, even for only a moment, and that is more beautiful than to spend one's whole life crawling on the earth.

But Joyce's Icarus never falls. Moreover, to the Irish poet the father is greater than the son; it is *his* name Stephen takes as his own. Daedalus is the more godlike in that he is a maker; it was he who invented and fabricated the wings, the labyrinth. Stephen Dedalus sees the poet as an artificer who hammers his work out of hard refractory matter, then stands aloof, a passionless deity, "The artist like the God of creation, remains within or behind or beyond or above his handiwork, invisible, refined out of existence, indifferent, paring his fingernails." The remote source of Stephen's artist-paradigm is the passage in Plato's *Timaeus* that tells how the Demiurge sets about his task of fashioning the world, impressing creative form upon matter, the principle of heaviness, sluggishness, inertia. Direct inspiration came from Joyce's own art-heroes Flaubert and Ibsen. Defending the impersonality of his writing, the author of *Madame Bovary* wrote to Mme. Chantpie, "The artist should be in his work like God in creation, invisible and all-powerful; one should feel him everywhere, but see him nowhere." Ibsen too regarded the artist as a Master-Builder; in *When We Dead Awaken* he offers Ulfheim's vision of the artist struggling creator-fashion with those marble blocks that fight against being hammered into life. So Stephen would declare his duty as an artist:

> . . . to press out again, from the gross earth or what brings it forth, from sound and shape and colour which are the prison gates of our soul, an image of the beauty we have come to understand—that is art—.

Stephen's view of the artist as "creator" is one to which we, as inheritors of the romantic tradition, instinctively incline. Our time's identification of the good with the "creative" has the status of an axiom, and popular belief enthusiastically supports Stephen's notion of artistic creation as part of the duty of the artist to "express himself." But this concept of the "creative artist" is the creature of a Platonism that is modern and romantic. Classical Platonism never held that the artist was a creator; Plato himself would not have known what it meant to say that the poet is "creative." Classical Platonism held, as did the philosopher himself, that the artist was an *imitator*. Rarely today do we come across a denial that the artist is primarily a "creator." Gerhart Hauptmann claimed never to have invented a single character, that all he could do was to transcribe them. In *Die Dämonen,* Heimito von Doderer sees to it that his young historian Stangeler agrees with the German dramatist:

> Everything "creative," René reasoned, was only imitation, and the whole "productive act" nothing but wholly free apperception, penetration of the world into a human being utterly without distortion. The thing was to remove every obstacle that tended to hinder this penetration.

Plato recommended that poets be sent into exile. Daedalus languished for a time in a foreign prison. But there is little in the identification of the artist with a mythical artificer, Demiurge or Daedalus, to suggest why the artist should be a self-banished man. The Demiurge did nothing to merit punishment; he was no Prometheus, but an agent of the blessed gods. As for Icarus, his judgment was to blame for what happened to him—not his wings. No, the theme of the poet's exile belongs more to Flaubert's and Ibsen's side of the fence than to the Greeks'. The note of self-banishment adds theatrical tone to the closing scenes of the *Portrait*, and strengthens Stephen's dramatic posture in *Ulysses*. But the motif of exile pervades Joyce's life and work so thoroughly that it cannot be fobbed off entirely on Stephen Dedalus, so often made scapegoat for ideological indiscretions alleged to be peculiar to Joyce's youth. In the *Portrait*, Stephen claims that his only arms in his fight for freedom to realize himself are "silence, exile, and cunning." When he wrote those lines, Joyce himself had already lived in exile ten years. He remained an expatriate until his death. Like his own Shem the Penman of *Finnegan's Wake*, Joyce, "kusky korked himself up tight in his inkbattle house . . . there to stay in afar from the life."

Ibsen, Joyce's master, had acted the part of the outlawed genius in his own life, had made a play of it as well in *An Enemy of the People*. Gerhart Hauptmann too had called Joyce's attention to the conflict between individual and society, sharply focused in the artist's situation. Stephen Dedalus had pored over Hauptmann's *Künstlerdramen:* Mr. Duffey of *Dubliners* kept an unfinished translation of *Michael Kramer* in his drawer. Behind Gustave Flaubert stood generations of French poets who made art of their alienation. Chateaubriand's René, Constant's Adolf, Sainte-Beuve's Delorme aroused a whole aviary from Musset's pelican to Baudelaire's albatross to croak sadly about the plight of the poet, lonely yet proud of his "otherness." Back of them all stood Rousseau who did so much to create the picture of the romantic hero ("I may not be better than other men, but at least I am different"). Jean-Jacques waxed lachrymose on the subject of his alienation from men and actually died mad. Hero-archetypes, solitary and estranged, predate the sensibility of the eighteenth and the *poètes maudits* of the nineteenth century. Hamlet, Stephen Dedalus's darling, is the very Platonic Idea of the isolated dreamer, the young man called to knowledge but not born to it. Shakespeare's gloomy prince paraded his madness first in 1602, only three years before the alienated knight of La Mancha made his debut in still feudal Spain.

In his schooldays, Joyce had treasured Byron and the early Yeats. Byron's Childe Harold was one of the grand models for the blighted poet of his century. Harold

> . . . knew himself the most unfit
> Of men to herd with Man, with whom he held
> Little in common.

The great Goethe, who had provided an earlier paradigm of sensibility with his Werther, made Byron the model of the Icarus-like Euphorion of the second part of *Faust*. The talented son of Goethe's friend Madame Schopenhauer admired Byron this side of idolatry; the young philosopher declared it was the poet's *knowledge* that alienated him from society. "Genius," said the author of *The World as Will and Idea,* "lives essentially alone. It is too rare to find its like with ease, and too different from the rest of men to be their boon companion. With the common man it is Will, but with him it is knowledge that predominates." Byron's Manfred (*cor anglais;* elegiacally) laments the loneliness of the exceptional man, while taking pride in its cause:

> They who know the most
> Must mourn the deepest o'er the fatal truth
> The Tree of Knowledge is not that of Life.

Byron's Cain was an outcast, a man with a sign on his brow to mark him kin to Lucifer, exiled from heaven because of pride. (*"Non serviam!"*) Pride too marks Stephen Dedalus—that "pride of spirit which had made him conceive of himself as a being apart in every order." Proud Parnell was betrayed and thrust forth; he stood coldly aloof as Catholic Ireland recoiled at the

revelation of his mortal sin. A Cain of lesser stature, Oscar Wilde
was an artist betrayed, disgraced, exiled. Yeats was no outcast,
although his earliest poems are sprinkled with self-admissions of
scornful otherness. ("They say I am solitary, yes, proud too!")
Unlike Joyce he took his poetic material from an imagined past of
Ireland. Stephen Dedalus recalls Michael Robartes who remembers
forgotten beauty and presses into his arms the loveliness which
has long faded from the world. "Not this," says the confident youth
who would forge in the smithy of his soul the uncreated conscience
of his race, "I desire to press in my arms the loveliness which has not
yet come into the world." Beneath all his "coldness," Stephen is
as sentimental as any Irishman. In the *Portrait* he hugs to his
heart the farewell of Yeats's Countess Cathleen to her two youthful companions before she signs away her soul to eternal exile in
return for the demons' pledge to restore those already bought up
in her famine-stricken land:

> Bend down your faces, Oona and Aleel
> **I gaze upon them as the swallow gazes**
> Upon the nest under the eave before
> She wander the loud waters.

Stephen changes the "she" of the last line to "he," for it is of his own
approaching exile he is thinking. "You're a terrible man, Stevie,"
says Davin to his young heretic schoolmate, "—always alone—."
Said the heresiarch La Mennais, *"L'exilé partout est seul."*

Unlike many of his brother poets in the romantic tradition,
Stephen Dedalus of the *Portrait* is quite willing to take the consequences of isolation. He never writes elegaic complaints about the
artist's lot such as Thomas Mann's Tonio Kröger inflicts upon his
patient Russian friend Lisaveta. Stephen belongs to the dominating
kind of romantic poet-heroes rather than to the retiring misunderstood type. Besides, he has no nostalgia for the ordinary. True, in
his schooldays he had experienced a fleeting impulse of concern
for his family.

He saw clearly, too, his own futile isolation. He had not gone one step nearer the lives he had sought to approach nor bridged the restless shame and rancour that had divided him from mother and brother and sister. He felt that he was hardly of the one blood with them, but stood to them rather in the mystical kinship of fosterage, foster child and foster brother.

But nothing came of it. Stephen takes something of the pride in his isolation that Joyce celebrated in his youthful pamphlet "The Day of the Rabblement," the first line of which invoked the tortured spirit of philosopher Giordano Bruno, heretic, outlaw, and "terribly burned"—

No man, said the Nolan, can be a lover of the true or the good unless he abhors the multitude; and the artist, though he may employ the crowd, is very careful to isolate himself.

Toward the end of the *Portrait,* as Stephen makes clear to Cranly that his coming exile involves parting from his Church as well as his mother, Cranly says, "Alone, quite alone. You have no fear of that. And you know what the word means?" But here Cranly is speaking less of Stephen's plight than of his own. It is not until we meet him in *Ulysses* that we find Stephen overtaken by loneliness. As the morning of that single day passes, his homeless state is borne heavily in upon him. He walks the strand near Sandymount meditating on the ineluctable modality of the visible, the shifting shapes and colors of sand, sea, and sky, murmuring, "I am lonely here . . . I am quiet here alone. Sad too." Later in the library episode, Stephen will read his own estrangement in the play of *Hamlet* and make an exile of the man Shakespeare:

The note of banishment, banishment from the heart, banishment from home, sounds uninterruptedly from *Two Gentlemen of Verona* onward till Prospero breaks his staff, buries it certain fathoms in the earth and drowns his book.

But alienation, exile, and loneliness derive only from the negative and less important side of Joyce's artist-theory. Self-realization, self-expression, and creation constitute the positive face of it. Neither Stephen nor his maker Joyce ever wanted exile simply to enjoy a posture of exalted misery. With them, it is never a question of freedom for its own sake, freedom *from,* but rather freedom *to—* freedom to work, to get on with the job to which one is called. Exile, for Stephen, is one of the arms he allows himself to use, a defensive weapon only. The pages of the *Portrait* that announce the theme of the artist's calling have a totally affirmative tone. Like young Moreau's strikingly similar experience in Flaubert's *Education sentimentale,* Stephen's artist-epiphany is keyed in a triumphant C-major; he wants freedom to bring his powers to fulfillment, to strike into existence something that was not there before, the uncreated conscience, the unborn beauty:

Now, at the name of the fabulous artificer, he seemed to hear the noise of dim waves and to see a winged form flying above the waves and slowly climbing the air. What did it mean? Was it a quaint device opening a page of some medieval book of prophecies and symbols, a hawklike man flying sunward above the sea, a prophecy of the end he had been born to serve and had been following through the mists of childhood and boyhood, a symbol of the artist forging anew in his workshop out of the sluggish matter of the earth a new soaring impalpable imperishable being?

His heart trembled; his breath came faster and a wild spirit passed over his limbs as though he were soaring sunward. His heart trembled in an ecstasy of fear and his soul was in flight. His soul was soaring in an air beyond the world and the body he knew was purified in a breath and delivered of incertitude and made radiant and commingled with the element of the spirit. An ecstasy of flight made radiant his eyes and wild his breath and tremulous and wild and radiant his windswept limbs.

The *Portrait's* closing pages, ring with confidence: in his apostrophe to his father, the old Artificer, Stephen feels secure and full of promise. Although in *Ulysses,* he is troubled by a remorse that reaches the pitch of hallucination, Stephen never wavers where his vocation is concerned. To that end in a single day he gives up his lodging in the Martello tower, quits his school job at Dalkey, and firmly declines Bloom's offer of paternal asylum at no. 7 Eccles Street. As Stephen vanishes from Bloom's sight in the dark of that early morning of June 17, 1904, he does not know exactly where he is going. But the reader is left in no doubt that he is off to begin the writing of *Ulysses,* and, what is more, that he will successfully finish it. In his high confidence of his own destiny as artist Joyce's Stephen contrasts so markedly with Michel, the hero of Gide's *Immoralist.* That passionate individualist too was reborn, but unlike Stephen's future, his own is so little worth betting on that he must call in his friends to advise him what to do with his "objectless freedom." The same comparison holds with Hans Castorp of Mann's *The Magic Mountain.* Although the German hero gives not only promise but also massive and objective evidence of his creative power, we are told by his narrator that the chances are none too good even for his physical survival. Proust's Marcel is a little closer to Stephen. Unlike the Irish youth, the hero of *A la recherche du temps perdu* is no longer young and has had a history of self-doubt and infirmity of purpose. Yet his story too closes on a note of high resolve as he begs Time to grant him leave to write down the immense novel he has just narrated. Stephen and Marcel are heroes of novels of self-discovery. Their genius will produce the books about them we are reading.

IV

James Joyce is the third member of a trio of absolutely exceptional men associated with the Catholic National University of Ireland, men different from one another in major respects (two of them English and former Anglicans), yet sharing common elements not the least of which is a certain participation in the nineteenth century romantic ideal of genius. John Henry Newman was a man who dwelt far above the snowline. By his conversion to Rome, he became one of England's loneliest men ("I became an exile in solitude"), for by that act he separated himself from family, from colleagues, from the communion of his childhood, from the university that he loved. Newman seemed a strong man who had to suppress part of himself. His love of nature tended to Wordsworthian pantheism. But his sensitivity to doctrinal heresy was exaggeratedly acute. His passion for music was such that he would cry out with joy after playing a Beethoven quartet part on his violin. Yet in his lectures he classified the playing of stringed instruments with bird-stuffing as mere elegant accomplishments having nothing to do with true education. As a convert, he was regarded with suspicion by his fellow Catholics who thought him eccentric or worse. His simple but aristocratic presence made the Pope himself feel ill at ease. As a Catholic, Newman's life was one official failure or embarrassment after another—the botched editorship of the *Rambler,* the muffed bishopric, the abortive Bible translation project, the mortifying Achille case, the near-sympathy with Modernism, the wrong side taken on Papal Infallibility, the red hat delayed until he was too old to do any more harm. Perhaps his most remarkable failure as a Roman Catholic leader was his first—as Rector Designate of the new National University of Ireland in 1852. The Irish bishops envisioned the new university as a fortress of Catholicism from which sallies could be made in force against the influence of Protestant Trinity and the secularized Queens colleges. For his part, Newman wanted no lay seminary, but a Catholic Oxford. Outmaneuvered for six years, he finally gave up and resigned his rectorship, contenting himself with the publication of his Dublin lectures we know as *The Idea of a University.* Not until 1883, the year after Joyce's birth, did the University College open in the old Georgian mansion on St. Stephen's Green in Dublin—and it opened under the direction of the Jesuits. Joyce put high value on Newman as a writer. We hear his voice on Vergil in the *Portrait,* and Stephen recalls his "proud cadence":

—Whose feet are as the feet of harts and underneath the everlasting arms.

One of the pastiches of the "Oxen of the Sun" episode in *Ulysses* is gotten up in Newman's prose style. Toward the end of his labors on *Finnegans Wake,* Joyce wrote to Harriet Weaver—"nobody has ever written English prose that can be compared with that of a tiresome footling little Anglican parson who afterwards became a prince of the only true church."

After his conversion at Oxford while still an undergraduate, Gerard Manley Hopkins visited Newman, and received the advice that his first duty was to show his friends that becoming a Catholic was no obstacle to scholarship. So the young man Professor Jowett called "the star of Balliol" got a double first in Greats. He had thought of joining Newman's Oratory, but the soldierly Loyolan Rule of the Society of Jesus attracted him. "Don't call the Jesuit disciple hard," said Newman in agreeing. "It will bring you to heaven." As a Jesuit, Father Hopkins was regarded as a mildly eccentric misfit, inadequate in rural missions, in parish work among the city poor, in fashionable Farm Street. When in 1875 he submitted to *The Month* that dragon of a poem inspired by the wreck of the steamer *Deutschland* carrying away from Germany six Catholic nuns exiled by the Falk Laws, the Jesuit editors rejected the prodigy with respectful dismay. A professorship in the new University College in Dublin seemed to the English Jesuits an admirable way to get the ethereal Father Hopkins out from underfoot and at the same time to put his undoubted erudition to work for the greater glory of God and the National University of Ireland. Hopkins was Professor of Classics in University College from 1884 until his death on June 8, 1889. On that day the aged Cardinal Newman sat waiting in his Birmingham Oratory. Death had not yet come for him. Nine months before, little James Joyce—aged "half-past six"—had entered the Jesuit school at Clongowes where Hopkins had written his sonnet "The Soldier." To Father Hopkins the College in St. Stephen's Green was "a sort of ruin and for purposes of study nearly naked." He did a minimum of teaching there, for most of his duties were taken up with setting and correcting national examinations. A special man of the "derailed" type, Hopkins was a spiritual exile, *un joli jesuit à la petite tache humide.* He belonged not to the race of romantic poets who are Promethean conquerors, but to the odd, self-effacing, and misunderstood variety.

He considered his Irish residence as exile ("now I am at a third remove,") and took his assignment to the Dublin college as final confirming of his lifelong isolation:

> To seem the stranger lies my lot, my life
> Among strangers.

Hopkins's sense of exile, his fiery vision, and passionate love of words (particularly Anglo-Saxon ones) mark a cousinship with Joyce by no means at third remove. Stephen Dedalus's line on the changingness of things in the "Proteus" episode of *Ulysses* ("I throw this ended shadow from me, manshape, ineluctable, call it back") is anticipated by Hopkins's words on the contingency of existence:

> Manshape, that shone
> Sheer off, disseveral, a star, death blots black out;

Long before young Dedalus was old enough to cock an appreciative eye at pied beauty ("A day of dappled sea-borne clouds") Hopkins had been praising God for dappled things as well as for

> All things counter, original, spare, strange.

Some commentators put Hopkins's inner conflict down to latent homosexuality; others say he was the victim of consuming tension between his art and his religion. Still others will have him a saint, prey to *acedia,* the spiritual torpor that troubled the souls of the ancient Fathers. At any rate Stephen Dedalus's God of the Roman Catholics struck him dead of typhoid at the age of forty-five, having given no visible sign of attention to his Job's pleading:

> Wert thou my enemy, O thou my friend
> How wouldst thou worse, I wonder than thou doest
> Defeat, thwart me. Oh the sots and thralls of lust
> Do in spare hours more thrive than I that spend
> Sir, life upon thy cause.

It is often said that Joyce's mind has an essentially Catholic construction. "Your mind," Cranly remarked to Stephen Dedalus, who is on another occasion to be mistaken for a spoiled priest, "is super-saturated with the religion in which you say you disbelieve." Joyce's first biographer Gorman said of his subject that "Catholicism is in his bones." George Every claimed that Joyce's mind remained essentially Catholic in its "pity for human weakness and frailty, and terror of a judgment to come." Mary Colum said "I have never known anyone with a mind so fundamentally Catholic in structure as Joyce's own or one on whom the Church, its ceremonies, symbols, and theological declarations had made such an impress." Less sympathetic readers of the Dubliner have put down his attention to copulation and excreta to "the Catholic twist" in his mind. Cecil Maitland reduced the Dubliner's wit to the "cloacal humor of the refectory" and his treatment of sex to the obscenity of a confessor's manual. H. G. Wells discovered the secret of Joyce's art to lie in his exploiting that fearful sense of split between the divine perfection of the supernatural order, in whose existence Catholics believe, and the natural messiness of the human animal who must urinate, defecate, menstruate, and copulate. Certainly this radical Joycean dualism between spirit and matter exists, although in what sense, if any, it is Catholic, is arguable. At any rate, much of the antic nature of Joyce's art is a function of the left-handed way he exploits his Catholic material. Just as Dublin gives his work its unique flavor of physical place, so the Catholic Church provides him with a ready-made spiritual and symbolical topography.

Joyce looked at Catholicism through multiple lenses—metaphysical and historical, devotional and local. The Church was two thousand years of history, heavy with learning and sanctity. At the same time it had become in Dublin at the end of the century a quasi-evangelical sect, a parochial, nationalistic puritanism. Polarized against England and Protestantism, the Catholic Church in Ireland had taken on many of the qualities it set itself against. For the greater part of two millennia, the Holy Roman Catholic Apostolic faith had been identical with Western Christianity. But in the small half-urbanized world of Joycean Dublin, those two thousand years seemed to contract to accommodate the urgency and venom of the local situation, reducing religion to a parlor bourgeois blue-nosiness in which morality was something about the length of women's dresses. In what seemed to him the stale atmosphere of priest-dominated woman-culture, the young author of *Dubliners* thought he detected the presence of a lethal gas which produced in its victims unaware torpor, spiritual paralysis, and death. All the same, the writer Joyce was fascinated by the concrete "existential" side of Dublin Catholicism—the wheezy hymns, the pious gimcrackery, the rosaries and scapulars, the First Fridays and Novenas. An ideal Joycean stage set is the bedroom with stiff white curtains, a brass-fitted connubial bed that does not quite conceal an orange chamberpot. Over the bed on which a man and woman will shortly lie in lust or troubled sleep there hangs a thorn-girdled, sanguinary Sacred Heart, disembodied and sword-pierced. It is part of Joyce's genius that he succeeds so well in communicating the flavor of kitchen- and parish-Catholicism to his readers who may have no more direct knowledge of it than they have with the Jewish props of a Malamud novel. For all its scandalous *double-entendre* ("Oops I never ope momouth before I put me food in it"), Shaun's discourse on chastity to the twenty-nine schoolgirls of *Finnegans Wake* hits off with astonishing accuracy the archness-cum-bellicosity of those priests given to Retreat-time sermons on purity:

I was asking his advice on the strict T.T. from Father Mike, P.P., my orational dominican and confessor doctor, C.C.D.D. (Buy the birds, he was saying as he yerked me under the ribs sermon in an offrand way and confidence between peas like ourselves in soandso many nuncupiscent words about how he had been confarreating teat-a-teat with two viragos intactas about what an awful life he led . . .)

. . . Don't on any account acquire a paunchon for that alltoocommon fagbut habit of frequenting and chumming it together with the braces of couples in Mr Tunnelly's hallways (smash it) wriggling with lowcusses and cockchafters and vamps and roadants, with the end to commit acts of interstipital indecency. . . . When parties get tight for each other they lose all respect together. By the stench of her fizzle and the glib of her gab know the drunken draggletail Dublin drab.

Father Arnall's famous sermon in the *Portrait*, to which Shaun's in the *Wake* forms a comic pendant, is not just a tape recording, but a highly imaginative creation. A literal transcription of any such performance is simply dull, as James T. Farrell has shown to the extent of ten pages or so in his *Studs Lonigan*. But sixty years after its composition Catholics will read Joyce's set-piece and swear they recall that very sermon from their childhood—they don't, of course, for there never was such a sermon. On the stage (I am thinking of Phoebe Brand's production of the *Portrait* in New York), the retreat-master's sermon sounds well too, lifted up as it is above the banalities of its fundamentalism by a certain authenticity of emotion. Thomas Merton is reported to have said that Father Arnall's sermon was instrumental in his own conversion—a fact of no literary interest, but evidence that men's lives have been changed by some oddly situated arguments. (In *My New Curate*, Canon Sheehan tells of a man who was converted from atheism by a chance encounter with the Ontological Proof!)

For all the parochial and vulgarized atmosphere of Dublin's parlor-bourgeois Catholicism, the Church for Joyce remained "those twenty centuries of authority and veneration"—although often that history seemed to him a nightmare. A single theological phrase, a line from the Mass could call up for him, as for Huysmans' Des Esseintes, a long procession of saints, martyrs, patriarchs, Popes, doctors, mystics, inquisitors and heresiarchs, waggling their beards, chanting *"Extra ecclesiam nulla salus!"* The spiritual exercises of his Jesuit schooling reinforced the personal and devotional side of his religion, his studies put him in touch with the intellectual tradition of the Church. True, the scholarship of some of his teachers at Belvedere and the National University probably did not go much beyond snippets of antique learning eked out by Scholastic manuals and Latin tags. But Joyce seems to have found this modest material enough for him to begin Cuvier-fashion to reconstruct in his own image the intellectual sophistications of the Western Church, the Christological debates, the speculations of the Schoolmen, the neo-Gnostic cosmogonies of the Renaissance magic-masters. While it would be too much to claim that Joyce's mind was "Jesuit-trained" in the manner of the intellectual discipline to which Descartes was introduced by the fathers of La Flèche, it is only fair to give Joyce's Jesuit preceptors some credit for disclosing to their talented pupil the *logos* inherent in the Catholic tradition. At least they provided stimulation to a gluttonous mind already shot through by a compulsive, almost pathological rationalism that co-existed with a surprisingly commonplace *petit sentiment* indulged at the time in mawkish pseudo-Elizabethan verse. Later he would supplement the slender pickings of the Dublin curriculum with considerable philosophical and theological reading on his own at the library of Saint Genevieve in Paris.

Statements concerning the Catholic element in Joyce's mind and art must be set down cautiously lest they be taken as claims for orthodoxy on Joyce's behalf. Against T. S. Eliot's early sympathy with Joyce's "Christian" sensibilities and training, and Hugh Kenner's more recent suggestion that Joyce's work cannot be understood apart from a basic traditionalism and orthodoxy, the fire of a battery of arguments to the contrary has been directed by a number of critics disturbed by apparent claims that Joyce was, after all, a good Catholic and a traditionalist at heart. William Empson considers Kenner's views all the more alarming because the swing to the alleged "orthodox" or neo-Christian interpretation of Joyce has been accomplished in only thirty short years since the first howls of execration greeted *Ulysses*. Goldberg notes that Joyce owed at least as much to Homer and Shakespeare as he did to Scripture, adding the (surely obvious) truth that "while he shared many values with the Church, there were others he did not." Ellmann's biography makes clear that to the end Joyce retained an intense and unremitting hostility to the Church. The fact that his grandchild was baptized had to be concealed from him. His belated marriage to Nora Barnacle was a no-nonsense civil affair. When he died, a wreath with an emblem of Ireland was laid on his grave, but no priest was allowed to follow him there. Certainly Joyce was neither wistful ex-Catholic nor crypto-traditionalist. While his manner of leaving the Church may not have lacked a suggestion of flounce, his determination to exile himself from the Catholic community was without equivocation and (as time confirmed) irrevocable. But one can make the claim that Joyce's mind and art show an indelible Catholic coloring without at the same time maintaining that Joyce was orthodox, a forgiveably errant son of Holy Mother Church, and a Thomist traditionalist at heart. In the light of a rereading of the entire Joyce canon, the first claim still appears to be supported by the facts of the case. In some queer way that has nothing to do with fidelity to dogma or discipline, the Church seemed to remain for Joyce a guideline for thought as well as an enormous repository of file cards for reference. Joyce's conversational and epistolary remarks about "the one true Church" and "The Holy Roman Catholic Apostolic Church" show something more than labored jocosity. To the end, Joyce retained, even exaggerated, his Catholic vocabulary and Scholastic pedantry. *Finnegans Wake* cannot be got around in this respect.

Contemporary critics and the reading public both tend to underestimate the *demonic* in Joyce, a quality that appears to be related in some basic way to his Catholicism. Even Father Noon, whose fine study examines much of the relevant doctrinal material, presents an amazingly deodorized Joyce. Today when college freshmen cut their teeth in English A on the *Portrait* and young girl graduates quote *Ulysses* in Class Day speeches to the benign approval of their elders, the temptation is to dismiss Joyce's naughtiness as "art" or as something people objected to a long time ago. With the American genius for turning everything into psychology, college lecturers introduce Stephen Dedalus to admiring youth as a typical young man with "problems." Onstage, he tends to a type—the attractive adolescent rebel. The Woolsey decision in 1934 that allowed *Ulysses* to be imported into the United States ushered in an era of liberal publishing practices concerning the printing of coarse words and mention of sex acts. The American reading public likes printed descriptions of sexual intercourse (probably a substitute for suburban adultery) and a flood of coital literature is poured out to suit their taste. But Joyce's initiative in these matters is not to be compared with the dreariness of Henry Miller's *Tropic of Cancer,* despite the recent opinion of Judge Marvin Dye who in defending Miller's book against the charge of obscenity likened it to *Ulysses,* describing the latter in a sympathetic (if mixed) trope as "a commentary on the inner lives of human beings caught in the throes of a hopeless morass." The devilry in Joyce is real, although like Berlioz and his *Requiem* with its orchestra, chorus, and four brass bands, he keeps his fortissimos very much under control. Joyce uses blasphemy and scatology as deliberate techniques to get artistic effects, and his Catholic element lends these devices a peculiar air of authority. To commit authentic blasphemy, a man must in some way move within the context of belief. When George Moore states, "The Irish like priests, and believe in the power of priests to forgive them their sins and to change God into a biscuit," he is blaspheming *materially,* as Stephen's Jesuit preceptors would say, but not *formally,* since he is an unbeliever. Joyce could do it both ways, and not alone through the irreverent mouth of Buck Mulligan:

> I'm the queerest young fellow that ever you heard
> My mother's a jew, my father's a bird.

Everybody knows that *Ulysses* begins with Mulligan's parody of the opening of the Mass ("Introibo ad altare Dei") and that Stephen enters the bawdyhouse district chanting (more politely) the Introit for Paschal time. Throughout *Ulysses,* prayers and devotions are comically parodied; in "Circe" the earlier adventures of Odysseus-Bloom are handily recapitulated by a burlesque of the litany of the Blessed Virgin; a take-off of the Credo enlivens "Cyclops." Travesties of Catholic devotions (some of them pretty crude) occur in virtually every third page of that theological fun house *Finnegans Wake:* "three patre-knocksters and a cuplet of hellmurries"; "Load help you Maria full of grease"; "Mother Mary Miserecordial of the Dripping Nipples"; and the rest.

Joyce's scatology may not, perhaps, be put down as easily as his blasphemy to the Catholic factor in him. Exaggerated interest in the nature and function of the organs of copulation and excretion are often found in societies where these matters are guarded by purely social taboos. But it is interesting to observe that Joyce (like Swift, whom he resembles in some ways) is almost totally lacking in joy of the body; he is devoid of that holy naturalism which inspired the heroes of Gide or Lawrence, the reborn young men who tear off their clothes and their morals with a cry of glee to the pagan sun. Surely it would be incorrect to link Catholic doctrine with belief that the body is incompatible with the spirit, since according to that doctrine the body is the temple of the Holy Ghost, destined to resurrection and a glorified state. It is tempting to compare Joyce's fascination with the smellier by-products of the human body, the intestinal concern pervading the most cognitive reaches of his art, to the writings of certain Churchmen like St. Augustine ("Inter faeces et urinam nascimur."), Odo of Cluny who for purposes of edification enumerates the horrors of subcutaneous man (and woman), Innocent the Third whose catalog includes "unclean generation, loathsome nutrition when in the maternal body, awful stench, secretion of spit, urine, and excrement"—or even Joyce's more nearly contemporary cousin, Baudelaire, that other Catholic *manqué* who begged God to allow him to contemplate that dung, his body, without disgust. But in the Irishman's case, there seems to be a closer analogy to certain medieval heretical dualists. Joyce is the last Manichee. The extreme polarity in his work between the lowly flesh and the cold heights of *logos,* an opposition H. G. Wells ascribed to the Dubliner's incorrigible Catholicity, is actually more nearly akin to that insane dualism between spirit and matter which more than three centuries before Bruno was "terribly burned" led thousands of Albigensians to an odd theology, odder vices, and in the end to the stake. The comparison becomes a shade less fanciful when we consider the Gnostic props and mock-Platonic cosmogonies of *Ulysses* and *Finnegans Wake* together with the Docetic and anti-Marian Christology put into Stephen Dedalus's mouth. Like the

Christ of the Manichees, Stephen's Jesus only *appears* to live, suffer and die, only seems to be the child of Mary. He is really the ghostly son of God alone.

V

We can suppose that the Catholic Church had something to do with Joyce's interest in symbols, cycles, and correspondences. He was not moved Protestant-fashion by the "aesthetics" of Catholicism, but the effect of the liturgy on him is perceptible throughout his work and particularly noticeable as his writing matures. Church liturgy moves according to cycles, calling attention to the timelessness of the events commemorated without denying their historical character, their occurrence in real time. Symbolism and literalness coexist in the Mass, for in the reenacted sacrifice the crucial signs—bread and wine—are at one with the things signified, the body and blood of Christ. As a born Catholic, Joyce had less to suffer from that sense of loss of a community of symbols which marks the agnostic culture to which today he stands a hero. Unlike Yeats, he did not have to get up a symbolism from scratch out of Celtic myth or hermetic philosophy, although he was not above picking the pockets of both. Moreover, a case can be made for the hypothesis that Joyce's intense interest in cycles, palingenesis, metempsychosis, and the rest of the apparatus a critic might dismiss as metaphysical scaffolding, actually masks a view of life that is essentially religious. One of the two central doctrines of Christianity (the first is the Incarnation) is the Resurrection. Now there is no doctrine of resurrection in Greek philosophy, but two of its teachings approach it. The first is metempsychosis or transmigration of souls, which the early Fathers like Tertullian and Gregory of Nyssa acknowledged to be the nearest *philosophical* approximation to the religious teaching of the Resurrection. The other teaching is the Stoic doctrine of palingenesis or regeneration, according to which every cosmic epoch is the duplicate of one previously destroyed, so that every person who died in one world will be regenerated in all succeeding worlds. Metempsychosis, palingenesis, and finally resurrection itself mark the stages of Joyce's road from the opening of *Ulysses* to the close of *Finnegans Wake*. Yet it would be ingenuous to conclude that Joyce's symbolism and correspondence-apparatus have predominantly Catholic sources. His youthful epiphany technique is far closer to Yeats or even to Mallarmé than to Dante, and the allegories of his early stories are not very different from those of Ibsen's plays or the French naturalistic novel.

Fairly simple emblems and correspondences account for much of the "symbolism" in Joyce's earlier work. Mrs. Riordan's green and maroon velvet-backed hairbrushes stand for Parnell and Davitt. Eileen's cool white hands put Stephen in mind of the Virgin's litany (*"Tower of Ivory. House of Gold.* By thinking of things you can understand them"). Later, Stephen fashions the birds whose flight he watches into tokens of loneliness and exile. In *Ulysses*, his ashplant stick will become an augur's rod, Mr. Bloom's hard hat a warrior's helmet. Galoshes hint broadly of the bourgeois fussiness to which Gabriel Conroy of "The Dead" has fallen victim unaware; in this respect Gretta's husband reminds us a little of Andreyev's Professor Storytsin.

It is perhaps strange, but I, a book-man, a professor in galoshes, a learned bourgeois, a rider in trolley cars, I have always been dreaming of beauty.

The old priest's paralysis in "The Sisters," suggesting the spiritual torpor of Dublin, is the sort of allegorical touch Joyce found in his master Ibsen who used trolls, dollhouses, and bad drains to similar ends. Plagues are hard-worked allegorical devices—Mann's "collera morbous" and Camus's Oran *peste* are obvious examples—and Joyce adepts know that the plague which threatened in Ibsen's *An Enemy of the People* actually broke out in Joyce's first and unpublished drama *A Brilliant Career*.

But Joyce had under his hat far more than these simple naturalistic parallels. Already in "Grace" of *Dubliners* he had made a tentative move to attach the parts of the slight story to the monumental di-

visions of The *Divine Comedy*. In the *Portrait,* Stephen identifies himself not only with the classical Icarus-Daedalus pair but also with
Lucifer who, as Promethean hero, takes his proud stand against a
deity thundering and remote. All the world knows that in *Ulysses*
the "disconnected and incoherent" patterns in the lives of Stephen
Dedalus and the Blooms are traced by correspondence to characters
and adventures in Homer's *Odyssey.* The lid is off in *Finnegans Wake*
where Icarus's fate is recalled by the fortunate fall of H. C. Earwicker, the Dublin pub-keeper whose life blurs into myth as he is
assumed into timeless identity with heroes of earth and heaven. For
his pattern-correspondence method, Joyce proposed the label "two
plane" although the tag fits the machinery of *Ulysses* better than
the *Wake* where the technique is multiplane. Unknown to Joyce, Hopkins had adumbrated the two-plane device when he suggested that
certain passages of Greek drama are marked by counterpoint of an
explicit "overthought" and a hidden "underthought." That classical
art and poetry in the West depended for its existence on a body
of mythological reference is an almost self-evident generality. More
particularly it was a stock theory of nineteenth century romantics
that great art must take its departure from mythology, that the
artist must seek inspiration in myth and legend, preferably those of
his own land. But making a modern story double the pattern of
classical myth seems to be a mark of certain literature of our century,
a literature which prefers allegorical significance to social-class rele-
vance. Shaw's comedy *Pygmalion* which precedes *Ulysses* by ten
years has it both ways, but O'Neill's tragic *Mourning Becomes
Electra,* nearly a decade after the Joyce novel, deals with the abyss of
human consciousness rather than the problem of Reconstruction in
New England. French drama has been redoing mythology along
classical lines for centuries, but Cocteau felt compelled to be even
more explicit, riding the Tristan legend as well as Heraclitean-Nie-
tzschean palingenesis in his *L'Éternel retour.* ("We know," said the
animals to Zarathustra, "that you teach all things eternally return and
ourselves with them.") T. S. Eliot linked his own and his fellow
poet's liking for classical myth exemplified in the life and mind

of modern man to the breakdown of class structure. In re-creating Homer's *Odyssey* through the adventures of Leopold Bloom, says the author of *The Wasteland*, Joyce imposed myth on a society losing its order.

The names of Joyce's two big books are "archetypal"—Ulysses for Bloom, Finn-Finnegan for Earwicker who is actually referred to in the text as an "archtypt," as well as "avatar," "patternmind," and "paradigmatic ear." How much do mythological characters and situations that serve Joyce as patterns for his correspondences owe to C. G. Jung's archetypes? Jung himself seems to have gotten the term "archetype" from hermetic sources as well as from the Platonic tradition. As a source, his disciple Jolande Jacobi cites the *Corpus Hermeticorum* as well as the treatise of the Pseudo-Dionysius on the Divine Names, although it appears that the Zurich psychologist had Augustine's exemplars (*"ideae principles . . . rerum stabiles atque incommutabiles"*). Jung's archetypes are mythic patterns, symbols of universal human history, deriving from the experience of all humanity. They resemble Platonic Forms, but have this difference: rather than subsisting apart from the sensible world as deathless originals of which mortal things are but copies, they are immanent in the dark root-realm of the collective unconscious of mankind. But Jung's archetypes are not only psychological models; they are metaphysical too, since they transcend consciousness. They transcend cultures too. The archetypes are found as common themes in all the mythologies and religions of the world—the Fall, the burial and resurrection of the god, the Great Mother, the World Tree, Prometheus, Hercules, the Mage, and so on. Their therapeutic value, Jung believes, lies in the fact that we are permitted to reconcile our own particular fantasy life with these exemplars.

Joyce did not like Jung, who seems to have read *Ulysses* without cracking a smile. Although in desperation he allowed the Swiss psychoanalyst to treat his mentally ill daughter Lucia, Joyce rarely lost an opportunity to poke fun at Jung whom he called "the Swiss Tweedledum who is not to be confused with the Viennese Tweedledee, Dr. Freud," an attitude typified by the remark in *Finnegans Wake*, "we grisly old Sykos who have done our unsmiling bit on 'alices', when they were jung and easily freudened." In any case, the debt does not seem to be a large one. While the mythological apparatus of the *Wake* may owe a surface something to Jung's archetypes—the motif of the Fall is treated in the novel with a cousinly psychological-theological ambivalence—the Joycean myth-apparatus seems on the whole to have been constructed independently. Appearing first in *Dubliners* (faintly) and in the *Portrait* (noticeably), the myth-fact correspondence, powered by metemphychosis in *Ulysses*, runs on the wheels of Vico's cycle theory to death and resurrection in *Finnegans Wake*. "My imagination grows," said Joyce, "when I read Vico as it doesn't when I read Freud or Jung." Neither Odysseus nor Peer Gynt are listed among Jung's archetypes, yet the adventures of both these wanderers suggested to Joyce patterns he repeated in the peregrinations of L. Bloom. It was a Viconian Ibsen who set Peer complaining on a surprisingly Earwickean rubbish-heap:

Forward and back, and it's just as far; out and in, and it's just as strait. Time wears away and the river gnaws on. Go roundabout, the Boyg said; and here one must.

Joyce was rarely content to fasten a major character to a single original. Stephen of the *Portrait* is not yet Odysseus' son; in the sequel he is Telemachus and Hamlet too. The paternity motif in *Ulysses* has considerable structural as well as emotional import, and the role of Telemachus is too formal and minor to support the burden of Stephen's orphaned and homeless state. So the Hamlet correspondence is introduced to reinforce the Homeric parallel. In turn, the philosopher-prince's ambiguous relation to his father is doubled by Stephen's own inclination to the paternity doctrine of the heretic Sabellius who taught that it was not a Jesus of flesh who died on Calvary but a phantom of God the Father. "Who is the father of any son," asks Stephen, "that any son should love him or he any son?" To young Daedalus, who left the house of his father after the flesh, paternity may have a high place in the theological order as apostolic succession or mystic state. But in the human order, it is only a necessary evil.

"Bruno's philosophy," said Joyce, "is a kind of dualism . . . every power in nature must evolve an opposite to realize itself and opposition brings reunion." In *Ulysses* the center of gravity shifts from Stephen Dedalus to his opposite, Bloom, alter ego of Joyce's middle age as Stephen had been of his youth. Stephen, fatherless, is the theoretical man, his besetting sin pride, deadliest of the seven. His antithesis, Bloom, sonless, a practical man, is throughout the day stung by pangs of lust. Their respective adventures on the same day are played off against each other in a dialectical counterpoint that would have pleased Hegel. At midnight, in turbulent cricumstances, they experience a transient synthesis; they meet, then celebrate their reunion over cocoa in Bloom's house, while his recumbent wife Molly, drowsily willing to assume both men to herself, stirs restlessly in bed. In sixteen hours, Mr. Bloom has fled Calypso, left Polyphemus blinded, mused on Nausicaa, joined forces with his lost son, and returned himself to Penelope who, faithful to him in her left-handed fashion, grudgingly admits at close of day her husband's modest preeminence. Prudent, resourceful, never at a loss at critical moments, he is indeed Odysseus.

He is also the Wandering Jew. "Ahasuerus I call him," growls the Citizen. "Cursed by God." Bloom is hardly an "archetypal" Jew like Feuchtwanger's mage Rabbi Gabriel, nor yet a stage Jew like Zero Mostel. He lacks Jewish texture and feel. Baptized three times, he has been successively Protestant, Catholic, and free-thinking Mason. He also experiences Christlike transfigurations, and although he declares in Kiernan's bar that "Christ was a Jew like me," Jesus is not a Jewish exemplar. It seems clear that Bloom's Jewishness is an outward sign of his homeless and estranged condition, that his wanderings are those of a pilgrim with dubious prospects. Bloom is Gabriel Marcel's *homo viator*, "itinerant man." More modestly felt than Stephen's dramatic sense of exile, his state of alienation is none the less real and poignant. A misfit at home, in his job, and in gregarious Dublin, Bloom is an extraordinarily alert and noticing person, one of those *men on edge* of whom the author of *Jew Süss* wrote:

To be a Christian, that was to be one among many. But there was only one Jew for every six hundred Christians. To be a Jew, that meant to be despised, persecuted, humiliated, but also to be unique, always knowing that all eyes were upon one, always to be on the strain, tense, gathered up, every sense alive and on the alert.

Thus, Joyce's Bloom is one of the originals of the Jew as Outsider in the literature of our century. In him the romantic image of the Jew as special man widens until Jew turns into man-in-general. Glancing in a mirror, Bloom sees there "the image of a solitary mutable man"; "Everyman or Noman," he calls himself, an "allaround man." The point of such portrayals, says Mr. Leslie Fiedler with Kafka as well as Joyce in mind, is to suggest that "we live in an age of rootlessness, alienation, and terror, in which the exiled condition so long thought peculiar to the Jew comes to seem the common human lot." In Mr. Bloom's loneliness the nineteenth century alienation as estrangement from society fuses with the characteristically twentieth century estrangement from the world as a whole. The heroes of Kafka, Camus, Sartre, Nathanael West, Beckett, and the rest, discover themselves not only out of place in "bourgeois" society, but out of joint with the cosmos as well. With Melville's Ishmael they proclaim that We are all sadly cracked about the head, Presbyterians and pagans alike. Their alienation is more religious than social; their condition smells to high heaven of some aboriginal catastrophe fatal to the happiness of the human race. The Existentialists take this calamity to reside in the fact of existence itself. Graham Greene interprets it as original sin. Two clichés betray us, says the novelist whose special men tend to be policemen rather than Jews, "Isn't it a small world?" and "I'm a stranger here myself." Vigor, the Sûreté chief of *The Quiet American* reads Pascal to while away the time. It was this same Pascal who recognized the conviction of exile in his own soul as an indelible mark of the human condition:

Man knows not where he belongs. He is plainly astray and fallen from his proper place irrecoverably. He goes seeking it on all sides, anxiously, vainly, in impenetrable darkness.

Throughout his day, the roving Bloom is treated as a bothersome nonentity by his associates, yet occasionally Dubliners concede that he has something different or special about him. "He's not one of your common or garden . . ." says Lenehan. "There's a touch of the artist about old Bloom." His wife Molly admits his difference from the common run of men, contrasting his sensitivity with the coarseness of Boylan and his sort. Citizens witness his kindly acts, although only Nosey Flynn seems to remember them—"He has been known to put his hand down to help a fellow . . . O, Bloom has his good points." In the course of his day, Bloom performs many corporal works of mercy—he visits the sick, buries the dead, helps the blind, feeds animals, gives to charity, aids a widow, rescues a fatherless genius from harm and offers him a home. "Bloom's justness and reasonableness should grow in interest," said Joyce to Frank Budgen. "As the day wears on he should overshadow them all." Thus, as a good man, Bloom is corporal of the awkward squad of those virtuous misfits of the twentieth century English novel whose ranks include two good soldiers, also wife-bedeviled, Captain Tietjens and Major Scobie. Joyce critics rightly object that excessive attention to Bloom's "archetypal" connections—Odysseus, Christ, Ahasuerus, Parsifal, Sancho Panza, and so on—obscures those concrete and human qualities of prime interest to novel readers. In Bloom's case these qualities include kindness and modest dignity, as well as a certain steadfastness that marks him off from his nervous foster son, a humble courage that proves him a hero after all. Unlike Stephen (*vide* the "Circe" episode), Mr. Bloom is not paralyzed by the idea of death, not even when he visits Hades. Oddly enough, in this respect he resembles Mann's Castorp who dwells in the kingdom of the dead yet allows death no sovereignty over his thoughts. Yet for all his virtues, human and novelistic, for all as well the mass of specificities concerning him, Leopold Bloom remains a somewhat abstract figure;

in some queer way he is deficient on the substantial side. Joyce seemed to lack part of the old nineteenth century talent for character making in the round, the talent that makes *Buddenbrooks* and *A la recherche du temps perdu* such "novelistic" novels. It may be a deficiency he shares with Flaubert. Still, the fact that Bloom is not as three-dimensional as a Proust character may preserve in him a certain vitality. Swann, Odette, Oriane de Guermantes, and the Verdurins are already on their way, as Nathalie Sarraute says, to the vast waxworks where sooner or later all literary "types" end up. Stephen Dedalus, Joyce's single contribution to the show, is there now.

VI

In *Myth of the Eternal Return,* Mircea Eliade claims that primitive thought and action are archetypal. To prephilosophical man, the success of a projected action was guaranteed by making it conform to a pattern—"an object or act becomes real only insofar as it imitates or repeats an archetype." According to this view, Plato's dialectic is a sophisticated development of the premetaphysical belief that reality can be reached only through repeating or copying some changeless model. Moreover, by means of this imitation of archetypes in primitive cult, *time is abolished.* The devotee's rite and gesture, modeled on a paradigm given and fixed, are lifted up out of time, so that his act becomes one with the eternal. "The work of two of the most significant writers of our day—T. S. Eliot and James Joyce," says Eliade, "is saturated with nostalgia for the myth of eternal repetition and, in the last analysis, for the abolition of time." Belief that Joyce is committed to a time-abolishing technique is interesting in view of that fact that an older generation of critics tended to find in Joyce's writing a "new" concept of time, which they took to be typical of the time-conscious twentieth century. Edmund Wilson drew analogy between Joyce's novelties and the world views of Einstein and Whitehead. Wyndham Lewis held Bergsonism directly responsible for Joyce's Bloom and Proust's Charlus alike, insisting in *Time and Western Man* that

Without all the uniform pervasive growth of the time-philosophy starting from the little seed planted by Bergson . . . there would be no *Ulysses,* or there would be no *A la recherche du temps perdu. . . .* In short, Mr Joyce is very strictly of the school of Bergson-Einstein, Stein-Proust. He is of the great time-school they represent. His book is a *time-book. . . .* He has embraced the time-doctrine very completely.

Now Proust's exploitation of time may or may not owe something to Bergson. The whole question of the relation between Bergson and Proust needs clarifying, since the alleged philosophical connection between them has long been a critical commonplace. Wilson claimed in *Axel's Castle* (1931) that Proust had been deeply influenced by Bergson. Harry Levin supports the connection in *The Gates of Horn* (1963) where he describes Proust as "Bergson's pupil" with particular reference to the novelist's preoccupation "with the perpetual flow that carries all things away." Now in so far as Proust treats time (and he does so treat it) as a perpetual flow that carries all things away, he is no pupil of Bergson. Proust's attitude to time is pessimistic. Obsessed with the *destructive* aspect of the passage of things, he regards time, like the poets of the Greek Anthology as "a perpetual perishing." To Proust time is an aging, a hurrying toward death. But Bergson's concept of time is optimistic. For him, time is never a falling away; it is one with the creative flow of all things into new-ness. In the case of Joyce, the distinction is even clearer; there is nothing at all Bergsonian in Joyce's cyclical and archetypal chronometrics. True, Joyce plays on time as on an accordion. All of Odysseus' adventures are compressed, as we know, into sixteen hours of the same day in Dublin, and in one of the episodes the entire development of English prose style is jammed into forty paragraphs corresponding to the forty weeks of human gestation. The characters in *Ulysses* are rather anxious about the time of day, and those of *Finnegans Wake*—in which universal history is suitcased into one nights dream—display analogous concern:

What age is at? It saon is late. 'Tis endless now senne eye or erewone last saw Waterhouse's clogh. They took it asunder I hurd them sye. When will they reassemble it?

But insofar as Joyce's working metaphysic of time is archetypal, cyclic, Viconian, and metempsychotic, it stands in flat contradiction to the premise on which Bergson's philosophy (and Whitehead's too) is based. That premise is *time is real and cannot be abolished*. By time, of course, Bergson means not the abstract and mathematical clock time which the intellect constructs in order to measure the behavior of material bodies and mechanisms it scissors out of its environment in the effort to control matter in collision with living forms, but *duration,* change, the passage of things, the irreversible thrust of life pushing on to real newness. It is an aspect of authentic creation, not mere transformation of what is already there, a repetition of a pattern already given. According to Bergson, all Platonism is rooted in the false belief that *time is unreal.* For if the world of our experience is real only insofar as it copies or participates in eternal and unchanging Forms, then change is phenomenal only, and time belongs to the world of appearance. If the sensible world unrolls itself according to an archetypal plan, it follows that time is unreal, for the future is already a *fait accompli* on that higher level.

The notion that time is unreal has been vulgarized to the point of science fiction in our day. But men of speculative imagination of every age have been drawn to the idea that cosmic or cultural history does not move in a straight line, but in a circular or spiral pattern. Following the legendary teaching of Heraclitus, the Stoics held that the material of the universe combines and recombines in fire-punctuated cycles to produce recurring worlds. The Alexandrian metaphysics postulated a two-cycle rhythm, the *Proödos* or outgoing emanation from the One and Eternal Being, and the *Epistrophe,* the return of all things to God. In the high Middle Ages, mystics like Heinrich Suso were absorbed by the idea of the *Kuklos.* Jakob Boehme said: "The right man who is in contact with God knows no time. His time is alike a round crown which has no beginning and no end." The concept of the Eternal Return is a corollary drawn from the Greek philosophers' idea of mortal time as governed by the circular motion of the cosmos. Announcing that time came into being with the creation of the cosmos, Plato declared that the cosmos moved in a circle "because it was the most beautiful way in which to move."

Greek philosophy had no idea of time as evolutionary duration, real novelty, authentic future. Despite the new sense of history pressed into human consciousness by the Crucifixion, medieval philosophers continued to follow the astrophysics of Plato and Aristotle, a cosmology based on the concept that time is fundamentally the measure of the circular motion of the universe. Another Bruno—Bruno de Solages, rector of the Catholic Institute of Toulouse—reminds us of the metaphysical implications of this doctrine. "Necessity, an eternal necessity, regulated this clocklike Universe. The Eternal Return with its Great Year which puts into place all the pieces of the huge mechanism was included in this necessity, as were human events. . . ." When we transfer the cycle-concept from cosmic process to world cultures, we get philosophies of history, professional and amateur, based on the proposition that nothing new can ever really happen. The historian may be a Teutonic world-pessimist, Spengler:

It is, and has always been, a matter of knowledge that the expression-forms of world-history are limited in number, and that eras, epochs, situations, persons are ever repeating themselves true to type.

Or Missouri optimist, Harry S Truman:

I began to see that the history of the world has moved in cycles and that very often we find ourselves in the midst of political circumstances which appear to be new but which might have existed in almost identical form at various times during the past 6,000 years.

In *Science and the Modern World,* Whitehead points out that the recurrences of things are very obvious in our ordinary experience. Days recur, lunar phases recur, the seasons of the year recur, beats of the heart, breathing itself. Apart from this recurrence, the philosopher reminds us, knowledge would be impossible—for nothing could be referred to our past experience. In *Ulysses* Bloom is constantly struck by the quality of recurrence in things and events. He expects a new moon that night, and the thought recalls to him the full moon he saw a fortnight ago in the company of his wife. A moment before he had been thinking of the time-ball at Greenwich and this led him to brief despair of the possibility of human knowledge penetrating to the causes behind the astronomer's universe. "Gasballs spinning about, crossing each other, passing. Same old ding-dong always." As he leaves Gerty McDowell on the beach that evening, Bloom tells himself that he wants the new, yet admits that there is nothing new under the sun. "So it returns. Think you're escaping and run into yourself. Longest way round is the shortest way home." All the same, Joyce takes care to qualify his hero's conviction that all things repeat by providing him with occasional intuitions of *nonrecurrence*. Gazing down at the Liffey that morning from O'Connell Bridge, Bloom meditates briefly on nature as a Heraclitean flux: "How can you own water really? It's always flowing in a stream, never the same. Which in the stream of life we trace. Because life is a stream." That there is a sense in which time *is* real, that the past is irreparable and the future unpredictable is sadly borne in upon him by his memory of the clown and the florin, a recall that comes to him right after Stephen Dedalus has declined his paternal offer of a home. Bloom remembers how once at a circus a clown pretending to be looking for his father announced that Bloom was his papa. He remembers too the time he marked a florin with three notches and put it into circulation "for possible, circuitous or direct return." The ensuing catechism reads:

> Was the clown Bloom's son?
> No.
>
> Had Bloom's coin returned?
> Never.

Santayana declares that attention to the double experience of mutation and recurrence, concern for time which scatters all yet recreates, is exactly what we should expect of a poetic nature touched by philosophy:

> One of the first things . . . that impresses the poet, the man of feeling and reflection, is that these objects that people the world

all pass away, and that the place thereof knows them no more. Yet when they vanish, nothingness does not succeed; other things arise in their stead. Nature remains always young and whole in spite of death everywhere; and what takes the place of what continuously disappears is often remarkably like it in character. Universal instability is not incompatible with a great monotony in things; so that while Heraclitus lamented that everything was in flux, Ecclesiastes, who was also entirely convinced of that truth, could lament that there was nothing new under the sun.

In the end, Bloom realizes, as did Stephen earlier, that history repeats itself, but it does so with a difference.

The Eternal Return reappears with a bang in *Finnegans Wake* where cycles revolve like pinwheels, types pullulate. Even those sluggards who have never read Joyce's macaronic dream-book (who has?) know that it is the circular story of the troubled slumber of the family of a Dubliner named H. C. Earwicker, a Protestant of Scandinavian ancestry who keeps pub at Chapelizod on the far side of Phoenix Park. Earwicker's uneasy sleep is kin to death, his waking resurrection. In his dream the publican leaps to merge with hod carrier Tim Finnegan (artificer, master-builder, Dedalus) who, as the ballad goes, "fell from the ladder and broke his skull" only to rise again when rioters at his wake splash whiskey in his coffin. Finnegan's fall, signaled by the primordial thunderclap that scared the bejesus into man, is the crash of Humpty Dumpty (Earwicker's first name is Humphrey) doubled by the *chute* of Adam-Everyman (his initials stand for "Here Comes Everybody"), redoubled by the tumble of philosopher Giambattista Vico, upon whose cyclic-historical method the book itself is patterned. United in his dream to his precursor Tristan, Earwicker makes guarded love to his daughter Isobel (Iseult-la-Belle; "Chapelizod" is a corruption of "Chapelle d'Iseult"), expands with his twin sons Kevin and Jerry to Shem the Penman (James Joyce) and Shaun the Post (his brother Stanislaus), gives rise to a host of further polarities including Cain and Abel, the Mookes and the Gripes, the Ondt and the Gracehoper, Mick and Nick (St. Michael and Lucifer) and others *per omnia saecula saeculorum.* Earwicker is the Norse invader of ancient Ireland. By a commodius vicus of metempsychosis, he is also the Irish hero Finn MacCool (Finn again!) as well as a giant sleeping by the river Liffey (Mrs. Earwicker in bed beside him) Anna Livia. Finn is a god, winged and terrible, manifesting himself at the end when Anna rushes out to her cold mad feary father, the Sea. But all the while he is just an old man dreaming of the past, the moribund hero of a raffish *Dream of Gerontius,* Joyce's aged father recalling his prime and muttering "My God! the times we had!" Nietzsche, whose Zarathustra taught the Eternal Return, said that in sleep and dream we work through the whole task of former humanity. So Earwicker's restless subconscious, the psyches of his wife and children cooperating, widens to a magic theater wherein the drama of all human history is played—in the words of Sir Thomas Browne, "a shadow and hieroglyphical image of the whole world." History, young Dedalus had told Mr. Deasy, was a nightmare from which he was trying to awake. As Earwicker's stifled consciousness struggles to free itself from the womb of sleep, the ontogeny of the publican's dream recapitulates the phylogeny of historical man.

At the age of seven Giambattista Vico fell headfirst from the top of a ladder to the floor, fracturing his skull, and remained unconscious for five hours. Observing his broken cranium, the surgeon predicted that he would either die of it or grow up an idiot. "By God's grace," says the philosopher, "neither part of his prediction came true." As early as 1905 Joyce was reading "Mr. John Baptister Vickar" who has the job of producer in one of the side-dramas of *Finnegans Wake.* Already Vico Road (which goes round and round) had appeared in *Ulysses.* In Vico, Joyce found something more than a congenial crank. He fancied the rhetorician in the Neopolitan jurist, his passion for clarifying tropes, the etymological speculation so reminiscent of Plato's *Cratylus,* the careful attention to Homer—for Vico was the first to suggest plural authorship of the Homeric poems. Like Vico, Joyce was morbidly afraid of thunder, and found much to his taste the Italian's curious theory of the co-origin of religion and family. The primeval thunderclap strikes both shame and fear of God into the beast-man copulating in the open so that he drags his random woman into the protective darkness of a cave which thus becomes the first home, housing the first wife and family. In contrast to the rigid Natural Law abstractions of Grotius and Hobbes, Vico's *Scienza nuova* postulates a universal law (*Diretto universale*) which arises from the conscience of mankind, changing as human consciousness changes. Vico saw a three-stage pattern in human history—an age of gods, an age of heroes, an age of men. These patterns repeat themselves for we may see in modern history recurrences of forms found in the exemplar-states of Greece and Rome. "This is the nature of principles," said the philosopher, "that things begin and end in them." Every nation follows a *Storia ideale eterna,* "the ideal history traversed in time by every nation in its rise, development, maturity, decline, and fall." To the order of *history* corresponds the order of *language*: in the divine age, gestures and dumb show; in the heroic, heraldry and emblem; in the human, popular tongues. On the hypothesis of an ideal history is built the concept of a mental language common to all nations. Confidently Vico looked forward to a pan-etymological dictionary of thought-words, a sort of rhetorical counterpart of Leibniz's dreamed-of universal and symbolic language. "Such a lexicon is necessary," said Vico, "for learning the language spoken by the ideal eternal history traversed in time by the histories of all nations."

The sometime Berlitz professor constructed his own ideal language for *Finnegans Wake.* He had approached it in the last third of *Ulysses.* Now he relentlessly crams portmanteau words with multiple meanings to achieve a verbal polyphony. A Viconian thunder roll announces Humpty-Earwicker's accident, and the Augustinian cry "O foenix culprit!" (O felix culpa!) echoes with endless reverberations in double—sad for Earwicker-Adam's fall, glad since it means eventual resurrection. ("O fortunous casualitas!") The *Wake* divides itself into four parts, the first three corresponding to the Viconian divine, heroic, and human ages respectively, the fourth a *ricorso* or dissolution of epochs so that the others may begin all over again. Subdivisions of the book are governed by this four-part cycle, the naturalistic genesis of which is the four-walled Earwicker bedroom. On one of the walls hangs a chromo of St. Michael and Satan that sparks the dream fight between Mick and Nick. In the course of the night the walls widen to the four provinces of Ireland, which give rise in turn to the four Evangelists, the fourth (Johnny McDougal) always lagging a little behind his Synoptic colleagues, Mat Tarpey, Mark Lyons, Luke Gregory. The narrative scheme of the *Wake* proceeds *circolarmente,* the last sentence:

A way a lone a last a long the

running into the first,

river run, past Eve and Adam's, from swerve of shore to bend of bay, brings us by a commodius vicus of recirculation back to Howth Castle and Environs.

Dreaming herself the river Liffey, patient Mrs. Earwicker traverses the ages of man in Viconian recurrence from the time of our first parents to the present, returning to her husband (as the river she sees him as Dublin Castle on the hill of Howth) when she wakes up. As Earwicker swings perilously through history that night, taking off from trapeze bars provided by the homely details of his waking life, the great bell of the Eternal Return vibrates to changes on "Teems of times and happy returns. The seim anew." Joyce urges his readers to mount their "wholemole mill-wheeling vicociclometer" and measure the dream miles rolled off by their "bisexicles" as they ride down the Vico road which "goes round and round to meet where terms begin." But the stouthearted reader must pedal hard Wonderland-fashion even to hold his own. At one point Shaun the Postman travels backward in the night through the events already narrated; his journey is marked by the Stations of the Cross, but it's really only a beer barrel drifting down the Liffey. For a reader's guide, Shaun himself suggests we read *Through Hell with the Papes* by "Denti Alligator." But *Finnegans Wake* has more circles than the Florentine exile's *Inferno*.

Of course, Joyce wildly exaggerates the "circular" aspect of Vico. That section of *Scienza nuova* titled "The Recurrence of Human Things" is the shortest of the work's five books. The corso-ricorso examples offered by Vico are modest, nearly all of them limited to *ad hoc* comparisons involving reference to the exemplar states of Greece and Rome, contrasted with the preceding ages of barbarism. The philosopher says little about cycles beyond identifying as "cyclical poets" those marketplace singers who chanted Homeric and other epics to "the base and large circle" of vulgar listeners mentioned by Horace in *Ars Poetica*. Even a superficial reading of Vico will show that Joyce took from the eccentric historiographer whatever suited him for the peculiar purpose of his own work at hand. The basic historical motif of *Finnegans Wake* is simple to the point of ingenuousness. We can find it in the Santayana lines on transiency and rebirth, or at the close of a Soviet war novel where the bright convolvulus twines itself upward through the hollow eye socket of a German skull lying on the Russian plain. Joyce found it in Edgar Quinet's sentence which is quoted in French in the "homework" section of the *Wake:*

Today as in the time of Pliny and Columella the hyacinth flourishes in Wales, the periwinkle in Illyria, the daisy on the ruins of Numantia; while around them cities have changed their masters and their names, collided and smashed, disappeared into nothingness, their peaceful generations have crossed down the ages as fresh and smiling as on the days of battle.

To distract attention from a simple sentiment, as well as to show off their erudition, Alexandrian sophisticates used to lace a poem with elaborate acrostics and make it read the same forward as back. In *Finnegans Wake,* Joyce covers up his simple sentiment with Himalayan hen-scratchings.

That dream-book is a *Heldenleben.* Not only does it commemorate Finn and through him the lives of all heroes, but it also celebrates itself and its author James Joyce under his alias Shem the Penman (Jim the Penman; Sheamus à la Plume) lest the reader be at a loss as to "who in hallhagal wrote the durn thing anyhow." Like Strauss's monster autobiographical tone poem, the *Wake* quotes with unabashed approval themes from the artist's earlier works, particularly his "ulylessly unreadable Blue Book of Eccles," and makes fun of the critics who may take the whole thing as

> The muddest thick that was ever heard dump.

As forger, Shem, the poet of the *Wake,* groans over his hermetic task in language that recalls the grim writing-machine to which the doomed of Kafka's penal colony are condemned:

the first till last alshemist wrote over every square inch of the only foolscap available, his own body, till be corrosive sublimation one continuous present tense integument slowly unfolded all marrvoicing moodmoulded cyclewheeling history.

Finnegans Wake constantly talks about itself, and this reflexive principle is carried through in the treatment of the words that compose it. For these words are meant to be taken both in their formal and material suppositions: not only are they carriers of multiple meanings ("in universal, in polygluttural") but they are also intended as objects interesting and valuable in themselves. Sometimes the effects are no more than tricks left over from *Ulysses*. Joyce used two hundred devices of classical rhetoric to make "Aeolus" windier, but twice that many river names make Anna Livia no wetter. Many of Joyce's second-order sound effects creak like Strauss's wind machine—"How mielodorous is thy bel chant, O songbird, and how exqueezit thine after draught!" Other touches, like the line that closes Earwicker's tavern, mingling a ship's sailing with the pub customers' stepping out into the clean night air, still hold a bit of the old charm we associate with Stephen's meditation on the protean strand:

> Now follow we out by Starloe.

Joyce's claque, encouraged by the master himself who entertained an exalted opinion of his last work's tonal value ("It's pure music!"), have made much of the melodic side of *Finnegans Wake*. But such testaments to the musical quality of the book generally end alike by floating downriver with Anna Livia Plurabelle.

"To all save a few learned and imaginative philologists," says W. H. Gardner, "the greater part of *Finnegans Wake* must remain an alluring enigma." Gogarty, less tolerant, presses a charge of deliberate irrationalism against Joyce, "This arch-mocker in his rage would extract the Logos, the Divine Word or Reason from its tabernacle, and turn it muttering and maudlin into the street." But Joyce's fault, if it is fault, lies not in irrationality, but in his excessive, almost theological rationalism. The entire surface of *Finnegans Wake* is tied up into tight hieratic little knots, left for the reader to pick loose. This done, bit by bit the entire intelligible structure— supposed to be apprehended as a simultaneity—discloses itself. Consider the short sentence from the "Letter" chapter that Mr. A. Walton Litz has so skillfully pulled apart:

From quiqui quinet to michemiche chelet and a jambebatiste to a brulobrulo!

"Qui qui" (Who? what?) is meant to remind the reader of the first of Vico's ages, the first questionings of the infant race of man. "Quinet" is Edgar Quinet, French historian, reader of Vico, outcast from the Sorbonne, and author of the key flowers-in-the-ruins passage cited above. Among its other signification, "michemiche" is a variant form of the leitmotiv "mishe mishe" ("I am I am") announced on the book's first page, and is linked with the second part of the Viconian cycle, the heroic. Taken with "chelet," "michemiche" gives us the name of Michelet, a second French historian and Vico's translator. The *individual* significance of the third stage of the Viconian cycle is death (the first is birth, the second, marriage) and the words "jambe" and "batiste" evoke the picture of cloth-covered legs, the shrouded body at the wake, while taken together they form the first name of Giambattista Vico. The four-part cycle is closed by "brulobrulo" *(brûler)* suggesting the hot fate of heretic Bruno as well as the destruction that must precede resurrection in the Viconian order.

The necessity for such scholarly decoding exasperates even those well disposed to Joyce, and his counsel of patience in the *Wake* ("above all things else we must avoid anything like being or becoming out of patience") usually falls on deaf ears. Joyce's notorious remark to Max Eastman that he expected his readers to put a lifetime on his works is another version of Beethoven's legendary reply to his violinist who complained that he found the A minor quartet unplayable: *"Schuppanzigh, do you think I write my quartets for you and your puling fiddle?"* Like the old Dalai Lama in Fosco Maraini's *Secret Tibet* (the *Wake* too is a Book of the Dead) Joyce felt the demons and the serpentiform gods squatting on his severe and powerful shoulders, requiring those who would read and understand him to share the burden. Everyone agrees that *Finnegans Wake* is excessive. But Thomas Mann's words apply: "It is better to ruin a work and make it useless for the world than not to go to the limit at every point."

Finnegans Wake took Joyce seventeen years to complete. *Ulysses* needed only the Biblical seven, while the earlier and relatively brief *Portrait* took ten years of intermittent writing. Of the three novels, the *Portrait* is strikingly compact, a White Dwarf in the Joycean galaxy compared to the Red Giants, its more diffuse successors. The *Portrait* lends itself without diminution to high school reading lists and off-Broadway dramatizations, as well as to those "meinherrs from Almany" who still grope "for deephid meanings in the depth of the buckbasket." ("For the people gay pictures," said Goethe, specifying two conditions of a masterpiece, "for the *cognoscenti* the mystery behind.") *Ulysses* stands as a mountain landmark, far less difficult now to climb and conquer than it once seemed. While those of its sections governed by artificial style give less pleasure now than they promised, the greater part of Bloom's story *reads* splendidly. Unfortunately the same cannot be said of *Finnegans Wake*. True, the grand design of this outrageous masterpiece has never been topped— the humble publican kicked up through a series of successively exalted types till he reaches the high rung as H. C. Everybody, the "homogenius man." The world of humanity does indeed owe Joyce the tribute he demanded "for having placed on the planet's melomap his lay of the vilest bogeyer but most attractive avatar the world has ever had to explain for." The execution of the complex blueprint plans of the dream-book, the mutual support and balance of the "simultaneous" section-forms is achieved with complete security and cunning. The rub lies in the matter poured into these forms. Some of this material is delightful, but these are the very parts, hacked out of the text in large chunks and small bites, that Joyce fans hold up over and over again—the opening scene, the closing monologue, Anna Livia, Shaun's sermon, and two or three other familiar parts. Throw in as well all the fine short clips and snatches from the entire holus-bolus:

> And not all the king's men nor his horses
> Will resurrect his corpus
> For there's no true spell in Connacht or hell
>   (bis)   That's able to raise a Cain.

Admirable! But so much of the content of the dream-book seems no more than *fill* for its "moodmoulds," an interminable piling of dump-heap junk to keep Earwicker's tiresome hen busy forever scratching over bits and scraps, old bedsprings, stained mattresses, broken shamrock pots, parts of lamps, tattered Missals, rusty pumps, torn Irish flags, dog-eared jokebooks, discarded trusses, tin cans, "stinkend pushies"—all strictly controlled, of course, by Joycean laws of association. The Dubliner seems to have counted too much on the grand design of his book to carry the weight of the prodigious litter he piled into it, as "Denti Alligator" before him relied on the strength of his *Divine Comedy*'s intricate structure to support its multiplicities of parochial feuds and Florentine gossip. Great though he is, Joyce is an imperfect Dante. For all the talk of its "music," the greater part of *Finnegans Wake*—before or after decoding—*does not read well*. It is also susceptible to a peculiar misuse. Joyce quite properly insisted that the *Wake* is, after all, a funny book ("It's supposed to make you laugh!"), but the laughter it raises too often reminds us of those self-conscious guffaws at foreign films by members of the audience anxious that others should know *they* got the joke. It's a dubious tribute to Joyce that the dream-book of H. C. Earwicker has been turned into a new *Alice in Wonderland*, a pandemonium of arch epigraphs, an inexhaustible source of coy asides for generations of academic Mrs. Minivers to come.

VII

Joyce revised Aristotle, steeled his soul in the school of old Aquinas. *Exiles* has been called the first existentialist play, *Ulysses* a metaphysical joke, and *Finnegans Wake* a poetic version of Wittgenstein ("The Fall is All that is the Case"). Joyce has been compared to his own favorite para-philosophers—Bruno, Vico, Cusanus—as well as to the Irish epistemologist Berkeley, the archdruid defeated by St. Patrick at the end of the *Wake*. Even *Time* magazine made of Joyce an Augustine "dying at the close of the Roman world to the echo of Vandal swords against the city gates." If we were to take Joyce *seriously* as a metaphysician—as George Moore insisted we must—the obvious choice of his exemplar would be Plato, a "Gnawstick" Plato adept in magic. The vision-epiphanies of his characters, their participation in eternal forms and mythical paradigms, their souls' transmigration in a world where the unreality of time is proved by the Eternal Return—all this is standard Gnostic-Platonic machinery to which Joyce was instinctively attracted. His hero, the gyrovague Bruno, preferred the Grand Artificer of hermetic Platonism to the *Primum Mobile* of Aristotle and Dante. Joyce himself compared his task of constructing *Finnegans Wake* to the cosmic job of the Demiurge of the *Timaeus*. Stephen Dedalus's exaltation of *stasis* or "arrest" as the supreme condition of the emotions in the aesthetic state recalls the *"nunc stans"* Schopenhauer associated with the Platonic Ideas, and we may fancy this quality confirmed by the peculiarly static impression conveyed by Joyce's writings that led critic Harry Levin to compare the Dubliner's art to frozen gargoyled cathedrals and mummified Pompeiis. To Arland Ussher, who sees in Joyce "a hyperborean incarnation of Plato," Leopold Bloom resembles less the wily Odysseus than he does the Platonic Socrates.

Yet it was Aristotle, not Plato, who made the point that poetry differs from history in that the former deals with the universal while the latter treats of the particular. At the same time he maintained against Plato, his teacher, that the universal can never be separated from the particular. Joyce's elaborate construction of types and correspondence for his characters and their adventures is *his* peculiar way of handling that old problem with which every poet must deal— how to make the particular manifest the universal, without causing the particular to lose its particularity. To Joyce, the supreme interest and value of any *this* did not lie in some separated *that,* however transcendent and superior the *that* may have been. It is not what Mr. Bloom stands *for* that makes him valuable, nor what Dublin *represents* that counts first. "For myself, I always write about Dublin," he told Arthur Power, "because if I can get to the heart of Dublin I can get to the heart of all the cities of the world. *In the particular is contained the universal.*" At any rate, this is true of *Ulysses* and remained part of Joyce's program in the making of *Finnegans Wake.* ("When a part so ptee does duty for the holos we soon grow to use of an allforabit.") Still, when we get into Earwicker's nightmare, the scale so nicely balanced in *Ulysses* shoots wildly up toward the universal and Platonic Idea. Under the double load of too much taken, whiskey and archetypes, the publican nearly suffocates in his sleep.

When George Russell or Yeats meditated on an esoteric or metaphysical doctrine, they did so with the question, "Is it true?" in mind, and persuaded themselves that it was. Joyce was less naïve in these matters. To him an idea had value only insofar as it served the work he had at hand. His question was not "Is it true?" but "Can I use that?" To some this may raise a status problem about the metaphysical or mythological analogues in Joyce's books. Are they Wittgenstein ladders to be kicked away when deemed of no further use to the climber? Is the Homeric correspondence of *Ulysses* a scaffolding only, the gantry supporting a rocket which will not need it in flight? (If so, why Joyce's fidelity to matching minutiae that recalls the dead-leaf butterfly's habit of carrying out its disguise to micro-

scopic and unnecessary detail?) Or is the *Odyssey* an integral part of
Bloom's situation on that ever more rapidly receding day of June
16, 1904? Does the Viconian cyclometer of *Finnegans Wake* do
anything more than stabilize, as it would a rolling ship, the historical
dream of H. C. Earwicker? Or is it part of that dream? Did Joyce
take Vico *seriously*? We know that when asked if he believed the
Scienza nuova was true, Joyce replied that he did not believe in any
science. Admitting that Vico and Bruno had stimulated his imagination far more than Jung or Freud, he said to Harriet Weaver, "I
would not pay overmuch attention to these theories beyond using
them for all they are worth." In the end, the status of Joyce's metaphysical references is as equivocal as that of Dame Philosophy
herself in the Middle Ages. To medieval theologians, philosophy was
a handmaiden (*ancilla*) and in this way myth and cosmology stood to
Joyce. But a handmaiden has instrumental value, as well as a certain autonomous worth of her own. Stephen Dedalus would recall
Aquinas' saying that an angel and a stone together are worth more
than an angel alone. Unless he were as drunk as he was on his death-
day, Tim Finnegan would never kick a ladder away. How would he
get down?

Simone Weil shrewdly observes that morality lies not in judgment,
but in attention. At the close with *Finnegans Wake* as well as at the
beginning with *Dubliners*, we find in Joyce's art a detached concern
for the troubled lives of ordinary people, a certain caring, at once
intent and remote, for the basic things of the human routine—birth,
marriage, work, sleep, death—the essentials which give to human life
its authentic cyclical rhythm. Such is his material, lifted up (*sursum
corda!*), transmuted, changed to make a story of it—but not "ideas"
at all, unless they serve him to his end. An artist who had to contend
in himself with both softening sentiment and deathlike coldness, Joyce
is most human when he touches the note of loneliness: Not the theatrical isolation of the existentialist hero, nor even the banishment of the
artist, the exile of the exceptional man—his own Stephen Dedalus,
his earlier self—but the loneliness of the ordinary man, the usual
couple, man and wife, their kissing days over, lying together in the

same bed, yet worlds apart, both lifted up in sleep by the flow of that stream bearing them on to death. Joyce totally lacks Mauriac's confidence that a key to the enigma exists, that each tear counts, each drop of blood. In the depths of Earwicker's night, a heart's wail pierces the muddled gloom:

> A cry off
> Where are we at all?
> and whenabouts in the name of space?
> I don't understand.
> I fail to say.
> I dearsay you too.

Once, the quality "philosophical" meant a disposition of the mind such as the ancient Stoics cultivated—attention to the inevitable ways of nature and life, accommodation of oneself to them with a soul untroubled by time and death, noting all things, marveling at nothing. Toward the close of the "Anna Livia Plurabelle" section of the *Wake,* we hear the muffled voice of a philosophical poet, the Stoic Valéry: "Der went is rising." We know the rest: *Il faut tenter de vivre!* There are the graves, the cold, and the eternal sea. But one must try to live.

2

André Gide

André Gide

᳓ *The role of ideas is to remain in the
service of beauty.*

Le Roi Candaule

ON THE SECOND of April, 1952, a little more than a year after Gide's death, the Holy Office in Rome issued a decree:

IN FULL ASSEMBLY OF THE SUPREME SACRED CONGREGATION OF THE HOLY OFFICE, THEIR EMINENCES THE LORDS CARDINALS CHARGED WITH THE CARE OF THOSE THINGS PERTAINING TO FAITH AND MORALS, AFTER A VOTE OF THE MOST REVEREND LORDS COUNSELLORS, CONDEMNED ALL THE BOOKS OF ANDRÉ GIDE AND ORDERED THEM PLACED IN THE INDEX OF PROHIBITED BOOKS.

The Vatican's *Osservatore Romano* added a comment: "The bitterness of this post-mortem condemnation will perhaps come unexpectedly and crushingly today, but it owes this to the fact that it now becomes irrevocable. Now that the author is dead, his work remains unchanged, henceforth fixed in its final aspect: in that way it is forever immutable, just as the author's face became rigid in death. . . . Gide's work from beginning to end is altogether orchestrated on a note of equivocal seduction, so consistent a note that it eventually bores and nauseates. Generations of young people came under his treacherous fascination; things which, before him would scarcely have been whispered among mature people became through Gide's fault a sort of boast—a filthy boast—of adolescents. He invented a way of negating Christ, taking advantage of chosen words of the Gospel, even quoted in Latin and as a sort of musical motif, and of attacking the Church while remaining in her very sanctuary. . . . André Gide, with that strength and sweetness of voice that occasionally recalls the loftiest voice of noblest France, dared to reduce to a problem whatever was most certain, most unalterable, most respectable—not indeed to come back to it and assert it with greater force and novelty, but with the purpose of shamelessly negating it and of damaging himself without infamy, thereby making for himself fame, an income, a prize."

The condemnation provoked appropriate shudders all over the Western world. Right-thinking people had forgotten that the Holy Office had survived the Inquisition, indeed that it *is* the Inquisition.

Even Graham Greene wrote to the *London Times,* "In common with many other Catholics, I have little regard for the Index in the rare cases when it deals with imaginative writing. The Roman Index is not an infallible document and sometimes makes mistakes as absurd and regrettable as British judges, juries and magistrates." Others recalled *Osservatore*'s oddly similar arraignment of Shelley (Gide had noted it in his *Journal* of 1931), regretting that "the little poet who had a gift for turning out erotic lines" had been born at all, since, had he not existed, "poetry would have lost but little, and great scandals would have been avoided." Most critics of Gide's condemnation accused Rome of sour grapes. She had angled so long for this precious soul whose capture had eluded the most zealous efforts of Claudel, Maritain, and the rest. With François Mauriac, she had hoped to the very end that the writer of *Les Caves du Vatican* would find some goat path to heaven. But now death had snatched this Christ-loving pagan from her grasp forever, and she could no longer control her anger. Mauriac, sad that "this elderly Faust who is so dear to us, should fix himself permanently in the definitive affirmation that man must be put in place of God," declined to associate himself with Gide's condemnation in this world or the next. To a journalist who asked him after Gide's death where he thought the incorrigible poet was now, the author of *River of Fire* replied, "I don't know. But wherever he is, it must be very interesting."

Unlike Gide's works, the writings of James Joyce—renegade Catholic, blasphemer, and scatologue—have never come under the Church's official ban. Indeed *Osservatore Romano* found things to praise in *Finnegans Wake,* contrasting its "spirituality" with the realism of the naturalistic novel. The most reverend Lords Cardinals had not read Joyce's youthful broadside, "The Holy Office," and even if they had, would have cared little, since the ribald verses in no serious way touched faith or morals. But if Joyce had the longer rope from the Church, he had the shorter life. A glance at the "extremities" in each writer's case underlines the measure of the Frenchman's span. When little James Augustine was born in 1882, André-Paul-Guillaume, already thirteen, had composed poetry, glossed piously on the New Testament, vowed himself to a life of holiness in the company of his beloved cousin Madeleine Rondeaux, yet was even then convinced the devil had his eye on him. Gide's young immoralist Michel breaks through his cerements twelve years before Stephen Dedalus spurns the graveclothes of boyhood. At Joyce's death in 1941, André Gide had still a decade of life ahead of him. Taste and temperament separated the two poets as well as culture and family background. Of the works of Gide he knew, Joyce cared only for *Lafcadio* and *The Pastoral Symphony*. For his part, Gide had no firsthand acquaintance with the Irishman's writings, although after reading Louis Gillet's book on Joyce in 1942 he wrote for *Figaro* an imaginary interview in which the characters discuss Joyce's "deformation" of language. Philosophies of history, Viconian or otherwise, made no appeal to Gide who claimed for himself an anti-historical nature. Although he loved Nietzsche, Gide found the doctrine of the Eternal Return abhorrent, and took Zarathustra's "Great Year" as a sign of the philosopher's incipient madness, an unverifiable hypothesis betraying a need of afterlife and eternity. Besides, the teaching of *l'éternel retour* contradicted one of Gide's favorite beliefs—he did not find it inconsistent with his "antihistorical" inclinations—the importance and reality of *progress*. "That resumption *ab ovo* of the long destiny of our 'earth',' he says of the Nietzschean cycle theory, "makes all progress illusory. And history cannot . . . begin all over again without the course of events being fatal." Gide insisted that his inbred bias against "history" was early reinforced by his youthful contact with the Symbolists, and the otherworldly atmosphere of Mallarmé's salon. Michel of *The Immoralist* turns his back on a historian's career; to him history means "books and ruins" and in the course of his moral Cartesianism he ends by avoiding both. "The noblest monuments of the past," says Michel in words that recall Quinet's ageless Numantian daisies and Illyrian periwinkles, "were less to me than those sunken gardens of the Latomie whose lemons have the sharp sweetness of oranges—or the shores of the Cyane, still flowing among the papyri as blue as on the day when it wept for Proserpine."

To his lack of historical sense, Gide attributed his distaste for politicians and social problems. At the age of twenty-four he set himself a rule that suggests Mann's nonpolitical Castorp, "Never indulge in politics and almost never read the newspapers." Toward the end of the First World War a quarter-century later he says, "To tell the truth, political questions do not much interest me." Twenty-two years after that he confides to his *Journal:* "The Social Question! . . . If I had encountered that great trap at the beginning of my career, I should never have written anything worth while." But, unlike Joyce, Gide never felt easy about his lack of interest in social questions. His sensitivity to the colonial exploitation of Negroes he saw on his Congo journey and his awkward descent into (and hasty climb out of) the public arena as a "comrade of the U.S.S.R." was evidence of his bad conscience toward the realm of social and political reform. Joyce was the true nonpolitical, perhaps the only great writer of the twentieth century who was from first to last totally indifferent to social questions—except as they might affect him personally.

Joyce's self-imposed exile involved a permanent pulling up of stakes, while Gide's African wanderings were like those of his Persephone, cyclic in character, going down year by year to a strange and delicious lower world—yet always returning to the sphere of light. Joyce had his Nora with him wherever he settled—Trieste, Zurich, Paris. Gide left Madeleine at Cuverville, although he felt like a man leaving part of his heart. In his youth, Joyce exploited his differentness from his schoolmates, rejecting neither the role of Byronic outlaw nor that of misunderstood genius. The young Gide complained of estrangement. *"Je ne suis pas pareil aux autres,"* he had sobbed to his mother as a child, "I am not like the others." But—as Klaus Mann points out—the time when words like "estrangement" and "solitude" and "isolation" appeared most often in Gide's writing was the most social time in his life. Gide knew everybody. His personal charm and talent, a certain gregariousness and love of "visiting"—later reinforced by prestige and editorial power—turned the list of his friends and guests into an almanac of *fin de siècle* and twentieth century literature—Mallarmé, Wilde, D'Annunzio, Claudel, Valéry, Proust, Thomas Mann, Malraux, and the others. To refuse a favor went hard with him. An article, a fore-word, an essay to be translated, a tribute to a musician, a preface for a new poet or catalogue of Polish art, were distractions for which he seemed almost grateful. The gentle phrases ("With all my heart . . . I am glad to . . . this small favor . . .") flutter down ungoverned by the rule that rings sternly through Joyce's correspondence—"I never write articles."

To Joyce, the novel is the end to which everything else is a means. Gide is a novelist only by the way. The Germans distinguish between the poet or creative writer *(Dichter)* and the man of letters *(Schrift-steller)* and never tire of telling how often the two are found com-bined in their great men from Goethe to Thomas Mann. Joyce is all *Dichter,* all poet. His "articles" belong to his youth. Gide's poetic gift is major, but tends to diffuse itself—appearing in concentrated form early in his career, later mingling with his "writing" in general, leavening it, lending to it the style and tone we associate with all his work. Gide's purely creative pieces tend to be of small dimen-sions. *The Return of the Prodigal Son* is a flawless miniature. We know that he did not consider books like *The Immoralist, Strait Is the Gate,* and *Pastoral Symphony* big enough to deserve the honorific title "novel." He called them *"récits"* instead, reserving *"roman"* for *The Counterfeiters,* his one all-out try at a large-scale work of fiction. Jean Hytier, whose commentary on Gide follows attentively the master's pronouncements on his own work, says that it is debatable whether Gide is a novelist at all. Like Gide, he holds that the novel should be of complex form, an affair of multiple destinies, a "meta-physics of the intelligence, regarding that pleasure proper to it as an intellectual pleasure." Thus defined, the novel stands in contrast to the more modest *"récit,"* a tale marked by no proliferation of episodes but rather by a singleness of contour, a simple *donné.* Of course, there is a certain arbitrariness in such a dichotomy. Before the word "novel" was applied to prose epics or to multivolumed chronicles of manners, it meant a short tale set within a larger work such as the parts of the *Decameron* or the story of Cupid and Psyche in Apuleius' *The Golden Ass*. In this sense, it is possible to define the novel etymologically rather than by length or complexity. A novel, *(Novelle)* Goethe remarked to Eckermann, should be about some unusual ("novel") event.

Gide and Joyce both were drawn to mythological themes, but handled them in quite different ways. From his childhood, the author of *Philoctetes* loved what he called "The Greek Legend," one of two teachings whose virtue he deemed inexhaustible. (The other was Christ's doctrine.) He admired the gods and heroes of Greece, applauding their initiative, their capacity for gratuitous action. But Gide never used the myth as *apparatus*. He was satisfied to update the old characters—Prometheus, Candaules, Oedipus, Theseus—to conform to the simple requirements of a moral fable, elegantly turned, but with a thorn left in it. There is no gigantism in Gide; his work has neither labyrinths nor multiple "levels." He owns no arsenal of symbols, no booby traps to shoot off plural meanings under his reader's nose. His language is chaste and flawless French, his symbols (if we now speak of the whole of his work) are graceful emblems—for fidelity, an amethyst cross; for conscience, a gnawing eagle; for moral falsity, counterfeit coins. Yet near the close of life the aged Gide designated the same symbol of the artist that young Joyce chose at the outset of his career. "Icarus," Gide says in *Theseus*, "Icarus was, before his birth, and remains after his death, the image of man's disquiet, of the impulse to discovery, the soaring flight of poetry—the things of which, during his short life, he was the incarnation. . . ."

Companion of Symbolists and *l'art pour l'art* men, auditor of Mallarmé's Thursdays, himself poet and critic of literature, André Gide quickly earned and kept throughout his life the reputation of moralist. It was a character he was anxious to decline. In the preface to *The Immoralist* he claims that he has not tried to prove anything by that ambiguous little work, only to paint his picture well and stand it in a good light. "In art," he says, "there are no problems—that are not sufficiently solved by the work of art itself." At thirty-five, he still maintains—as did his Ménalque, Oscar Wilde, decades before—that ethics is but an annex to aesthetics. Near fifty, he insists that his work can be judged soundly only from the aesthetic point of view. At sixty, he compares those who look for moral messages in works of art to certain prostitutes who before giving themselves ask, "How much is your little gift?" *("At once my first impulse is to get away!")* Nevertheless two generations of young students of university age rose to what Klaus Mann calls Gide's "moral leadership." For twenty years, initiate and sensitive souls in France as well as many beyond her borders took the dithyrambic *Fruits of the Earth* to their young hearts as a testament of grace and of personal liberation. From *The Notebooks of André Walter* of 1891 to the between-wars *Counterfeiters,* Gide played pied piper variations on the theme of abandonment to forbidden pleasure, counterpointing with injunctions to self-transcendence and even sobs of Christian renunciation. The youth of France followed him—at least, those with spirit. Their elders too believed in the reality of Gide's moral influence, but considered it pernicious. *"La Nature a horreur du Gide,"* punned Henri Béraud who had read *Corydon.* "His work is the most flagrantly unpunished intellectual and moral scandal of the century," said René Johannet in *La Revue Française.* In 1940, the Vichy-controlled *Le Temps* denounced Gide as a public danger by reason of his influence over youth, citing two of his books, *The Immoralist* and *The Treatise of the Narcissus*—published respectively thirty-eight and forty-nine years before—and Gide noted with satisfaction that accusations of *corrumpere juventutem* are more likely than praises to assure fame. In Germany, after it was plain he would not lend himself to their plans, Nazis proscribed his work. Even in America, and as late as 1953, Agnes Meyer—liberal newspaper publisher and disciple of John Dewey—wrote of Gide: "His magnificent style is proof that literary genius can result from a dominating love of evil. . . ." Mrs. Meyer was contrasting Gide with Claudel whose style, she says, springs from love of good. That same Claudel, once Gide's friend and correspondent, lived to denounce him as a poisoner: "How many letters have I not received from young men who have gone astray! At the beginning of their downfall there is always Gide."

It is often said that the French expect moral instruction from their poets, whom they tend to regard as authorities more reliable than politician or priest. The last two have their *parti pris,* while the artist is still free to choose. Gide was peculiarly fitted for the role of moralist-poet because of his talent for dramatizing elements taken from his own personal conflicts. Although his stories are by no means simply "confessions," his characters, with all their ambiguities and tensions, were born from his own adventures, those moral situations he encountered as he shuttled Hermes-fashion between the worlds of spirit and flesh. Gide is no spectator-novelist, no observer of "society." All his best work bears the unmistakable mark of having been written *from the inside.* His morality of mobility instantly caught the attention of bourgeois youth, and this gave him an immense pedagogical advantage. The two generations in France to whom Gide spoke most directly—that of 1890-1914 and the postwar youth—had each in its own way experienced a bringing-up that was stuffy and oppressed by externals. The first generation found in Gide's books the discovery of personal freedom, the second the justification of it. Any pedagogy based on purifying the heart, then following it, has a perennial attraction for the young. And where there is art to back it up, resistance is disarmed. The morality of impulse and self-realization that flowed through *Les Nourritures Terrestres* of 1897 is even today a wine that will stand much watering.

II

A lyricism of the senses and their satisfaction breathes fervently through Gide's writing from first to last. Jean Hytier goes so far as to say that the poetic work of Gide turns almost *exclusively* about the theme of desire. In Gide's *"Nourritures,"* the object of desire is identified entirely with pleasure, and pleasure is construed as satisfaction of the senses. These senses of ours are the very gates of truth. "I have no use for knowledge that has not been preceded by a sensation," says the poet of *Fruits of the Earth.* Later he found himself confirmed by Nietzsche's dictum that from the senses originate all trustworthiness, all good conscience, all evidence of truth. Moreover, pleasure certifies the moral worth of the deed from which it springs. "The pleasure I feel in an action I take as a sign I ought to do it." To young Gide, every desire had a right to be satisfied, if not, show why not. William James announced this as a moral rule, but unlike the American philosopher, Gide could think of no reasons why not. Nature herself gives Nathanaël's teacher the clue that man is born for pleasure. Desire makes the plant burst its seed, stocks the hive with honey, fills the human heart with love. "Nathanaël," cries the young hedonist, "I will teach you that there is nothing that is not divinely natural." But, like all opportunities, chances for the satisfaction of desire often knock but once, and the poet of *Les Nourritures* begs his unknown comrade to seize the precious moment that may never come again. "Nathanaël, ah! satisfy your joy while it gladdens your soul— and your desire of love while your lips are still sweet to kiss, and while your embrace is joyous."

Yet he liked to think that the intensity and duration of desire could be increased by holding back from the satisfaction of it. The hero of *The Notebooks of André Walter* refuses himself a visit to the Grande Chartreuse lest the pleasure of touring the monastery fall below the delight of its anticipation. In *Fruits of the Earth,* the formula reads: "What we want, Nathanaël, is not so much possession as love." But in his *Journal* of 1930 Gide scolds himself for this "André-Walterism," locating it in a part of his youth which he has presumably outgrown. "That was the period when I kept from touching what I most wanted. This amounted to plowing up the field for the demon and already sowing fine regrets for later on!" Yet three years later we find him writing in the same *Journal* that he *still* finds more pleasure in the effort than in the object sought. "Not to make every effort toward pleasure, but to find one's pleasure in effort itself is the secret of my happiness." Pater, of course, had said much the same thing in his dictum about preferring experience to the fruits of it. Again Gide returns to the theme in the 1935 sequel to *Nourritures* —"And yet how often on the point of gathering joy, I have suddenly

turned away from it as might an ascetic." And he tells his readers
that it was not diminishing desire that he felt with the approach of
old age, but the fear of too rapid draining of pleasure by his greedy
lips. "Thus I came to prefer thirst itself to the quenching of it."
With *Nourritures,* says Jean Delay, biographer of Gide's youth,
André Walter became André Gide. True. But the aspiring hedonist
never lost the Walterish feeling that the hunt was worth more than
the quarry.

To a younger moralist-poet, Gide's cries of desire to prolong the delicious experience by withholding complete surrender seemed ca-
pricious and repellent. At sixteen Albert Camus had been put off by a
first reading of Gide to which he had been recommended by his
uncle. He did not enjoy squeals of pleasure: *Oh! Oh! Oh! Oh! cette
petite volupté qui passe!* Nor did he admire Gide's hints of forbidden
passions under the date trees; Arab place names left him unmoved.
"Blidah! Blidah, fleur du Sahel! petite rose!" Says the author of
L'Étranger grimly, "Alas, I knew Blidah." Yet the solar delight that
vibrates in Camus's writings (particular noticeable in his earliest)
owes something of its heat to Gide as well as to the African sun:

How many hours spent trampling underfoot the fragrant herbs,
caressing the ruins, trying to accord my breathing with the tumul-
tuous sighing of the world. Submerged among the wild odors and
somnolent concerts of insects, I open my eyes and heart to the in-
tolerable grandeur of that sky gorged with heat.

What most irritated Camus in Gide's writing was his poetizing on the
need to hold desire in check to make it keener. This "André-Walterism" put Camus in mind of that class of brothel patrons known to
habitués as "the cerebrals." Ovid also knew them: *Sustentata venus
gratissima.* But Gide's preferring of passion to its object is more
than perverse caprice; it is a rather special manifestation of what
critics have perhaps too grandiloquently called his Faustian spirit. It
is certainly related to Gide's lifelong obsession with the ideal of
progress. Not only is desire itself preferable to desire's satisfaction;
the pursuit of Truth is of more value than truth itself. As a young

man, Gide had admired to the point of copying out the well-known
lines of Lessing:

If God held enclosed in his right hand all of Truth and in his
left the eternal aspiration toward the Truth (with the certainty of
never attaining it) and if he said to me "Choose!" I should humbly
seize his left hand, saying "Give, Father, for pure Truth is only
for Thee."

Gide applied the same formula to his own personal search for God.
Progress toward the Beatific Vision rather than attaining it remained
his religious ideal. Alissa of *Strait Is the Gate* cannot imagine heavenly
joy other than in an infinite and perpetual drawing near to God. Indeed, she cannot imagine *any* joy that is not progressive. Twenty
years after he wrote the lines on Alissa's death, Gide restated his
faith in the outline of a sermon that tries hard to center on
Truth but finds itself nostalgically backsliding toward Desire. His
metaphor would have distressed poor Alissa:

But the full embrace of Truth, my brethren, is refused us; and
moreover it would give our soul a less keen satisfaction than its
pursuit, just as free access to a naked body often disappoints the
hand that took such delight in slipping between flesh and frock. . . .

That little passage shows Gide's ideal of progress toward Truth to
be an intellectual corollary of his André Walter's philosophy of desire, itself a poetic variant of an idea which was to become a meth-
odological axiom of the twentieth century's first half. What counts is
not so much the object of method, but method itself. What is important to philosophy is not certainty but search. Not knowledge,
but the ways of it. Science does not employ inquiry; it *is* inquiry.
Amusing to think of the hero of Gide's early *Urien's Voyage* (1893)
returning from his quest in the Sargasso Sea to find his dear young
lady Ellis sitting on the lawn under an apple tree where she had
waited fourteen days for the tardy voyagers, having returned before
them by the quicker land route. Clad in a *robe à pois,* with plaid scarf
and cherry-colored parasol, she is eating an endive salad while read-

ing Kant's *Prolegomena to Any Future Metaphysics*—the work which proclaimed to the world the philosophical futility of any search for the Absolute.

So far as pleasure is concerned, adepts of André-Walterism risk sharper jabs from those thorns of memory that trouble even ordinary hedonists in advancing years. Desire is mortal, and dies before we do. One must deal with regrets in old age, regrets so keen that for some only religious conversion can stifle them. In the same year that young bourgeois Frenchmen warmed themselves in the fervor of Gide's *Nourritures,* another poet-seeker after deviate pleasure, Constantine Cavafy, was writing in Alexandria:

> In the inner room of the noisy café
> an old man sits bent over a table;
> a newspaper before him, no companion beside him.
>
> And in the scorn of his miserable old age,
> he meditates how little he enjoyed the years
> when he had strength, the art of the word, and good looks.
>
> He knows he has aged much; he is aware of it, he sees it,
> and yet the time when he was young seems like
> yesterday. How short a time, how short a time.
>
> And he ponders how Wisdom had deceived him;
> and how he always trusted her—what folly!—
> the liar who would say, "Tomorrow. You have ample time."
>
> He recalls impulses he curbed; and how much
> joy he sacrificed. Every lost chance
> now mocks his senseless prudence.
>
> . . . But with so much thinking and remembering
> the old man reels. And he dozes off
> bent over the table of the café.

So too the aging Gide. His saddest thoughts are about lost opportunities, pleasures missed. "Some days," he writes at sixty, "the memory of all I did not do and might have done obsesses me." At sixty-five, "Regrets? I regret *not* having yielded to temptation," and then goes on to mourn that at an age when desire is at its keenest, our youthful and austere souls are best able to inhibit it, and all too often do so.

III

But the Gidean *morale* is far more than a simple ethic of desire. From his earliest works emerged a poetic teaching of self-realization and self-transcendence, pointing to a dynamic and internal morality as opposed to one static and external, a morality which could be defined only in terms of mobility and spontaneity. This is an individualism oddly yet by no means inconsistently linked in spirit both to the immoralism of Nietzsche and the ethic of the New Testament—an individualism whose highest value is sincerity, yet a sincerity that can express itself only in ambiguity, in doubleness. Its end is freedom—to be oneself. Its twin mottoes: *"Become what you are!"* and *"Go beyond!"*

From first to last, Gide defines the good in terms of mobility. His exaltation of mobile values takes so many forms as to elude classification. It was through its motif of *disponibilité* that *Fruits of the Earth* reached the children of the bourgeoisie. To become what we really are, it is first necessary to detach oneself, to hold oneself in readiness to accept what opportunities come along, to embrace whatever vital and promising occasion chance throws our way. One must not ask that the outcome of such adventures be assured in advance; it is the morality of the office clerk to count the cost. Better (as Keats said) to be imprudent movables, than prudent fixtures. Inclined to mobility by temperament and instinct, Gide turned it into an ethical value and poetized about it. "Never have I been able to settle in life," he said. "Always seated on the edge, as if on the arm of a chair; ready to get up, to leave." Self-detachment is a necessary condition of self-fulfillment. So in his *Prometheus* of 1893, Tityrus says to Angela:

"Leave my oak-tree! How can you think of such a thing?"
"Isn't it nearly big enough to grow by itself?"
"Yes, but I'm attached to it."
"Detach yourself," replied Angela.

Gide's counsel of *disponibilité* was made to order for the young, whose vital energy and natural suppleness fit them so well for adventures in a world new to them. But Gide noted sadly that youth cannot wait to throw away its birthright, to trade in its precious deposit of individuality and freedom for the false security of the *type*. Youth smothers itself by sinking into the protective mold of husband, father, wife, mother, businessman, teacher, magistrate. To go over to *the others*—to the official class, to those who live by rules and fixed postures! Look at these young people, smiling, tense with love of life. How different from their parents who have pulled down the corners of their mouths forever, who are settled, done for. Yet out of the tired wisdom of middle age, the parents advise the young to declare themselves early, to throw in their hand before they've played it. "The temptation that is hardest to resist for youth," says Gide at seventy-seven, "is that of 'committing oneself,' . . . Everything urges them to do so, and the cleverest sophistries, the apparently noblest, the most urgent motives. One would have accomplished much if one persuaded youth that it is through *carelessness* and laziness that it commits itself . . . that it is essential—not to be this or that, but to be." Of Camus, Simone de Beauvoir says that he, like Sartre and others of her generation, moved from individualism to commitment. Gide, their elder and teacher, never made that shift.

His call to unrest, like all counsels of perfection, was both seductive and difficult of fulfillment. To leave one's family ("Families, I hate you!"), to say farewell to one's parents ("Let the dead bury the dead!"), not to stay in one place, not to love anyone in particular— This last is especially hard for the young who burn to give themselves. But that's just it, say Ménalque, the young diarist's spiritual director, don't give, but *lend* yourself. Why should you deprive another of the joy you bring to the first? Gide's lifelong suspicion of women sprang not so much from his sexual anomaly as from his conviction that women are by nature sworn enemies of *disponibilité*. Even Angela is not a contradictory instance. For understandable biological and social reasons, women want to tie a man's feet, to domesticate his instincts, to put him in slippers. This may ensure the stability of society and family, but it is fatal to the creative initiative of youth. "You imagine you are here," says Ménalque to his young friend, "But the best part of you is confined elsewhere; your wife and children, your books and studies hold it prisoner, and God is robbed of it." More than forty years after *The Immoralist*, Gide's surviving heroes are still sitting on the edge of their chairs ready to jump up and be off. In *Theseus* of 1946, the conqueror of Pasiphaë's Minotaur is uncomfortable with the devoted Ariadne who longs to be with him in life and death. She warns her mobile lover against risky adventures like Icarus' flight, while he in his turn shies away from the thread she insists on attaching to him before he enters the labyrinth. Even his first night of love with her bores him a little: "The hours passed slowly for me, I must admit. I have never been good at staying in one place, be it even in the very bosom of delight. I always aim to break free as soon as the novelty has worn off." Of course, Gide was not the first to pipe that tune; Baudelaire knew it by heart:

Mais les vrais voyageurs sont ceux-là seuls qui partent
Pour partir; cœurs légers, semblables aux ballons
De leur fatalité jamais ils ne s'écartent
Et, sans savoir pourquoi, disent toujours: Allons!

And D. H. Lawrence would pick it up: "*What next?* That's what interests me. 'What now?' is no fun any more."

To detach oneself is the first condition of rebirth, says Gide. This Descartes of the emotions who would burn the books and start afresh told his readers that he brought back with him from his first North African adventures "the secret of a man newly risen from the grave." All Gide's fervent heroes enjoy the experience of being reborn. Early on they have found that all education tends to negate itself, that everything surrounding a young person's growing up—books, teachers, conscience, duties—conspires to produce an artificial self. One must get rid of this fabricated "I" by stripping off the accumulated scribble that conceals the true nature. The young writer of *Paludes* cries out against the cerements that choke him, asks his Angela whether they ought to try once more to lift the stifling wind-

ing sheets or to accustom themselves for the rest of life to scarcely
breathing. As his cousin, the Immoralist, would shortly do in his more
sinister fashion, the innocent dithyrambist of *Fruits of the Earth*
joyfully celebrates his resurrection: "I awaited a second puberty.
Ah, if only my eyes could see with new vision! If only I could cleanse
them from the soil of books, make them more like the skies they
look at—skies which today have been washed bright and clean by
the recent rains." His wish came true. "I fell ill," he records, "I
travelled, I met Ménalque, and my marvellous convalescence was a
palingenesis. I was born again with a new self, in a new country; and
among things which were absolutely fresh."

To bring to birth one's real self, that which one shares with no
other, is the entelechy of youth. In poetry or truth, conviction that
his individuality is the most precious thing about a man is never
absent from Gide's writing. It was his own irrepressible ego that rose
up in protest against the thought control he found in the U.S.S.R.
in those days when even he, André Gide, believed for a time he was
"committed." Conversely, the Gidean sin against the Holy Ghost
was early defined as anything that prevents that individuality from
breaking through to the surface. It is written (and Gide took
Scripture seriously): *If the salt hath lost its savour, wherewith shall
it be salted?* Failure to discover the self—or to create it, which is
the same thing—leads to spiritual death by boredom. In a moment
of exalted scruple, Pascal had cried out, *"Le moy est haïssable!"* But
Gide declared that, for his part, he rather fancied his ego. He would
find it charming if he chanced upon it in someone else; why should he
hate it in himself? To critics like Barrès, who saw in Gide no more
than an intellectual playing with his own sensations, this was sheer
spiritual narcissism. But if Gide's individualism was a *culte du moi*,
it was not simply moral flabbiness. He believed that it had its own
hard rule. Courage is needed to act on the precept, *"Dare to be
yourself,"* since it means breaking patterns, and patterns are comfortable things to live by. It means being prepared to abandon one's
"principles," so often but external rules by which we measure moral
judgments as if they were so much yard goods. Scratch a man of

principle and you find a Pharisee. ("Ah, how true!" murmured Gide's readers, the young bourgeois *collégiens*, as they took scornful thought of their parents.) Daring to be oneself must issue, not in resisting our heart's deepest desires (even though these may seem anti-ethical), but on the contrary in giving way to them. To the Christian egoism that counseled salvation of one's own soul as man's primary concern, the young Gide of the North African journeys compared the egoism of self-abandonment—to abandon oneself to danger, even to the point of letting oneself perish—and found it no less wise. He stopped calling his desires temptations and followed them.

Despite the metaphors of *uncovering* he uses in describing the process of self-realization (graveclothes, palimpsests, hidden selves), Gide did not believe individuality or unique selfhood to be an endowed quality, an element forever fixed within a man like the natures of Plato's citizens of brass or gold. It is part of Gide's ethic of mobility that a man discovers and preserves his individuality by *acquisition*. Impossible to define oneself without moving, changing, developing, even negating oneself. That a person is provided with a fixed and a priori nature is not a modern belief; it is Greek, and Gide knew this. "Pagans," he says in his essay on the theater, "rarely considered qualities of the soul as goods that could be acquired, but rather as natural properties like those of the body. Agathocles was good, or Charicles courageous, quite as naturally as one had blue eyes, the other black." The Gidean exhortation to realize oneself cannot be fulfilled unless one can break away from what one is at any given moment. Thus understood, the Goethean motto *"Become what you are"* is a counsel of mobility, the first maxim of a dynamic categorical imperative—and had not the voyageurs come back, Urien's charming Ellis would have read this into her next diversion, *The Fundamental Principles of the Metaphysics of Morals*. Self-realization implies self-transcendence; becoming what we are entails going beyond. This is Gide's paradox, his variant of the Christian exhortation to "die to self." It is a peculiarity of Gide's hedonism that it contains within itself the key to its own overcoming.

Les Nourritures closes with two of Gide's most striking pages. The first shows that, by its own logic, individualism cannot be promulgated through personal example. Here we meet the famous *"Jette mon livre,"* an injunction summing up Gide's early perception of the need of detaching oneself as a necessary condition of individuality and self-realization: "Nathanaël, throw away my book; do not let it satisfy you. Do not think *your* truth can be found by anyone else; be ashamed of nothing more than of that. If I found your food for you, you would not be hungry for it; if I made your bed, you would not be sleepy." Individualism is like pluralism; it cannot be preached as "the only way," for then it contradicts itself:

> Throw away my book; tell yourself that it is but *one* of the thousand possible postures for confronting life. Seek your own. What another might have done as well as you, do not do. What another might have said or written as well as you, do not say or write. In yourself cleave only to what you feel to be nowhere but in you and make of yourself, impatiently or patiently, ah! the most irreplaceable of men.

Even more graceful is the passage dedicated to his young wife Madeleine, the woman who embodied so much of Gide's "beyond";

> She turned her eyes toward the rising stars.
> "I know all their names," said she . . .

By her constant and beloved presence in those old days, the saintly "Emmanuèle" reminded the young poet-philosopher in love with desire of that individualism which transcends its own negation, the "I" flowering on the grave of an ego renounced, a self surrendered to God. He loved this angel, yet felt no desire for her.

It is often said that Gide's "Dare to be yourself" is a maxim of *sincerity*. But what is sincerity? To be oneself, to push aside all that is factitious and external, to let the real, the unspoiled self (even if it is the old Adam) break through to the surface—that is to be sincere. So also, to be a man with no guile, a poet who writes without fakery. ("Oh, to be utterly and perfectly sincere!") Ancient moralists defined sincerity as the property of *"the man without doubleness."*

Now Gide was the last man on earth of whom it could safely be said that he was, morally speaking, all of a piece. His life and art overflow with doubleness. He calls himself "a creature of dialogue" and boasts that everything in him is conflicting and contradictory. "I am merely a little boy having a good time," runs one of his favorite quips, "compounded with a Protestant minister who bores me." He enjoyed reminding his readers that his ancestry was both Huguenot and Catholic, that his father came from sun-baked Uzès in the south, while his mother's family was rooted in rainy Normandy. Discovering that on his birthday (November 21st) the earth leaves the influence of Scorpio to enter that of Sagittarius, he asks, "Is it my fault if your God took such great care to have me born between two stars, the fruit of two races, of two provinces, and of two faiths?" (The year of that question is 1935; he no longer talks of *his* God but of yours.) In any case, he followed his two stars—Cuverville and Biskra; the New Testament and *Arabian Nights;* Emmanuele and young Mohammed; *agape* and *eros.* Simultaneously he gathered in his ego and renounced it; concentrated his spiritual powers and squandered them; saved his life and threw it away. Yet throughout his career he made sincerity his ideal. "A man *'in whom there is no guile,'* he writes at sixty-two, "I know nothing that has dominated my life more than this word of the Gospel."

Paradoxically, sincerity is an equivocal virtue. It is the moral ideal of ascetic and saint, yet it is also the virtue ranked highest by the burgher and suburban citizen. The characteristic vice of the bourgeois (in French literature, at least) is hypocrisy, Phariseeism. Yet the bourgeois always *professes* sincerity in himself and admires it in others. Ask a girl of the middle classes why she esteems her husband-to-be, and four out of five times she will reply, "Because he is honest and sincere." In this usage, "sincerity" points to the trait of a man of unimaginative linear virtue, a character which, in a moment of exasperation during the first Eisenhower-Stevenson presidential campaign, philosopher Irwin Edman called "simple, stupid integrity." As friend or foe, the sincere man is always in one sense easy to deal with; he does not *elude,* he will not slip from one's grasp. The bourgeois knows where he stands with a man whose personality is strong but uncomplicated, who has a single soul in his stout breast, who stands straight and free from twists or loops which double back on themselves. It is the *shifty* ones who bother him, those whose vision of life or art filters through a kind of squint, the sort that cannot be comprehended by frontal encounter, but must be approached on an angle. It never occurs to the bourgeois that it is these shifty ones who carry on much of the world's work in art, religion, science, and politics too. Of course, the solid citizen is right in claiming that humanity could not get along without the first kind. There are times when "simple, stupid integrity" comes in handy. The men of Thermopylae stuck to their posts, even though they knew

> That Ephialtes rises in the end
> And at the last the Persians will get through.

Gide was not a man of Thermopylae. He was one of the shifty ones. Yet he made the maxim *"Purify thy heart,"* his own.

As a moral excellence, sincerity is subject to further limitation. It is not as difficult a virtue as is commonly supposed. Indeed in most instances where it shows itself sincerity is not a virtue at all, but a mark of the character of wicked or weak men. During a splendid "high conversation" in Thomas Mann's *Joseph in Egypt,* the noblewoman Mut-em-enet, vainly trying to stifle her budding passion for Joseph, replies to her husband who has argued that we must live in sincerity:

> Sincerity . . . is easy, and therefore it is not lofty. What would become of men if each would live only in the sincerity of his own desires, claiming for them the dignity of truth and unwilling to be strict with himself to his own improvement? The thief too is sincere, and the drunkard in the gutter and likewise the adulterer. But shall we by reason of its sincerity pass over their conduct?

Gide's most *abject* character—Amédée Fleurissoire of *Lafcadio*—is sincere. Michel of *The Immoralist,* his most egotistic character, is sincere. His most lofty heroine, Alissa of *Strait Is the Gate*, is sincere. Their sincerity is a function of a single-minded commitment which leads in each case to failure and disillusion. In constructing Michel and Alissa, Gide drew out from his own doubleness one side of himself; in this way he was able to make characters whose fatal flaw *resides* in their sincerity.

IV

In composing *The Immoralist* (1902) and *Strait Is the Gate* (1909), Gide exploited his doubleness. A pair in contrast, each tale contains as well its own internal dualism. Hero and heroine have their way, but in the end the reality of their triumph is slyly called into question. The Immoralist gets what he wants—his freedom—but doesn't quite know what to do with it. Saintly Alissa, who by her spiritual exertions has surely earned the grace of a happy death, finds herself forsaken in the end. Coleridge said that one of Shakespeare's modes of creating characters is "to conceive any one intellectual or moral faculty in excess, and then to place himself, Shakespeare, thus mutilated or diseased, under given circumstances." Gide remarks (and all his critics echo him), that in the composition of each tale, he took *one* of the simultaneous and contradictory impulses of his own mind and heart, isolated and exaggerated it by turning it into a leading character (Michel, Alissa), then sonata-fashion played the contrasting value off against the primary theme by means of a second character (Marceline, Jérôme). The result is an external equilibrium between the two works and a balanced tension within each. By his claim of manufacturing opposed characters out of conflicting elements in himself, Gide took his stand as a writer on the side of his admired Dostoevski, whom he made fashionable reading in France. The author of *The Brothers Karamazov* did not write novels with heroes who, thinly disguised, stand in for the author. Ivan, Alyosha, Mitya, the rascally old father, the epileptic Smerdyakov—he found them all in the equal and opposite tensions in his own nature. Neither Dostoevski nor Gide had any use for the hero who is all of a piece or for the stock type—the soldierly soldiers, the senatorial senators, the volcanic lover, passionate mistress, kindly father *à la Traviata*. Such characters are predictable, mechanical rather than vital; they lack the Epicurean "nameless element," that *exiguum clinamen* which gives human nature its swerve. They are not *"interesting."* Further, by drawing his characters out of his own conflicting impulses, Gide was able to separate himself from those novelists whose talent lies in objective and spectator-like description of men in society or war. He puts himself with those writers who draw everything from themselves and their personal spiritual autobiographies. Such a novelist "is the sole guarantee of the truth he reveals and the sole judge. The heaven and hell of his characters are in him. It is not himself that he paints; but what he paints he might have become had he not become everything himself."

The fervent voice of *Fruits of the Earth* was all too naturally that of young Gide. *The Immoralist* is much more of a novel than the earlier book, although Gide calls it simply a tale *(récit)*. By bearing down hard on one side of his nature in the writing—the pagan individualism, the desire for sun and naked flesh—Gide managed to construct an artificial thing, a miniature Leviathan, near-perfect. Despite his use of the creaky device of the confessional testament (like certain French novelists, of whom Mauriac is one, Gide never outgrew a weakness for letters and diaries as props), he made of *The Immoralist* a work of art rounded off into itself, a self-contained entity, fully shaped. In *Nourritures,* he had tended to pant down the reader's neck. But in *The Immoralist* for all its autobiographical parallels Gide succeeded in putting the necessary distance between himself and his book as well as interposing it between book and reader— distance to the point of purged horror, objective, aesthetically satisfying.

Every moral incitement of *Nourritures* is present in Michel's story. There is the old motif of *dépaysement*: a heady wave of irresponsibility, an exhilaration of personal freedom surges over Michel hard upon his sudden detachment from home and duties by his honeymoon trip to the desert. Again the theme of desire—reinforced by Pateresque injunctions to seize pleasure on the wing. ("Every joy is like

the manna of the desert which corrupts from one day to the next.
. . . : let every moment carry away with it all that it has brought.")
The young scholar shudders with delight as he discovers the Arab
boys, the African sun on their naked bodies and his own. Rebirth!
His old self discarded as a useless fiction, Michel's new ego emerges as
the precious writing of an ancient palimpsest reveals itself beneath the
pedantic valueless inscription on the parchment's surface. There is
the joy of daring to be oneself, of asserting that unique and irreplace-
able "I" instead of walking paste-up of things learned from family
and stuffy books, a collage of everybody's "principles" including one's
own. Carried over from the earlier tale is the Wildean *alter ego*—
Ménalque, ambassador of hedonism and the dangerous life. Plying
the young bourgeois with Shiraz, Ménalque exhorts his all-too-apt
pupil to break out of a shell already cracked by desert convalescence,
praises those who have the courage to discard patterns and stand up
to their fates, accepting the isolation society metes out to those who
dare to be themselves:

The pleasure I feel in an action, I take as a sign that I ought to
do it. . . . If only the people we know could persuade themselves of
the truth of this! But most of them believe that it is only by constraint they can get any good out of themselves, and so they live
in a state of psychological distortion. It is his own self that each of
them is most afraid of resembling. Each of them sets up a pattern
and imitates it; he doesn't even choose the pattern he imitates; he
accepts a pattern that has been chosen for him—and so they don't
find themselves at all. I detest such moral agoraphobia—the most
odious cowardice I call it. Why, one always has to be alone to invent
anything—but they don't want to invent anything. The part in each
of us that we feel is different from other people is just the part that
is rare, the part that makes our special value.—And this is the very
thing people try to suppress.

What is new in the emphasis of *The Immoralist*—if we compare it with Gide's earlier book—is an exploitation of the idea of
identification of moral right and strength, a link historically associated with the names of Callicles and Nietzsche. It does not take

Michel long to learn the need of ruthlessness in brushing away the claims of others if they stand in the way of his self-fulfillment or threaten to block the release of his demonic energies. New too is the stage manager's introduction of a real, though overlight, counter-weight to all this high egoism—Marceline. Hers is the Christian ethic of renunciation of self, finding one's being by losing it for others. The saintly girl nurses her tubercular husband back to health under the desert sun only to have him brutally push her aside when he fancies she is trying to stand between him and Lachmi's golden nudity. He makes a few halfhearted attempts to deny his newly discovered self, to *immobilize* himself by tying himself down to his estate in Normandy, an apartment in Paris, a lectureship at the Collège de France. But in the end he drags his sick wife back to the desert to die so that he may be free to discover the mysterious source of the delight he associates with the native boys. Then there is the remarkable *devaluing* of Michel's ideal at the story's close. The scholar reborn senses obscurely that his freedom has turned into dust and ashes in his hands, that what he has suppressed in himself to give his wayward impulses full sway will one day avenge itself. Still, the tale Charles Du Bos called Gide's "masterpiece of luminous cruelty" does not simply return a verdict in behalf of virtue and against vice or the other way around. While *The Immoralist* may be construed as a moral fable, it is first of all a work of art; as such, it has its own internal equilibrium, solves no problem, draws no con-clusion. Marceline's ideal is deflated as well as Michel's, although the little brushstroke Gide paints in to show this is almost imperceptible. Michel's young wife patterned her life after Christ. As she lies dying, her husband tries to restore her beloved rosary to her hands. But twice she drops, and deliberately, the chain of beads from which hangs the image of her crucified Saviour to cling instead to the man whose love for her struggles against his mortal disgust.

Readers of *The Immoralist* usually are quick to spot the parallels to Nietzsche, particularly in Michel's identification of "right" and "strength." "I quite understand your doctrine," says his wife, "—for now it has become a doctrine. A fine one perhaps . . . but it does away with the weak." A section of *Beyond Good and Evil* (one of the first books of Nietzsche's Gide read), in which the philosopher laments Ménalque-fashion the difficulty of disengaging oneself from the net of ordinary duties, is headed "We Immoralists," and in *Ecce Homo* the now demented genius shouts, "I am the first Immoralist." Key concepts in Gide's tale—the isolation of the exceptional man, the idea of sickness as opportunity for a fresh creative start, the exaltation of health and joy, as well as the invectives against religion as neurotic escape, weakness decked out as "Christian humility," impotence calling itself renunciation—they are all there in the German philologist *manqué* whose delicate childhood in the bosom of a female family is so strikingly similar to Gide's own. Like Gide's Michel, the earlier Immoralist handled sick women roughly—"The sick woman especially; no one surpasses her in refinements for ruling, oppressing tyrannizing," and the ailing misogynist goes on to say that in the eternal fight of the sick against the healthy, she spares nothing living, nothing dead, for all her "spiteful grimaces of patience." But a lamb like Marceline? Even such lambs. Nietzsche says he is not surprised that lambs should bear a grudge against the great birds of prey, but that is no reason for blaming the birds of prey for taking the little lambs.

Nietzsche's death preceded the publication of *The Immoralist* by less than two years. Gide had read the German poet-philosopher with enthusiasm, but denied that his ideas had influenced the writing of Michel's confession. "Nothing is so absurd," he complains to his *Journal,* "as that accusation of *influence* in which certain critics excel every time they note a resemblance." He gently discouraged a young friend from writing a thesis on the subject of Nietzsche's influence on his work. Was not *The Immoralist* composed entirely in his head and heart before he read Nietzsche? He admits that his study of the philosopher was helpful insofar as it enabled him to cut out of Michel's story a lot of theoretical material that would otherwise have made it top-heavy with ideas. According to his own account, Gide found in Nietzsche's writing confirmation of insights he had already experienced rather than inspiration for new work. All the same, Nietzsche's talent for doubleness delighted him. In *The Birth of Tragedy* the philosopher had attributed to the ancient Greeks *simultaneous* drives toward frenzy and order. Gide found in his own soul the dualism celebrated by Nietzsche under the slogan "Dionysius versus Christ!" He agreed with the author of *Genealogy of Morals* that the Christian ethic tends to isolate the good from the instinctive, thereby depriving virtue of its dynamism. Certain lines from Gide's 1904 lecture on the theater have a peculiarly Nietzschean ring: "Those over whom their desires are victorious do not find it difficult to believe in the gods. Desires are true gods so long as they rule. . . . It was *the invention of morals* that turned Olympus into a desert."

Not only did Gide share with Nietzsche a creative energy that worked best out of inner crosscurrents of thought and feeling; like the philosopher too he defined his personal ethical ideal in terms of self-transcendence. The attitude toward illness in *The Immoralist* is quite Nietzschean in this respect. Michel scorns his colleagues at the university because "Not one of them has managed to be ill." Nietzsche said, "It was sickness that brought me to reason." Disease shook Michel out of his stupor; during his convalescence he was reborn. In itself, sickness has no value; the good lies in *overcoming* it. Nothing great, Nietzsche remarked, comes into being except in despite. To transcend oneself, to find in the moment of passion the necessity of *going beyond,* is Gide's ideal—as it was Nietzsche's and Goethe's before him. Gide did not have to read the Germans to construct his *Prometheus.* The hero of that quasi-surrealist *sotie* of 1899 comes to terms with his eagle, later overcomes it (the eagle represents his conscience) and has the bird cooked and served for dinner. Moreover, Gide's treatment of self-surpassing usually elicits more harmonies of renunciation than we would find in Nietzsche's vainglorious dithyrambs. "What one undertakes beyond one's strength," says the wounded exile of Gide's *Philoctetes* (1899), "that is what is called virtue." In the end the poor man gives away his most precious possession, his bow, once the weapon of Hercules. The hero of *King Candaules* (1901) surpasses himself to the point of incredible altruism; he shares *his* most precious possession—his lovely wife—with a fisherman. In whatever form it takes, Gide's "passez outre" retains to the end its individual character. In the late *Theseus* (1946) we hear the call to go beyond combined with the old Gidean theme of *disponibilité:* the conqueror of the Minotaur let neither Perigone nor his handsome son by her detain him long on the road to Athens, "— breaking free, as usual, and anxious not to lose any time. I have never allowed the past to involve or detain me; rather have I been drawn forward by what was still to be achieved; and the most important things seemed to me always to lie ahead."

Gide himself never seems quite to have made up his mind about the odor of Nietzsche alleged to hang about *The Immoralist*. Thirty years after the little novel appeared, he confides to his *Journal* that his ratiocinations of the period of the story's composition were "Nietzschean," and tells how he objectified these arguments by presenting them in exaggerated fashion through his hero Michel. Yet hardly a year earlier (1932), we find him agreeing with critic Henri Drain that an abyss separates the story of Michel from the exhortations of Nietzsche's prophet: *"Zarathustra* displays a triumph; *L'Immoraliste* relates an error, a failure, the very parody of a Nietzschean triumph. One is a book of propaganda; the other is a book of warning." Hard upon the actual publication of *The Immoralist,* charges of Nietzscheanism (hence of pro-Germanism) were made against it by critics who reacted naïvely to the story, assuming that the voice of Michel was Gide's own—an assumption reinforced by Gide's method of first-person narrative. Gide's early anxiety to disassociate himself from his repellent hero shows more than a trace of nervousness: "Everything that he [Michel] does that is not childish," he protests in a letter of 1902 to Arthur Fontaine, "is cruel or lamentably vile . . . he debauches himself; he covers himself with vermin; he kills his wife." Subsequent references to Nietzsche in his *Journal* make it clear that while he admires the philosopher's great strength, he, André Gide, has too much sympathy for other people to follow his hard line: "How I feel constantly hindered by my sympathy. Constantly feeling that my thought can and must bruise those I love. Those who go forward without fear of hurting others, I admire and envy." Nietzsche argued that the Christian religion sacrifices the strong to the weak. But, Gide asks, cannot that strength best express itself in bringing help to weakness? As for the book *Zarathustra,* he could never abide it— although he read it seven or eight times: "Impossible! The tone of this book is unbearable to me. And all my admiration for Nietzsche cannot succeed in making me put up with it." It is in *Zarathustra,* he says, that we find a reason for Nietzsche's torment—he is jealous of Christ. Mad though it is, he much prefers the philosopher's last work, *Ecce Homo.* As for Gide himself, after Michel of *The Immoralist,* he created no further suspect Nietzschean characters. There is one exception—Strouvilhou of *The Counterfeiters:* "When we take care of the poor, the feeble, the rickety, the injured," growls this latter-day Immoralist, "we are making a great mistake; and that is why I hate religion—because it teaches us to." But little Boris's corrupter hardly counts in a discussion of Nietzsche and Gide. He is no more than a painted devil.

In his excellent book on Gide, Albert Guerard warns against the easy tendency to overplay the Nietzschean individualism in *The Immoralist,* pointing out that the strength of the little novel lies rather "in its art and psychological understanding, and its controlled transposition of personal experience." Too much concentration on the theoretical or ethical side of the tale, says Guerard, has led critics to neglect its psychological aspect, the fact that it is basically a story of implicit homosexuality. He reminds Gide's readers that nowhere in the story does Michel commit an overt homosexual act, that only toward the close of his adventure does it begin to dawn on him that what he really wants are boys rather than women—although this was earlier made rather clear to the reader. (In the story's closing line alone is there a qualified admission of his anomaly by Michel as he mentions that his Ouled-Naïl girl has told him she believes he prefers her little brother Ali to her: *"Peut-être a-t-elle un peu raison."*) Guerard insists that Michel's anarchic actions cannot be understood unless we see in them the expression of his sexual frustration. Against his conscience and public disapproval, the repressed hero is irresistibly drawn precisely to those things most irrational, most forbidden.

Thus we see in *The Immoralist* a Freudian drama objectifying a moral conflict between id and superego—a struggle rooted in Gide's own life, now transposed to a work of art.

Perfectly true. Or very nearly so. To construe *The Immoralist* simply as a fable of Nietzsche individualism is to load back upon it that burden of abstraction Gide himself tells us he got rid of by reading Nietzsche. As far as the *theory* of right-through-strength goes, the German had stated it brilliantly; why restate it? Michel's homosexual development lends concrete interest to Gide's tale; it accounts for the peculiar *bite* of the story. At the same time, it is easy to commit the opposite error in commenting on *The Immoralist* by playing up the particularities of Michel's pedophile tendency to the exclusion of Gide's clear exploitation (for purposes of art, of course) of the idea of individualism and its implied ethical question. Both elements are present in the tale, and any possible tendency to abstractness in the second is killed off in advance by the scorpion's sting of the first. (Gide *could not* be abstract; think of that clot of blood!) A critic's itch to comment on *The Immoralist* may lead the unwary to a choice of extreme interpretations—one turning the little work of art into a problem in moral philosophy, the other reducing it to a Freudian case history. Guerard's argument against an intellectualistic approach to Gide's story is sound enough, but his own way of handling it has a touch of that psychological reductionism practiced by certain American critics, a bent confirmed when he goes on to suggest that Thomas Mann's *Death in Venice* is also "really" a story of homosexuality, and that all poor Aschenbach's philosophizing about the artist-nature is just so much theoretical window dressing.

V

Against the Immoralist whose pagan cries of abandon made even his creator uneasy, Gide placed in the balance Alissa's tears of renunciation. *Strait Is the Gate* of 1909 followed Michel's testament after a seven-year interval during which Gide apparently gave much time to spiritual self-examination. In *The Return of the Prodigal Son* of 1907, he had arranged (in very beautiful language) a reconciliation between the wanderer and his father, but even so the mobile youth urges his younger brother to follow his example and get away. In Alissa's case, self-detachment takes the form of the Christian ideal of progressive separation of self from all that is not God—even to the extreme of life itself. For this exceptional woman, Christ's counsels of perfection are binding imperatives. The command "Sell all that thou hast," means to her that she must offer to God as a sacrifice the prospect of a normal and happily married life with her beloved. The too-passive Jérôme accepts a series of separations, receiving his final dismissal at the little garden door she closes between them. Only when he reads her diary after her death does he realize the depth of her love for him, and with it the extent of her renunciation. The last entry suggests that she knows the vanity of her sacrifice, that in the end she finds herself forsaken by God—the one love alone to whom she has offered up her marriage and her life:

". . . a pang of anguish pierced me, a shudder of my flesh and soul; it was like the sudden and disenchanting *illumination* of my life. . . . Even now I am writing to reassure myself, to calm myself. Oh Lord! may I reach the end without blasphemy!

I should like to die now, quickly, before again realizing that I am alone."

Like *The Immoralist*, Alissa's moving—if somewhat lachrymose—testament lends itself to psychological as well as to ethical interpretation; Gide was clever enough in the writing of the stories to set out the seeds of both. Throughout *La Porte étroite* he seems to hint very faintly that neither Jérôme nor Alissa really wants to get married. Jérôme's reluctance is conveyed through his invertebrate passivity in the face of Alissa's heroic dismissals (does he share Michel's anomaly?). For her part, Alissa seems to have acquired a distaste for the physical side of marriage as partial result of her mother's penchant for adultery—a fastidiousness that calls into question the clarity of her motives. Nevertheless, the theme of self-sacrifice is handled in the story with so much care and love that it is impossible

to believe the author has inflated Alissa's religious ideal only for
the fun of pricking it flat with a psychological pin. Hytier classifies
La Porte étroite as one of Gide's *ironic* tales. But the term "irony"
does not apply to Gide's writing here in the same sense as it does to
the stories, say, of Thomas Mann—who in *The Magic Mountain* will
introduce his readers to an extraordinary youth with the assurance
that he is ordinary. Although Alissa's story contains a *critical* element,
its sentences do not say one thing and mean another in that way.
The tongue-in-cheek effect we associate with *Lafcadio* and *The Counterfeiters* is totally absent from *The Immoralist* and *Strait Is the
Gate*. Gide did not smile as he read over the Pascal-like lines of
Alissa's diary; he wept. The ideal of self-renunciation which he took
to be the core of the Christian ethic was closer to his heart than it
was even to Dostoevski: *"Verily, verily I say unto you. Except a
grain of wheat fall into the ground and die, it abideth alone: but if
it die, it bringeth forth much fruit. He that loveth his life shall lose
it: and he that hateth his life in this world shall keep it unto life
eternal."* Gide glosses that text in his little commentary on the Gospels, *Numquid et tu*, "He who loves life, his soul—who protects his
own personality, who is particular about the figure he cuts in this
world—shall lose it; but he who renounces it shall make it really
living, shall assure it eternal life; not eternal life in the future, but
shall make it already, even now, live in eternity." Gide is one of very
few major writers of fiction in the twentieth century to whom the
religious ideal of a life of perfection *meant* something. Claudel saw
this; so did Maritain and Mauriac. On that ground they based their
hopes for Gide's conversion.

Alissa is a Christian heroine of rare and difficult breed—the
Protestant saint. Her scripture-searching, the scrupulosity with which
she examines her motives, her vision of destiny as a stark confrontation of the soul alone with God without intermediary, her
stubborn insistence on the sovereignty of her private judgment—all
these are qualities which Gide, proud of his Huguenot ancestry,
valued in Protestant Christianity. True, he is anxious lest the reader
of *Strait Is the Gate* be unduly impressed with Alissa's sacrifice, fail-

ing to notice on first reading that the tale is, like *The Immoralist,* a "plunge into the excessive," that Alissa's life is a failure, that her heroism, like all Protestant heroism, is "gratuitous" and therefore productive of error. (Claudel, thus informed, grumbled that if Alissa had been a Catholic as she damned well should have been, she would have found her proper place—in a convent.) All the same, Gide says, heroines like Alissa can teach us real nobility. In his autobiography, he recalls the lonely death of Anna Shackleton, the Scottish governess and tutor of his childhood who later became a member of the Gide family, "I was haunted for weeks and months by the anguish of her solitude. I imagined—I heard—that loving soul of hers utter its last despairing cry and sink back again, forsaken by all but God; and it is that cry that re-echoes in the last pages of my *Porte étroite.*" Forsaken by all *but* God? Alissa finds herself forsaken by God as well. It is she, not Anna, who has the right to that last despairing cry. Critics have pointed to Alissa's final diary entry as proof-text of Gide's deflating the ideal his book portrays, of devaluing the life of a person who has lived according to the choice he has made. Yet they do not seem to have noticed that Alissa's experience of abandonment in her last agony makes her death *more* Christian rather than less, and really implies no failure at all—if the term "Christian" is used in the pure and primitive sense to which Gide and his Alissa incline. "My God, my God, why hast thou forsaken me?" was uttered by the man whom Nietzsche calls the last Christian—the one who died on the cross.

Gide's work bears permanent impress of the ideal of commitment he found in the New Testament; yet his own attitude toward that ideal is ambiguous. In his earlier work, he warned the young against *any* commitment on the grounds that giving oneself too early means a choice taken, hence freedom lost. Commitment can be the end of mobility, of *disponibilité;* one is no longer free to detach oneself, to move on. ("I have always understood," Gide's wife wrote to him in a crucial letter," . . . your needs of *déplacement* and liberty.") Living one's life according to an absolute choice made may easily be followed by aberration and self-defeat. Yet giving over one's life is the very spirit of the Gospels. Such a life, as in Alissa's case, may create authentic heroism. How can one warn against extremes without seeming to counsel prudential morality? Smilingly Gide took refuge in the phrase *extrême milieu;* and it may not be straining too much to say that this "stand in the extreme middle" is a more modest version of that taken by Mann's metaphysical hero who can be "lord of the counterpositions," without being reduced to moral fence-straddling for fear he might get hurt or find himself compromised. Despite his occasional nervous shying at the "excesses" of his own characters, Gide held the ideal of commitment too close to his heart ever wholly to give it up. He had the living example of Madeleine to contemplate. Besides, amused contempt for the committed life was too closely associated with the bourgeois ethic for Gide ever to be at ease in the presence of the usual arguments against moral extremism.

For the concept of complete commitment, of going all out, is antibourgeois. That is why the reading of Gide's books, as well as those of Nietzsche and Dostoevski, aroused the *children* of bourgeois families to such enthusiasm. The ethic by which the sensible and enlightened man lives is always a matter of moderation, of *nihil nimis.* Aristotle and the Stoics were the classical formulators of this perennial ethic of the prudent man in whom virtue stands in the middle as a balance, an equilibrium between excess and defect. The morality of moderation easily adapts itself to bourgeois requirements. In the religious ideal of denial of self, the bourgeois finds as much oddity, as much individualistic extremism, as he would, say, in the fantastic egoism of Gide's Immoralist. To the bourgeois, the notion of voluntary poverty seems no more than a harmless eccentricity. He would amend Christ's merciless injunction to the rich young man to give up all that he had—qualify it at least to the extent of permitting the youth to keep a decent competence for himself. The bourgeois ethic knows no counsel of perfection. It cannot urge dying to self, for it must justify self-love, as do today those books by popular moral-psychiatrists who bring such comfort to the urban *déraciné* middle classes—books in which self-love is not only restored to respectability but advocated as a therapy. The bourgeois is concerned, not for the perfection of his own life, but for the stability of society. He is the defender of marriage, the family, and the domestic virtues. His *beau idéal* is the good citizen—a socially indispensable being who indulges his own ambitions, yet tempers them with a decent regard for the aspirations of others. He equates the good with the lawful, looks before he leaps, avoiding any line of behavior which will risk his neck or make him look ridiculous. His virtues are necessary to ensure that order without which human society could not exist. But the corruption of his virtue reduces order to rigidity, the living to the mechanical, the spirit to the letter. At his best, the bourgeois is the foursquare man on whom for two hundred years in Europe all order and progress depended. At worst, he is the hypocrite misreading his own motives, the Pharisee who mistakes external conformity to law with inner rightness of the heart.

VI

Exaltation of mobility and impulse *(Fruits of the Earth; Immoralist)*, warnings to "purify thy heart" *(Strait Is the Gate; Pastoral Symphony)*, identification of the good with the vital and spontaneous, association of the elasticity of youth with freedom and inner value, the rigidity of age with external law *(Lafcadio; Counterfeiters)*— all these marks of the Gidean ethic place it in the category Henri Bergson called *dynamic* as opposed to *static* morality. Not that there is any evidence of Bergsonian "influence" on Gide. Bergson had no copyright on the subject of the two moralities, one of heart's impulse, the other of constraining law. A long series of French moralists from Pascal to Camus play variations on that theme. Moreover, Gide did not care very much for Bergson, and had difficulty plowing through his books. A study of the philosopher by Cresson convinced Gide that he had "long been a Bergsonian without knowing it," but the remark loses something of its force when we remember that four years earlier he had made the same *mot* about Freud. Although he admired the philosopher's pragmatic account of intelligence, Gide believed that Bergsonian evolutionism owed its success to fashion. "I greatly mistrust," Gide writes in his Congo diary, "a system that comes so pat in response to the tastes of the period and owes a great part of its success to flattering them." All the same it is surprising how well the moral spirit we associate with Gide's writing finds its philosophical justification in the author of *The Two Sources of Religion and Morality.*

Bergson's popularity began with a lecture on the comic given in Clermont-Ferrand in 1883, a discourse later expanded and published under the familiar title "Laughter" ("Le Rire"). In this essay Bergson tried to answer the question why we laugh by positing a radical distinction between life and matter, a dualism later to be disclosed as fundamental to his system of emergent evolution. *Mobility* is the specific characteristic of organic life, as it is indeed of reality itself, while *rigidity* is the mark of matter and the mechanical. "A really living life," says the philosopher, "should never repeat itself." When a living being behaves with gross inelasticity, the rigidity of habit overcoming sensibility and awareness (the professor who put out his wife at bedtime and kissed the cat is a caricature of it), we laugh— or at least we smile. The object of laughter, says Bergson, is always "something mechanical encrusted on the living . . . some rigidity or other applied to the mobility of life." Now the victory of inflexible habit over supple vitality is recognized by us obscurely as a little dangerous; so we neutralize the threat by laughter, which is a form of social censure. Novelists and men of the theater take full advantage of this power of the comic as they turn even vice into material for laughter. The misers of Molière and Balzac are comic. So inflexible have they become about money and goods that they no longer act like living men but as mechanical dolls. Men's actions are laughable in proportion as they remind us of a machine.

Bergson delivered his discourse on laughter when the young initiates of Paris were reading Gide's *Notebooks of André Walter.* The philosopher's *Two Sources of Religion and Morality* appeared six years after *Counterfeiters.* In his last work, Bergson carried the dualism between the mobility of life and the rigidity of mechanism worked out years before in *Creative Evolution* into the moral order, where the dualism shows itself by a distinction between two kinds of morality, internal and external, open and closed. The morality of society, imposed on us from without, is the means by which the social hive preserves itself as an organism. Essentially legislative, this morality demands selfless cooperation of members of the social group—in extreme cases, to the point of antlike obedience, despite the promptings of intelligence which always counsel egoism and self-benefit. Opposed to the morality of accommodation to law ("static") is the inner morality of love ("dynamic"), its selflessness a refinement of vital and spontaneous impulse, of movement from the heart of life itself, rather than of obedience to a code imposed from without. The morality of *caritas* has the power to transcend bondage of the social group, the closed societies of family, tribe, nation—to extend itself to all men. Certain religions owe their universal appeal to the legacy of their founders who not only preached but practiced a life that went beyond obedience to active love. Thus the morality of the New Testament includes that of the Old but transcends it. The dynamic absorbs the static which becomes then only a particular instance of the dynamic. Opposition and interplay of these dual moral principles must be conceded, says the author of *The Two Sources,* "if we want to understand not only how society 'constrains' individuals, but again how the individual can set up as a judge and wrest from it a moral transformation."

Of course, there is no hedonism in Bergson, no cult of self, no philosophy of desire—at least of the luxuriant and fleshly sort that pants through *Nourritures* and its sequels. Love for Bergson is *agapé,* not *eros;* like Mauriac's *un seul amour,* God is the object of Bergsonian desire. Moreover, through those years in which Bergson became progressively more absorbed in mysticism, Gide was doing his best to get rid of the residue of mysticism in himself. ("Mystical ideas" (he says in 1929): "I can slip into them as into old slippers; I feel at ease in them; but prefer to go barefoot.") But the writing of both men is marked by a sustained interest in the tension between two poles of value—the internal ethic of the authentic self against conformity to legislative morality, the freedom of vital impulse contrasted with anti-individualistic social constraint. Each in his own way, metaphysician and novelist are drawn to the idea of mobility, the creative novelty of life versus static mechanism, the automatism of routine.

Mobility is the key concept of *Lafcadio's Adventures (Les Caves du Vatican)* in which Gide stages an amusing contest between a supple and creative youth, and the rigidities of the conventions he despises. Here again, as in *The Immoralist* and *Strait Is the Gate,* a moral ideal is pushed to an extreme, then called into question. But the poetic subjectivity of the older *récits* is missing in *Lafcadio* (it will come back once more in *Pastoral Symphony*) and its place is taken by comic detachment, a new impersonality of wit. Instead of the solemn confrontation of two souls, characters proliferate merrily through this chronicle of the Vatican confidence game, and several divisions of the story are required for the play of their interlocking destinies. With *Lafcadio,* Gide found a novelistic format he was to make work hard for him years later in *Counterfeiters.* Young Lafcadio has the *disponibilité* of the earlier Gidean hero, raised to comic power. He is young, fancy-free, and illegitimate (his birth and background recall Apollinaire's); thus in his case even the normal tie to family does not exist, and he lives alone, except for a casual mistress. Poverty is the sole brake on his mobility and he is rescued from it by a legacy from his natural father. Thereafter Lafcadio moves agilely through the story like Stendhal's Fabrizio, full of the aimless energy and flexibility of youth. With a schoolmate Protos he had formed a club in the old days, *les subtils,* setting themselves defiantly against *les crustacés,* the solid, predictable ones who obeyed regulations and went over to the officials when they came of age—carrying their "principles" outside on their backs like the protective shells of snails and crayfish. In the story Protos reappears as a swindler; he has exploited his flexibility to promote a career of crime in which he dons and doffs identities like masks. Disguised as a cleric, he goes about bilking rich Catholics on the pretense that the Pope has been kidnaped and hidden, an unholy alliance of Freemasons and Jesuits having set an imposter on the throne of Peter in his place. Before the amused gaze of his two pliant darlings, Lafcadio and Protos, Gide sets up a basket of *crustacés* of whom the most hard-shelled specimen is the arthritic Armand-Dubois, behaviorist psychologist and anticlerical. Cured of his stiffened joints by an apparent miracle, the rigid atheist rebounds like a billiard ball into an equally doctrinaire Catholicism. Later, troubled by suspicions that God may be as bogus as the Pope, and disillusioned by the return of his ailment, he caroms straight back to his rats and reflexes, mechanically planning fresh reviews for the freethinkers' journal.

The opposite of action by Pavlovian reflex is genuine spontaneity. *Lafcadio* is most often associated with Gide's notorious contribution to literary morals, *l'acte gratuit*. From his childhood Gide had admired the kind of act which, seeming to spring from the heart without calculation, reveals a man's nature at a stroke. The absence of external compulsion seems to reveal such an act as free; its lack of calculation makes it sincere. "Our sincerest acts are also the least premeditated," he says as he reflects on his own decision to marry Madeleine Rondeaux. Could there not be a "pure act," disinterested in that it is an act for its own sake, done for nothing outside itself? This autonomous quality Gide found in the doings of the Greek gods for whom instinct was a better guide than reason. In a quite different way, the love of the God of the Christians for man is pure act, since it is wholly spontaneous and unmotivated, a spilling over of the divine energy, as the Greeks would say. Divine grace is gratuitous; God's love is unmotivated. The waiter in Gide's *Prometheus* once defined man as "the animal capable of the gratuitous act." But Gide believed that such acts, if they existed at all, would be rare indeed. Since every man fears being made to look ridiculous, he holds his acts in cold storage until he counts the cost. Thus his deeds are deprived of spontaneity. It is the exceptional man, indeed the solitary one, who is not afraid to be himself, who does not hesitate to reveal himself before men in an uncalculated gesture. "I tell you, Ulysses," says Gide's Philoctetus, "only since I have lived apart from men do I understand what is called virtue. The man who lives among others is incapable, believe me, incapable of a pure and really disinterested action." Supposing the possibility of such a deed, the "pure act" would emerge spontaneously from the depths of a man's being, unconditioned and autonomous like the Kantian goodwill— except that it need not be a deed society would call virtuous. While the gratuitous act might well be ethical, logically it could just as well be nonethical, even what society might call a crime.

In *Lafcadio,* Gide pushes the idea of the gratuitous act to see how far it will go. It goes as far as murder. The defenestration of Amédée Fleurissoire is Lafcadio's second yielding to impulse. Earlier, without taking thought, he had shinnied up the water pipe of a burning tenement to save two children. He had also toyed Dostoevski-fashion with the idea of strangling an old woman he was helping across the street. Nothing came of that. But in the Rome-Naples express he cannot resist acting definitively once again, although, unlike the fire incident, he has time for forethought. So poor Amédée is pushed to his death, innocent victim of a chain of circumstances that made him the unwilling messenger of the Vatican swindle gang. Only later does Lafcadio discover that Amédée was the brother-in-law of Count Julius de Baraglioul, son of Lafcadio's natural father. Baraglioul, it seems, is a novelist; in fact he is writing a smart book in which the hero is a young man who performs a gratuitous act, the results of which are criminal. The novelist insists on discussing his subject with Lafcadio who is already apprehensive concerning the consequences of his own fine gesture. That act *had* consequences—just disagreeable enough to cause him to question his new-found freedom. For the deed Lafcadio performed for the sheer joy of acting definitively, the wrong man (Protos) is arrested and charged, not before he has strangled the girl he believes has betrayed him. In the end Lafcadio finds himself confessing his crime to his hitherto despised half-brother who is horrified by the boy's revelation, despite his own literary cleverness about motiveless crimes. "And to think I was beginning to love you!" says Julius who, for all his success-hunting, seems to have preserved a shred of authenticity. In this way Gide succeeded in ending his novel on an unresolved chord, once again devaluing the moral ideal his equivocal hero seemed to embody —mobility, spontaneity, personal freedom. With his predecessor Michel, Lafcadio is left standing like the little boy in Ravel's *L'Enfant et les sortilèges* who, after breaking the furniture, smashing the clock, and twisting the cat's tail, cries, "I'm free! Naughty and free!" But Michel and Lafcadio, at least, have their doubts about it.

The disapproval that met the apparent cynicism of *Les Caves du Vatican* on its first appearance was more tempered than the roar of outrage which greeted *The Playboy of the Western World* on its Hibernian debut seven years before, but there were analogous grounds for criticism. Christy Mahon had murdered (he thought) his da, and the villagers gloried with him in his parricide. Lafcadio Wluiki had gaily carried out an apparently motiveless assassination of an innocent man. The passing years rendered Synge's fantasy more acceptable even to the Irishmen who had at first recoiled from it. But Lafcadio's lighthearted homicide has never gone down easily with Gide's readers. Even the sympathetic Hytier is shocked by it. Gide fell back on his complaint that those who accused him of corrupting the youth always insisted on identifying him with the personages of his novels. But he himself was always a little uneasy about his connection with the gratuitous act, and years after *Lafcadio* finally disowned it, at least in its absolute sense—"I myself do not at all believe in the gratuitous act," he wrote in 1928, "that is to say an act not motivated by anything. It is essentially unthinkable. There are no effects without causes. The words 'gratuitous act' are a *provisional* label that seemed to me convenient to designate acts that elude the ordinary psychological explanations, the deeds not determined by mere personal interest. . . ."

Sartre would agree. All action is in principle intentional. Lafcadio knew what he was doing. He intentionally realized a conscious project, even though he did not foresee all the consequences of his act. His *motive* in pushing Amédée out of the train was to do something definitive, to change the shape of the world. The *reason* (cause) of his action was the superfluous presence of the squalid little man who stood there exuding unattractiveness. But motives and causes are correlative; it is we who confer significance on them. Lafcadio's show of deliberation before the assault was a fake. When we deliberate, says Sartre, *"les jeux sont faits."* Despite Lafcadio's self-admission that his miasmic fellow traveler irritates him by the probable total otherness of his values, the supple youth styles his projected act as a crime without motive. Yet the attraction of the irreversible quality of the act draws him consciously to its commission. The slightest push, the merest inclination, and—the chips are down! Says Lafcadio:

In life one corrects oneself—one improves oneself—so people say; but one can't correct what one does. It's the power of revising that makes writing such a colorless affair. . . . That's what seems to me so fine about life. It's like fresco painting—erasures aren't allowed.

Sartre could illustrate human inability to escape even from a single act by citing Conrad's Lord Jim. The case had occurred to Gide, although he records it long after *Lafcadio:* "Noteworthy," he writes in his *Journal* of 1930, "that the fatal irresponsible acts of Conrad's heroes (I am thinking of *Lord Jim* and *Under Western Eyes*) are involuntary and immediately stand seriously in the way of one who commits them. A whole lifetime, afterward, is not enough to give them the lie and efface their mark." But Sartre would quarrel with the world "involuntary." Lord Jim *could* have chosen otherwise. So, for that matter could Amédée Fleurissoire. There are no accidents in the world of *L'Être et le néant,* nor are there any innocent victims. The bourgeois conformist is no more determined than the bohemian individualist; the crustacean is as free as the subtle. It is simply a question of choice. Amédée may have chosen differently from Lafcadio, but he chose all the same.

In *The Counterfeiters* (*Les Faux-Monnayeurs*, 1926), Gide made a second and final experiment with a novel built on the structural principle of intersecting circles of several individual destinies. Gide strained every nerve to complete the book, told his friends he had poured everything into it. *Counterfeiters* was to be his first *real* novel, and a big one—a "novel of ideas" in which the themes of appearance and reality, of real versus apparent motives, of the claims of the morally authentic against the morally false, would be made concrete by a subplot concerning the passing of counterfeit gold coins by a group of schoolboys. The result was a story considerably longer and more complex than the *Lafcadio* of twelve years before, although kin to it in spirit. At first Gide had planned *Counterfeiters* as a sequel to Lafcadio, with the hero of the earlier novel reappearing as one of the leading characters. Bernard—who took Lafcadio's place —is a character in the same style, particularly as we see him in the opening Stendhal-like chapters of the novel. In his preface to *The Charterhouse of Parma,* Balzac classified Stendhal's story of Fabrizio Del Dongo as a "novel of ideas." In Gide's novel, the "ideas" are edged forward only after the Fabrizio in Bernard has been allowed to cool off.

Readers of Gide know that *The Counterfeiters* is the story of two young students, Bernard and Olivier, and their successive relations to a novelist, Edouard, who is the uncle of Olivier. After the first few chapters in which Bernard is allowed the center of the stage, Edouard takes over the story, dominating it to the end as interlocutor and commentator. He is writing a novel to be titled "The Counterfeiters," and keeps a diary of its composition as did Gide with *The Counterfeiters.* Through the young men's connections to parents, siblings, friends, teachers, lovers, mistresses, and through the ties of these in turn to other parents, siblings, friends, and so on, characters proliferate like squirrels through the novel which runs to 550 pages in the *Oeuvres Complètes.* Among other personages, there are crustacean fathers and flexible sons, rascally boys and a saintly little girl, a good pederast and a bad one, a lachrymose Em-figure and a *femme fatale,* a uxorious young husband and a wife-hating old one, an amateur psychologist, and a professional villain. Intermittently the story stops for a reading of Edouard's journal, and at one point the author halts the tale archly to review his characters.

The most promising of this mixed lot is young Bernard who at the outset of the story displays all the old Gidean sincerity and *disponibilité.* After his accidental discovery that he is not the legitimate son of his father (a hypocritical bourgeois once diddled by his pious wife), Bernard refuses to bear his false name (Profitendieu) any longer, and detaches himself from his family to seek his fortune. Lafcadio-like, he formulates individualistic maxims appropriate to his exceptional self:

If not me, who? If not now, when?

Retrieving a baggage check Edouard dropped by chance, he claims the novelist's valise at the station, helping himself to Edouard's money and diary. But for all his brave beginnings, Bernard's career does not fulfill the promise of his initial bounce. As the permissive Edouard's secretary *pro tem,* the youth's energy dwindles—for he has nothing to fight against. The best he can do is to fall in love without desire with Laura, Edouard's ex-mistress whom the novelist is sheltering until *her* illegitimate child (by none other than Bernard's older brother Vincent) is born. In the end, the Lafcadio *manqué* fades into the penitent hero of *The Return of the Prodigal Son.* Resigning his secretary's post to make way for Olivier, his school friend, Bernard slips back to the house of his pseudo-father whose love for his wife's bastard son turns out to be the only genuine thing about him.

Some of Bernard's *disponibilité* is assumed by Edouard in the course of the story. In his journal, the novelist attacks the institution of the *family,* lamenting the hampering effect of "that cellular system" on the young born to freedom. Later he has opportunity to put his sentiment to the test by gently detaching the youth Olivier from his tearful mother, first having had to unstick him rather more rudely from the Comte de Passavant, bad homosexual and false novelist. After his first night with Edouard (a good homosexual), Olivier's joy is so great that he attempts suicide in an endeavor to forestall the inevitable diminution of happiness time will bring—a near-fatal action tied to an earlier conversation between Olivier and Bernard on Dimitri Karamazov's notion of suicide through sheer exuberance.

During his nephew's convalescence, Edouard is happy with his dear Olivier ("My breath, my life comes to me from him—through him"), yet he is not so immovably committed to this source of joy as to forget that he has another nephew, one he has not yet seen but is soon to meet, Olivier's younger brother Caloub. Edouard's concluding line, "I feel very curious to know Caloub," brings *The Counterfeiters* to a close on a typical Gidean unresolved chord, its brevity owing not so much to the mobile Edouard's need-to-move-on as to Gide's desire to finish off a story the length of which had begun to bore him.

"The work of art is the exaggeration of an idea," says Gide. In *Pastoral Symphony,* that simple tale of a Protestant pastor who mistakes *eros* for *agape* in sheltering a blind girl, Gide had played on the idea of real versus apparent motives. Now in the more ambitious *Counterfeiters* he subsumes the double-motive concept under the broader philosophical dualism of appearance and reality. Lest the obtuse reader fail to appreciate the polarity forming the ideational skeleton of the novel, Gide has his characters announce it from time to time. Young Bernard constructs the distinction out of his own passion for sincerity, using the metaphor of real and false coin: "I should like all my life long at the very smallest shock, to ring true, with a pure authentic sound. Nearly all the people I have known ring false. To be worth exactly what one seems to be worth, not to try to seem to be worth more . . ." Ironically, Bernard's younger brother George is one of the schoolboys used by the counterfeiters to get their bad money into circulation. Although we never meet the actual coiners, we know their intermediary is Strouvilhou. This corrupt Nietzschean is the personification of gratuitous evil in the book, an ambassador from hell; yet he too has a passion for sincerity. He informs Passavant that he will edit the latter's review only if in its pages he is allowed to demonetize fine feelings: "We live upon nothing but feelings which have been taken for granted. . . . These feelings ring as false as counters, but they pass for good coin." It is Edouard who gives the dualism its metaphysical formulation, finding in the opposition of appearance and reality the "deep-lying subject" of his novel— ". . . the rivalry between the real world and the representation of it which we make to ourselves. The manner in which we try to impose on the outside world our own interpretation—that is the drama of our lives." The rivalry between what is and what appears is not resolved by the cheap phenomenalism of Passavant who succeeds temporarily in indoctrinating Olivier with the belief that the artist is "the man who consents to take merely the outside of things, that their secret is their form and that what is deepest in man is his skin."

The appearance-reality play is carried over into the action of the novel by an ingenious variety of means. The false coins are emblems of all kinds of mistakes of seeming for being. The reunion of Edouard and Olivier is long postponed, because each has misinterpreted the other's self-consciousness at the railroad station. Bernard passes by his mourning schoolfellow out of shyness, but the boy thinks it is because Bernard feels only contempt for him. (Proust's characters are constantly guilty of such misconstructions.) Deception includes self-deception. The secret motive of Laura's marriage to the good Douviers and her consequent infidelity to him with Vincent is disclosed to be her love for Edouard. In the *ménage à trois* the novelist sets up in Switzerland while she is awaiting her confinement, Laura feels the least she could do is to repay his kindness by sleeping with him. But she drapes this sentiment with such delicate reticence that Edouard takes it for coldness. Edouard in turn believes that he has recommended little Boris to the Azais school only out of a sincere wish to offer the boy a safe harbor and to bring him near his doting grandfather. But what really impels him is curiosity to see what will happen to the disturbed child in that ambiguous place, a curiosity painfully gratified by the forced suicide of the little boy in the classroom. The dualism moves up to the level of meta-novel in Edouard's journal as he analyzes the problem of style in the writing of his "Counterfeiters." The naturalistic novel tries to describe things as they "really are," yet in some way fails to hit the truth. On the other hand, highly stylized art often succeeds in touching something universal in common experience. Racine's Mithradates, says Gide, talks with his two sons in a way no father would ever do in actual life, yet it is a scene in which all fathers and all sons can see themselves. To Edouard, the alternative to naturalistic fiction seems to be the philosophical novel, an airy stage for the light interplay of thoughts, a kaleidoscope of concepts, a crossroads of ideas. But the risk here is one of losing oneself in abstraction. "It's always dangerous to put intellectuals in novels," Mme. Sophroniska tells him. "The public is bored by them."

All Gide's cleverness with "ideas" leaves *The Counterfeiters* a strangely defective novel, despite the honors that have come to it. Perhaps the appearance-reality dualism *is* too abstract a distinction on which to hang so much particular and miscellaneous material— although Proust exploits a similar distinction with success. Gide himself was defensive about *The Counterfeiters*, alternately accusing himself of too great concern for "art" in the composition of the novel, then his critics' supposed lack of imagination in receiving it. It occurred to him that the *elliptical* quality of his book could not possibly satisfy readers conditioned to the explicit and linear chronicles of the naturalistic novelists. *Les Faux-Monnayeurs* was dedicated to Gide's friend Roger Martin Du Gard, his favorite among contemporary naturalistic chroniclers. It was the author of *Les Thibaults*, Gide says, who persuaded him to weave the several tales of his Lafcadio sequel into a single novelistic design. It may be that Gide has so many subplots to manage in his novel that he cannot avoid resort to distracting coincidences. Or perhaps *The Counterfeiters* shows the strain of a work by a writer who, standing at a critical junction in a late stage of his career, cannot resist the temptation *to throw everything in*. Allowing for differences, both Joyce's *Finnegans Wake* and Mann's *Doctor Faustus* are cases in point.

The style of *The Counterfeiters* has been singled out for praise by critics who have somehow fallen under its spell. "The elusive immaterial quality of *Les Faux-Monnayeurs*," says Lawrence Thomas in his study of Gide, "is precisely that of music." But it is precisely the style of the novel that abounds so irritatingly in nonmusical protuberances. The intermittent affectation of the historical present

("Olivier admires his friend with immense fervor. He knows him to be resolute" . . . and so on.) is too suggestive of Jean de Brunhoff's immortal chronicle of Babar, the elephant. ("Babar admires his friend, the old lady. He knows her to be kind" . . . and so on.) The homosexual passages in *The Counterfeiters* are embarrassing not for moral reasons, but because they produce some of the most sentimental blushings, sighs, and arm-squeezings this side of Dickens. Young Olivier's sobbings, swoonings, and "Take me aways" are more appropriate to the perfumed plush of *ottocento* melodrama than to the atmosphere, presumably cold and dry, of a twentieth century "novel of ideas." Passages like that of the twelfth chapter where Olivier and Edouard hold hands ("His hand fluttered in mine like a captured bird") are totally absent in *The Immoralist*. In his treatment of emerging sexual ambiguity in Michel's story, Gide put a fine aesthetic distance between reader and hero, a distance which enhances the effect of the (then) new and powerful theme. Michel's unconscious homosexuality is both a real and a symbolic attribute of his exceptional nature. But in *The Counterfeiters* there is no ambiguity whatever about the sexual bent of the principals, nor of the author's attitude toward it. From the beginning, Olivier's fondling of Bernard plus his confession that he felt no desire for the woman he slept with make it quite clear to the reader where the youth's preferences lie. As for Edouard—he has hardly debarked from his train before we realize that Olivier's uncle is (as Proust would say) an Auntie or (as Queneau's Zazie would say) a "hormosexual." Thus the handling of boy-love in *The Counterfeiters* has no advantage of distance; the sympathetic closeness of the author to the theme pushes it over into sentimentality and unconscious funniness. In fairness, it must be admitted that the silliest patch in the novel occurs in a heterosexual exchange—the improbable *pajama ex machina* scene between Lilian and Vincent: "In the cupboard," says Lady Griffith to her lover who has just jumped out of bed, "On the right hand side of the bath, you'll find a collection of burnouses and haiks and pyjamas. Take anything you like." Twenty minutes later, Vincent reappears "dressed in a pistachio-colored silk jellabah."

The shrewdest guess as to why *The Counterfeiters* misfires occurs in the text of the novel itself. Edouard confides to his journal that he has been reflecting on the criticism that a certain X (Du Gard?) has made of his plan for his (Edouard's) "The Counterfeiters," and admits that his advice is always salutary. But while X thinks Edouard's difficulties are attributable to the temptation besetting every novelist of ideas to be led astray by the very excess of his "ideas," Edouard himself believes that his trouble springs from a deeper source—his inability to use any longer the personal problems of his life as material for his art:

> He is afraid that my work may be too factitious, that I am in danger of letting go the real subject for the shadow of the subject in my brain. What makes me uneasy is to feel that life (my life) at this juncture is parting company from my work, and my work moving away from my life. But I couldn't say that to him. Up till now— as is right—my tastes, my feelings, my personal experiences have all gone to feed my writings; in my best contrived phrases I still felt the beating of my heart. But henceforth the link is broken between what I think and what I feel. And I wonder whether this impediment which prevents my heart from speaking is not the real cause that is driving my work into abstraction and artificiality. As I was reflecting on this, the meaning of the fable of Apollo and Daphne suddenly flashed upon me: happy, thought I, the man who can clasp in one and the same embrace the laurel and the object of his love.

As early as 1911, Jacques Rivière noted that Gide's fiction had begun to move away from life, seeing in the novelist's *Isabelle* of that year a transitional work the theme of which had not been drawn from the personal experience of the author. But we must resist the temptation to exaggerate this shift in the center of gravity of Gide's work. *The Pastoral Symphony*, after all, appeared eight years after *Isabelle,* and it is just the kind of tale we expect of the writer of *The Immoralist* and *Strait Is the Gate,* a story in which we still feel the beating of his heart. Moreover, Gide had no dearth of personal material to write from in the years leading up to *The Counterfeiters;* he fashioned the novel while under the spell of young Marc Allégret, and the Edouard-

Olivier relationship in the novel reflects this. The scene in which Edouard gently tries to reconcile Mme. Molinier to the idea of her son living with him must have had its counterpart in certain exchanges between Mme. Allégret and Gide who once mentioned to her how much the virtues of Greek and Christian teaching had meant to him, adding piously, "And that Christ's is of an infinitely superior kind I hope one day to convince certain of your sons." Gide occasionally gave the impression of confusing pederasty with the spirit of the New Testament.

Gide's lifelong insistence that his work be judged solely from an aesthetic point of view balanced an awareness on his part that the material of his best and most characteristic fiction was drawn from the moral conflicts of his own life. The young men who sat at Mallarmé's feet (Gide was one) construed the Symbolist credo to mean that the poet should turn his back upon life, even his own. But Gide was much too fascinated with life, and most particularly his own, to make a good Symbolist on those terms. He simultaneously affirmed and denied that an effect of his own art was to teach. This coexistence of *l'art pour l'art* with the moral, even the didactic, element in his soul sets up in Gide's best storytelling a tension that gives to it its peculiarly "Gidean" tonality. *The Counterfeiters* was written in those years of Gide's life when he had moved well away, not from personal conflicts, but from that part of his life when these conflicts were one with his awakening and self-discovery—his youth. *Les Faux-Monnayeurs* was Gide's first and last attempt to write a "pure" work of art on the grand scale, a brilliant philosophical novel that would secure his eminence as one of the great twentieth century creators of fiction. A final clue as to why the attempt failed lies in a remark Gide made at the time he was searching for the form of *The Counterfeiters*: "There are moments when I lack the courage to face the idea of creating characters of a novel," he said. "My own life has been too interesting." As a novelist, Gide will probably survive in his earlier, smaller works, their characters still projections of personal tensions not yet relaxed by advancing years. For all his talk that his job was only to paint pictures and to stand them in the best possible

light, this irony remains: when Gide is at his most moralistic, most
didactic, most "warning," his work is aesthetically most satisfying.

VII

After *The Counterfeiters*, his last major work of fiction, Gide had
still a quarter century to live. Nearly all of his writing of any interest
in this long final period of his life lies in his diaries—either in the
Journals proper or in the separate records of his Congo trip and
journey to the Soviet Union. As a novelist, he was finished. *The
School for Wives*, its sequel *Robert*, and the later *Geneviève* read
like bad Mauriac stories. *Œdipus* is slight, and the *Persephone* he
wrote for Ida Rubinstein so that she might dance to Stravinsky's
music is no more than a sketch. His last tale, the little *Theseus* of
1946 shows a spark, but that soon flickers and goes out. Only through
the *Journals* did Gide manage to keep a toehold on his reputation
as a major literary personality. These diaries trace his journey to the
Congo and Lake Chad regions, his recognition by the literary Left
when his mild observations on colonial abuses appeared in print, his
sudden and public affection for Communism, and the disillusioning
visit to the U.S.S.R. in 1936, followed by his hasty disengagement
from the embraces of the Russian bear. His retirement to Tunisia
after the fall of France to sit out the war, reading Goethe and making
acid comments on the Americans, did not strike the French Com-
munists as sufficiently patriotic, and *Les Lettres Françaises* howled
for his head. But General de Gaulle graciously accorded him a
victory interview in Algiers, and soon after the belated laurels of the
Nobel Prize descended on the still handsome bald cranium, now constantly protected from drafts by the rumpled beret.

In the end he admits it was the residue of mysticism in him that
brought him to Communism, in which for a moment he thought he
had found his ideal—a society without the family, a religion without
a mythology. That, plus his bourgeois bad conscience for having had
since childhood so much more than the others. ("Just as we owed it to

ourselves to have a porte-cochère . . . so we owed it to ourselves always to travel first class".) He strikes out at mysticism with anger,
proclaiming it mankind's worst enemy, the abdication of reason. Once
he had held it to be a peculiarly Protestant excess; now he blames it
on the Catholic Church. He who had more than once considered conversion ("Thank God, a few converts among my friends took care of
this, however") now cries *Écrasez l'infame!*—"It is in the very name
of Christianity that we must combat the church." The mystical bent
of his poor wife, he claims, turned her soul toward Rome in her
declining years. ("The slow progress of Catholicism in her soul; it
seems to me that I am watching the spreading of a gangrene.")
Naïvely he complains that Christianity is a failure because Christians
have failed to live up to the teachings of Christ. (He had never heard
Chesterton's remark that Christianity could not possibly have failed,
for it had never been tried.) He snarls at priests; a school of them
passes him on the road—"not the slightest spirituality, not the slightest flame"—as the Christian Brothers had once tramped by Stephen
Dedalus. "Oh, how well off everything would be if we dealt with
Christianity! But religion is not Christianity, it is the priest." With
the Sisters, he is gentler. At sea he writes, "Through the open door I
watch at length two kneeling nuns whose faces I cannot see, as far
away from the altar as the width of the room allows; very simple,
very beautiful bearing. . . ." God? For a long time, he notes, he used
the word as a kind of dumping ground for all his vaguest concepts.
Now it strikes him that perhaps God has not yet begun to be, but is
in the process of emerging from the universe. Perhaps God needs
man's belief in him to exist at all. The man who had smilingly rejected Nietzsche's *L'Éternel retour* as a refuge for the mystical, writes
at Sidi-bou-Saïd in 1942:

As soon as I had realized that God was not yet but was becoming
and that his becoming depended on each one of us, a moral sense
was restored in me. No impiety or presumption in this thought, for
I was convinced at one and the same time that God was achieved
only by man and through man, but that if man led to God, creation,

in order to lead to man, started from God; so that the divine had its place at both ends, at the start and at the point of arrival, and that the start had been solely in order to arrive at God. . . .

Then a week later, this note:

But how slow God is in becoming! . . .

The theistic speculations and doubts of Gide's advancing years are of small interest. They play no part in what poetic inspiration is left to him. They have little originality. The theodicy colored by a perennial exaltation of progress (God himself must progress) is as dated as the emergent evolutionism of Lloyd Morgan and Alexander. His fideism skates close to the trite—an honest God is the noblest work of man. In the end, he gives it all up anyway. There is the God of the philosophers, the first cause, lord of the cosmos. Then there is the Christ of love. The first is no more than a word for Nature. The second an ideal around which we may center our lives. The final volume of the *Journals* gives way to a frank naturalism, rescued from banality only by the strangely moving entry near the end—the long passage that opens with the terrible recollection of his sister-in-law's still-born child. Memory of the bloody little wreck made beautiful for burial by the pious hands of the gardener's wife, the sweet small face beneath the empty cranium, forcibly reminds him of the error of Platonism that would forever cut soul from body in contrast to the wisdom of the Church's doctrine of the resurrection of the flesh, the ordained reunion of matter with the spirit that longs for it. But immortality? No, the soul is only the glow that surrounds the phosphorus. Images of his wife in her last sickness break for a moment into his epiphenomenalism. He recalls how she lay there, his Emmanuele, "like a Jansenist painting by Philippe de Champaigne." In her, Spirit had risen incomparably above Nature. But without its natural root, there can be no Spirit. He remembers Valéry's line from *Le Cimetière marin*:

Chanterez-vous quand serez vaporeuse?

Old age had come to him. He has serenity, that state he once called "the virtue of an old man." Though he never liked the Stoic's stiff upper lip, he welcomes his fate, saying with his Theseus, "My city stands. After I am gone, my thoughts will live on there forever. Lonely and consenting, I draw near to death." *Death fixes the outlines.* So Du Gard had said in his *Thibaults,* and so too Sartre in Existentialist variation on the theme of essence and existence. So as well the commentator in *Osservatore Romano.* Only at death do we become all essence, for then alone is *what we are* completed; the brush of the self-portrait toiled over for a lifetime is at last laid down. But Gide himself is not so sure of this. Years ago he had written of Du Gard's claim, "What a wonderful novel could be written that would make us realize this is false." All the same, he is listless, longs for some unexpected rebound. At seventy-two he still feels the stirring of desire:

The shortest night of the year.
The last four days have been more beautiful than one can say; more beautiful than I could endure. A sort of call to happiness in which all nature conspired in a miraculous swoon, reaching a summit of love and joy in which the human being has nothing further to wish for but death. On such a night one would like to kiss the flowers, caress the tree trunks, embrace any young and ardent body whatever or prowl in search of it till dawn. Going off to bed alone, as I have nevertheless to decide to do, seems impious.

At last, all desire fades, even the desire to live. *Anorexia.* The word fascinates him. A Stoic in spite of himself, he has achieved even against his will the *summum bonum* of the ancient philosopher—apathy. The poet of desire is at the end forsaken by his own. From time to time memories of his first African wanderings trouble his repose—the cool water drunk under a burning sky, the oleanders of the oases, the naked young bodies, superb joys of the flesh. They assail him now like the taste of colocinths, fruit filled with bitter ashes, yet beautiful as they lie on the golden sand. Dying, he scribbles between comas: "What will remain of all this? . . . of all that is being written today, in France and elsewhere. What will remain of our culture, of France itself, of what we have lived for? Let's make up our minds that everything is destined to disappear." A sad echo of Lucretius mourning the fate of this vast world, condemned to death and ruin.

"Biskra, I think of your palm trees—Touggourt of your sands." Not long after Gide's death, officials of the French *Bureau de Recherches du Petrole,* heavily guarded against surprise attack by Algerian rebels, watched engineers in a freight yard at Touggourt throw open the valves of a pipeline carrying oil from the Hassi Messaoud fields in the Sahara. *"Lassif . . . Bachir . . . Ashour . . . Moktir. . . ."* Dressed now in heavy western-style work clothes, black with petroleum, they stack the *tubes de sondage* along the route. *"Chetma . . . El Kantara . . . Chegga . . . M'rayer. . . ."* On its way to the Mediterranean coast the pipeline passes through Biskra. More than 800 kilometers southwest of Touggourt, the old caravan route to the Niger passes a restricted area near Adrar. At its edge one winter day in 1960 some Bedouin camel drivers stopped at a thunderclap and the sight of a cloud mushrooming into the pure blue:—at Zaouiet Reggan, France had contrived her first atomic explosion. On the day the flash burst over the wilderness of sand, André Gide had been dead nine years. But could even death have brought him rest? More likely that he wanders today—as once at Cuverville in harvesttime—like a madman amidst a peace as arid to him as the desert.

≈§ 3 §≈

Thomas Mann

Thomas Mann

✒ *A work of art may and often does con-
tain a metaphysical idea; yet it is not
necessary that the reader, nor even the
artist at the moment of creation, be
aware of this.*

MANN

✒ *Psychopaths, suicides, fanatic ego-wor-
shippers, wild dreamers, and tuberculosis
patients with the heightened self-ab-
sorption of sickness, were the majority
of the great poets whose names are
synonymous with German romanticism's
artistic conquests; for it is true that the
threat of destruction of personality in
insanity or death very often stimulates
gifted individuals to heightened productivity. It literally looks as if such a
threat, of early death or madness, is
necessary before German talents can
produce something above sheer medioc-
rity.*

UNDSET

"Do YOU KNOW what's needed to make a scamp out of an honest man?" asks the pseudo-professor Defouqueblize of young Lafcadio in Gide's *Les Caves du Vatican*. "Take him out of his country, remove him from his familiar element . . . just a cessation of continuity, a simple interruption of his current will do." Like Gide's, Thomas Mann's dislodged heroes tend to lose their moral bearings when loosed from home and normal routine. Aschenbach comes to grief on holiday in Venice. Away from home and linden tree, Leverkühn makes a fatal misstep in Leipzig, signs on with the devil in Italy. It was on a trip to Amsterdam that Thomas Buddenbrook pledged himself to the exotic Gerda with whose death-marked child the Buddenbrook's dynasty will pass away; even Thomas's sister Toni, summering in Travemünde, is tempted for a moment to forget what she owes to herself and her family. By the second page of *The Magic Mountain*, the voice of the narrator of Hans Castorp's story has taken on a warning tone:

Space, like time, engenders forgetfulness; but it does so by setting us bodily free from our surroundings and giving us back our primitive unattached state. Yes, it can even, in the twinkling of an eye, make something like a vagabond out of the pedant and suburban citizen.

Allowing for the difference in scale, Gide's *Immoralist* and Mann's *Zauberberg* are not unlike; both stories grow from the same root idea—the dislodgement of a young man, and his rebirth in questionable surroundings. Of exactly the same age as Michel, Hans Castorp is also an ex-student, a youthful bourgeois with tubercular weakness whom illness detains in an exotic vacation spot beyond the time of his appointed stay. Michel used the figure of a palimpsest to describe his rebirth; he felt a precious occult text coming to light within him beneath the mediocre surface writing. But German Hans is not content to compare his self-discovery to a mere affair of the written word; he cites his *Steigerung,* the hermetic elevation of creative spirit within the alchemical retort of disease and death. Moreover, Michel's ethical disintegration profits him less than Castorp's: the ex-engineer succeeds, after all, in fashioning a *Lebenskunst* in high romantic style out of his deck-chair dreams. But neither one hero nor the other fulfills the complete promise of his vision. Jolted by Marceline's pitiful death, Michel is forced (too late) to admit that he does not know what to do with his objectless freedom; and at the end of Hans's story he finds himself sunk in a meditative torpor so profound that only the external shock of the 1914 war can (too late) arouse him. Like Gide's fable of Michel, *Der Zauberberg* is a cautionary tale; its author described it as a "withdrawal from dangerous sympathies, enchantments, temptations."

A novel of *dépaysement,* then. Critics love to discover categories for Mann's Davos story. It is a pedagogical novel, the chronicle of a young man's education for life, a *Bildungsroman* after the fashion of Goethe's *Wilhelm Meister.* Just as young Wilhelm seems to his friend like unto Saul, the son of Kish, who went to seek his father's asses and found a kingdom, so too Hans Castorp, who came to Switzerland for three weeks, stayed there seven years to find a kingdom within himself. The poet Novalis said that *Wilhelm Meister* was a Candide story. So is Mann's *Zauberberg.* Like Voltaire's ingenuous hero, honest Hans acquires a tutor of encyclopedic learning, he experiments in love, has marvelous adventures, learns about life at very nearly the price of his skin. The very title of the story is made for a romantic fairy tale; it has all the standard ingredients—an enchanted castle, magic spells, a beautiful princess, kindly and malevolent wizards, dwarfs, giants, ghosts. And, of course, it is a novel of ideas; at least its dialectical method and high ideological content qualify it for that label, even though its classification as such would not satisfy Balzac who ruled that a novel of ideas must be concise, move rapidly, and avoid discussion—a limitation appalling to think of in connection with *The Magic Mountain*'s thousand discursive pages.

A cinematographical novel. One for the movies. Mann sets his hero's adventures against the background of the high Alps where the very scenery seems unreal. (Wasn't Bompard's Tartarin persuaded that all the natural marvels of Switzerland—waterfalls, avalanches, and the rest—were activated by elaborate machinery hidden under the rocks?) In Hollywood, where for years a libidinous interest has been shown in the novel, *The Magic Mountain* is classified as a promising

"Grand Hotel" story. Back in the twenties, the device of a luxurious international hostelry enabled Vicki Baum to bring together multiple human destinies in her novel, besides furnishing a spacious lobby for her grotesques to parade across. More recently, Katherine Anne Porter, updating old-German Sebastian Brant (as well as Sutton Vane) found that an ocean steamship provided suitable allegorical setting as well as legroom for the assorted personages of her Teuton-ophobe *Ship of Fools*. ("We are all on the passenger list!") Thomas Mann's sanatorium Berghof is his Grand Hotel, sheltering one hundred phthisic characters under one roof, allowing him to move his garrulous monsters through dining hall, salon, X-ray room, bed-chambers, and balconies. One advantage of a Grand Hotel novel is that it enables its writer to deal with high life; a story whose characters do not have to work for a living is always more fun to read than a tale of less fortunate mortals who must sweat for wages. In an access of social awareness in 1953, Mann reminded the readers of his Davos novel that a sanatorium of the order of Haus Berghof with its pampering care, stunning meals, and accessible females, was a capitalist-bourgeois phenomenon peculiar to the prewar period, a danger to the young, an incitement to idleness and sexual disorder. With the disappearance of families who could afford to keep a patient up there in such style, Mann observed, most of the Swiss sanatoria have become sports hotels.

Most, but by no means all. Despite the pressure of international sport and the decline of tuberculosis, to this day there survive near Davos a number of hospitals and sanatoria for the tubercular. Even those turned into resort hotels tend to keep the glass-fronted balconies of the old days, the *chaises longues* complete with rolled blanket for the comfort if not for the health of the guest. But it is true that tuberculosis is today a fading disease. With the aid of antibiotics, a surgeon can now get at the apex of an infected lung without the fear of spreading infection which compelled the patient of Castorp's day to submit to long months, even years, of rest cure. Most tuberculosis patients are victims of poverty and malnutrition. (The Second World War sent the death rate soaring in Europe, particularly in the

East.) A much smaller, although still well defined group of consumptives comes from the adequately nourished middle class. In many patients of this category, tuberculosis specialists note that the onset of the disease often coincides with a crossroads in the patient's personal life—a major decision to be faced concerning marriage or change of job, resumption of civilian life after a long period of military service, any imminent necessity of setting out on a new stage of career. This is as true today as it was more than fifty years ago when Hans Castorp found himself with a moist spot on his lung.

A long tradition links *tuberculosis pulmonum* with the development of genius. Claims of positive correlation between the disease and the poetic gift have been supported by partisans with citations of lists of ailing geniuses from Milton to Albert Camus—although skeptical physicians are inclined to credit the productivity in such cases to the leisure enforced by the cure which gives the patient opportunity to cultivate his talent rather than to the disease itself. Interest in illness as creative, in suffering as redemptive, in death as a powerful stimulus to art and life, is a mark of German romanticism from the romantic-biological rhapsodies of Novalis to *Wozzeck*'s poet in love with death. Himself tubercular, Novalis believed that sickness of the flesh may be rooted in spirit, that life itself is a disease. Long before Dr. Krokowski ("I have never in my life come across a perfectly healthy human being") and Nietzsche ("Man is the *sick animal*"), the poet of *Hymns to the Night* had declared that "The idea of perfect health is interesting only from a scientific point of view. Sickness is necessary to individualization." How much Franz Schubert owed his morbid fancies to a literary fashion that pushed *Sympathie mit dem Tode* to the point of sentimentality, how much to anxiety over his terrible disease, is hard to determine. At least we have the D minor ("Death and the Maiden") quartet and the great C minor quintet to point to, as well as Hans Castorp's favorite deathditty "Der Lindenbaum." The American Hawthorne read the German romantics (particularly Tieck), and the psychogenic theory of disease that emerges from Roger Chillingworth's diagnosis of Dimmesdale's ailment in *The Scarlet Letter* strikes a note familiar to readers of *The Magic Mountain*:

He whom only the outward and physical evil is laid open knoweth, oftentimes, but half the evil which he is called upon to cure. A bodily disease, which we look upon as whole and entire within itself, may after all, be but a symptom of some ailment in the spiritual part . . . a sickness . . . a sore place . . . in your spirit, hath immediately its appropriate manifestion in your bodily frame.

In the face of Hegel's mighty Reason and the scientism of the Positivists, the romantic philosopher Schopenhauer restored death to a position of metaphysical dignity. His pupil Nietzsche, the very Platonic Idea of the suffering genius, claimed illness first woke him to reason, going on to say that to an intrinsically sound nature, "illness may even constitute a powerful stimulus to life, to a surplus of life." Richard Wagner struck a more theatrical attitude: he tells his friend Röckel that his nervous system is in bad shape and getting worse, but explains this as the "necessary result of my abandoning myself to that passionate and hectic sensibility in virtue of which I am the artistic being that I am." Freud, Mann thought, was the reaper of this harvest; he took the Viennese to be, like himself, an heir to the romantic genius which adumbrated the whole idea of the psychic root of disease, the power of the irrational, neurosis as frustrated Eros. At the time he began to compose *The Magic Mountain,* Mann knew Freud only by hearsay; nevertheless he fabricated his own psychoanalyst for the novel, Edhin Krokowski, who tells Hans Castorp and the assembled patients, "All disease is love transformed."

Fever, excitement, the sense of love without an object—these are the first outward signs of Hans Castorp's response to his displacement, the sudden translation from his comfortable North German home to the Alpine height with its cold and stimulating air—its *Höhenluft,* as Nietzsche would say. Castorp's pulmonary lesions form the stigmata of his exceptional nature as well as signals of his emerging libido. In the Davos novel, Mann divides the outlandish inhabitants of his sanatorium into two well defined classes of unequal size. The majority of the patients are trivial and uninteresting. Like Hermine Kleefeld and her fellow members of the Half-Lung club, they use their disease to escape the responsibilities of living. The serious and interesting people at the sanatorium, Hans's seven teachers—Joachim, Clavdia,

Settembrini, Naphta, Peeperkorn and the two doctors—constitute a small but distinguished minority whose sickness is a function of their talent, the effect of some inner split which makes them "interesting." At first, the narrator's affectionate irony conceals Hans Castorp's exceptional nature; he makes all that talk about the engineer being just an ordinary young man (*ein einfacher junger Mensch*). Yet everyone young Hans meets at the fantastic sanatorium takes a sharp look at him, inspecting him far more thoughtfully than his unassuming youth would seem to warrant. Even the ouija board obliges with higher order phenomena the moment Hans is introduced to it. The process of metamorphosis set in from the first day, and before the novel is done Hans has emerged as an official representative of his social class, of Germany, of genius, and humanity itself. Although his German-bourgeois emblems are faithfully described—the good leather bags, the expensive clothes, his discreet gargle, the cigar, his sense of decorum, the eating of those good meals out of self-respect rather than appetite—Castorp's burgher self shows through the X-ray as weakened and cracked from the start. He is no more an authentic engineer than Kafka's "K" arriving in *his* strange village is a genuine land-surveyor. Both have left their equipment behind. In the long flashback in which Hans's childhood and youth at Tienappel's are so carefully described, we are told that the lad once painted a picture of a ship, a piece of work recognized by a stranger as manifesting real talent. To be sure, Hans and his uncle had smiled together at the thought of an artist's life for him—queer clothes, garret, irregular living, and the rest. All the same, Hans *had* painted a picture. As if these hints of latent gift were not enough, the narrator gives the show away in the early key passage:

A man lives not only his personal life, as an individual, but also, consciously or unconsciously, the life of his epoch and his contemporaries. . . . All sorts of personal aims, ends, hopes, prospects, hover before the eyes of the individual, and out of these he derives the impulse to ambition and achievement. Now, if the life about him, if his own time seem, however outwardly stimulating, to be at bottom empty of such food for his aspirations . . . a certain laming of the personality is bound to occur . . . a sort of palsy, as it were, which may even extend from his spiritual and moral over into his physical and organic part. . . .

In a letter to his friend Rohde, Friedrich Nietzsche, defending himself, prewrote Mann's defense of his Hans:

The man who has only a few moments a day for what he regards as most important, and who has to spend the rest of his time and energy performing duties which others could carry out equally well—such a man is not a harmonious whole; he must be in conflict with himself and must ultimately fall ill.

Tubercular and gifted, Hans Castorp is the central figure in a line of ailing heroes that goes back in Mann's work through Aschenbach and Tonio Kröger to Thomas Buddenbrook and his son Hanno. Less clearly, he prefigures Joseph. "It is almost impossible to discuss *The Magic Mountain*," Mann insisted, "without thinking of the links that connect it with other works; backwards in time to *Buddenbrooks* and *Death in Venice*, forward to the Joseph novels." In the early pages of *Der Zauberberg*, just at the moment the reader's curiosity is aroused by the initial description of Hans's reaction to the impressions made on him by the sanatorium and its denizens, the narrator drags his attention away with a long excursus on Castorp's childhood and youth, so that he may realize the importance of the young man's cultural roots. So too at this point it may be useful for us, if we are interested in Mann's "ideas" (*philosophische Erkenntniskraft*) as well as his "art" (*dichterische Kunst*), to turn back for a last look at those earlier works before going on with the mountain climb.

II

There are a number of astonishing things about *Buddenbrooks*. Granting that he had read the Goncourts, Maupassant, and the Russians attentively, how could a young man in his early twenties have carried out such a flawless performance to the length of two volumes? How could he in his own writing have hewed so close to the actual history and personalities of his own family, and yet have given the novel a completely independent life of its own? How could he have blended Schopenhauer's dualism of *Will* (Life) and *Idea* (Spirit) so smoothly into the mixture that his German bourgeois reading public was not for a moment put off by such *idées,* but on the contrary swallowed the heroic dose holus-bolus and demanded more? *Buddenbrooks* was a hit from the beginning, making its author a classical example of *the successful writer.* It is Thomas Buddenbrook who is that novel's exceptional man, the merchant-citizen with a weakness for beauty, a suppressed tendency to Catholicism. He is able and ambitious. But to do something, one must be something—and if a man has a bad conscience about what he is doing, it will not be long before external events shape themselves to conform to inner doubts. In the end, his business failing, his wife withdrawn to her music, his weakling son capable of nothing but dreamy improvising at the piano, Thomas Buddenbrook experiences the awful solitude of the Protestant soul standing naked before God. Yet he is an unbeliever. Shortly before his sudden and premature death, he finds consolation in a chance reading of Schopenhauer; this moment of high revelation stands to *Buddenbrooks* as Hans Castorp's snow dream to *The Magic Mountain.* Both epiphanies bring in their train a dramatic resolution of moral and metaphysical—even religious—conflict. In both men, too, the exaltation fades quickly; the experience itself is soon forgotten. Thomas Buddenbrook had asked, "What was Death?"

The answer came, not in poor, large-sounding words: he felt it within him, he possessed it. Death was a joy, so great, so deep that it could be dreamed of only in moments of revelation like the present. It was the return from an unspeakably painful wandering, the correction of a grave mistake, the loosening of chains, the opening of doors—it put right again a lamentable mischance. . . .

Organism! Blind, thoughtless, pitiful eruption of the urging Will! Better, indeed, for the will to float free in spaceless, timeless night than for it to languish in prison, illumined by the feeble, flickering light of the intellect!

Have I hoped to live on in my son? In a personality yet more feeble, flickering, and timorous than my own? Blind, childish folly!

What can my son do for me—what need have I of a son? Where shall I be when I am dead? Ah, it is so brilliantly clear, so overwhelmingly simple! I shall be in all those who ever, do ever, or ever shall say "I" —*especially, however, in all those who say it most fully, potently, and gladly!*

Arthur Schopenhauer died at Frankfort, Goethe's birthplace, only fifteen years before Thomas Mann's birth. Like *Buddenbrooks*, the philosopher's masterwork, *The World as Will and Idea*, was a young man's book, its first and basic volume appearing before the author was thirty. The essay "On Death and Its Relation to Personal Immortality," which Thomas Buddenbrook read with such rapturous concentration, was not a part of the initial volume, appearing first in the edition of 1844. The music-loving metaphysician's world view was well calculated to appeal to the romantic and aristocratic inclinations of young Thomas Mann, convinced as he was that the German bourgeois inclined to pessimism by nature. Schopenhauer took his place in Mann's gallery of German "brothers" as the metaphysician of the German Romantic movement. Later, the novelist would rate Wagner its musician, Nietzsche its "delicate child" and philosophical critic, Freud its psychologist, and Hitler its (perverted) politician.* The prime ingredient in all romanticism is the exaltation of the instinctive side of man, the raising up of feeling, desire, will, over intellect, cognition, consciousness. Schopenhauer elevated desire to cosmic status, positing as *primum mobile* a metaphysical principle which usurped God's place as Absolute, a first cause all-powerful, yet mindless and blind. At the same time he downgraded Intellect to the level of servant of Will, and reduced the individual conscious personality to an illusion. Since the full force of the cosmic Will works through each one of its individual and temporary organisms, the number and intensity of desires in each human being are created out of all proportion to the possibility of their ever being satisfied. Thus, suffering is the normal human condition. Like those metaphysical saints, the Indian Buddhists, Schopenhauer taught that release from

* Mann was eight years of age when Wagner died, twenty-five at Nietzsche's death, sixty-two at Freud's, seventy at Hitler's.

suffering can follow only upon extinction of desire. This may be accomplished in two ways—through art and through consecration. The second and more difficult path requires freeing oneself from the illusion of selfhood. The first, for moments at least, brings us in touch with a Platonic realm of universal Forms, arching like a rainbow over a roaring torrent, standing forever timeless and beyond death. As we lose ourselves in contemplation of a work of art, time stops, decay and death fall away:

> Then all at once the peace which we were always seeking, but which always fled from us on the former path of the desires, comes to us of its own accord, and it is well with us. It is the painless state which Epicurus prized as the highest good and as the state of the gods; for we are for the moment set free from the miserable striving of the will; we keep the Sabbath of the penal servitude of willing; the wheel of Ixion stands still.

These words the youthful Thomas Mann learned by heart, and could recite them to the end of his days.

In pre-1914 Munich, Thomas Mann took to his heart the aristocratic corollaries of Schopenhauer's pessimism—ideas of the autonomous supremacy of art, the nobility of lonely and knowledgeable genius whose merit is inborn, not earned by democratic sweat. And he was entranced to learn that his music-hero Richard Wagner had experienced a Schopenhauer *aperçu* similar to his own. Wagner at forty was tired out and discouraged with his prospects as a music-dramatist, as well as frustrated in his attempts to sleep with young Mathilde Wesendonk. Happening on a copy of *The World as Will and Idea*, the composer read big swatches of the treatise and wrote to Liszt in ecstatic terms, "This philosopher is the first to make it all clear to me!" ("*Aber es ist so leuchtend klar . . .*" says Thomas Buddenbrook in his Schopenhauer revelation.) Wagner promptly wove Schopenhauerian metaphysics into the Tristan poem he was writing, matched his *Sehnsuchtsmotiv* with the eternal longing of the World Will. Having touted Schopenhauer's philosophy effectively to his wide circle of acquaintances, Wagner sent to the none-too-appreciative philosopher a copy of his *Ring* poem inscribed "With reverence and gratitude." But Wagner was too absorbed in himself and his projects to remain a disciple of Schopenhauer for long. Besides, he based his personal metaphysic on a notion of his own that ran in fearful contradiction to Schopenhauer's first principles—the idea of Salvation through Woman, a belief the composer shares, according to Cecil Gray, with all typical rakes. Schopenhauer's impress on Thomas Mann was more lasting. From the author of *Die Welt als Wille und Vorstellung*, the young novelist learned "psychology," that is, knowledge of the ways Will has of slyly getting around Idea. The theme of every important work of Thomas Mann up to and beyond *The Magic Mountain* is exactly that—the victory of Will over Idea, of instinct over reason, life over mind. In Schopenhauer, Mann found formal confirmation of his youthful belief that the high elements of Germany's *Bürger* culture (he included himself as a typical representative) tended to pessimism and to estrangement from the political sphere. He liked to tell about the cool way the nonpolitical Schopenhauer handed over his opera glasses in 1848 to an officer of the Austrian army the better to direct his fire—against Germans. More than this, Mann found in Schopenhauer metaphysical justification for his own, very German-romantic obsession with the idea of death. In *The Birth of Tragedy*, Nietzsche had said that a cheerless solitary wanderer could choose for himself no better symbol than Dürer's Knight with Death and the Devil—"the mail-clad knight, grim and stern of visage, who, undisturbed by his gruesome companions, yet without hope, pursues his terrible path with horse and hound alone. *Our Schopenhauer was such a knight.*" The author of *Buddenbrooks* found this knightly concern with death completely in harmony with his own belief that love of death is an occupational hazard of the poet. "A philosopher once said" (of course it is Schopenhauer), "that philosophy would hardly exist on earth without death." Nor, adds Mann, would poetry exist on earth without death—"Where is there a poet who is not aware of it daily, in fear and with longing? For the soul of the poet is longing, and the last, the deepest longing is for deliverance." If Schopenhauer is right, the poet's longing for death is

explained. Death is release from the painful condition of individualization; a sinking back into the Absolute, the end of an illusion.

It is Nietzsche's shadow rather than Schopenhauer's that falls
slantwise on *Tonio Kröger*, Mann's early meditation on art and life
which has today nearly dislodged Storm's *Immensee*, from the anthol-
ogies for students reading German. Tonio, the young merchant-son,
is a Hamlet figure, but he is Hamlet seen through Nietzsche's eyes.
"Knowledge kills action—it is this lesson that Hamlet teaches," said
Nietzsche, and Tonio echoes him, diagnosing the artist's condition
as a state of chronic sickness of knowledge (*Erkenntnisekel*). "Such
was the case of Hamlet, that typical literary man," Tonio tells Mme.
Chauchat's young sister Lisaveta. "He knew what it meant to be called
to knowledge without being born to it." Tonio means that "art" kills
"life," that the poet's vision turns his eyes cold, causing good normal
folk with warm hearts, the Hans Hansens and Ingeborg Holms of this
world, to back away from him in uneasy awareness of his differentness. "Originality," said the young novelist Radiguet, dead before
twenty, "consists in trying to be like everybody else—and failing."
Tonio Kröger is a North German *poète maudit*. To him literature is
not a calling, but a curse; he would like to be one of those artists
Nietzsche calls "burnt children," poets on the model of Byron, Musset,
Poe, Kleist, Leopardi, Gogol—all of them "endowed with souls wish-
ing to conceal a break." The split in Tonio's honest soul is that between poet and burgher's son. This Tonio-doctrine that knowledge
unmans, that art is at best a melancholy business, is very German;
and there is a Dürer picture to fit Tonio's case too—the "Melancolia."
Surrounded by symbols of art and knowledge, by the emblems of
loneliness and madness too, the brooding old-German damsel is
really (as Panofsky says) a "Melancholia artificialis," or "Artist's
Melancholy." Still, in the end *Tonio Kröger's* admirable sob comes
neither from Dürer nor from Nietzsche, nor yet from Theodor Storm
or Fontane, but from the youthful German soul of Thomas Mann.
Tonio is his *Siegfried Idyll*, something beautiful, yet calculated to
indulge that weakness Nietzsche identifies as "a taste doubly
dangerous among Germans for quiet lyrics and intoxication of the

feelings." It was his nostalgia for the *Siegfried Idyll* that forced from Nietzsche the cry, "Music and tears . . . I can scarcely tell them apart." *Tonio Kröger* is Thomas Mann's *Portrait of the Artist as a Young Man,* a lyric of vocation discovered, creativity affirmed, the reborn young soul's high resolve to bring into existence what is not yet. Stephen Dedalus wants to press in his arms the loveliness which has not yet come into the world; Gide's Michel prays to his dark new God to grant him knowledge of other, newer races, unimagined types of beauty. For his part, Tonio writes a letter on good paper to the girl who correctly sized him up as a *bourgeois manqué.*

As I write, the sea whispers to me and I close my eyes. I am looking into a world unborn and formless, that needs to be ordered and shaped; I see into a whirl of shadows of human figures who beckon to me to redeem them; tragic and laughable figures and some that are both together—and to these I am drawn. But my deepest and secretest love belongs to the blond and blue-eyed, the fair and living, the happy, lovely, and commonplace.

Thomas Mann always held that the burgher element in his nature stood from the beginning as a counterweight to the creative impulse in him, and that out of the precarious balance between the two came his works of art, as well as the parallel series of his critical writings. To his *grand bourgeois* inheritance Mann believed he owed both help and trouble. Its good effect was discipline, a governing control that kept his creative power from running off the rails, dissipating itself in bohemianism and frittering away. From his ancestors' sober discipline, he fancied, derived the compulsion to finish his books, the follow-through necessary to bring to completion the long series of literary projects, their giant dimensions more typical of the nineteenth than of our own century. But this *Bürger* nature caused him anxiety and doubt. From his ancestry and upbringing, he believed, came his bad conscience about art, the small voice reminding him that for all the artist's pretensions, he is simply an entertainer such as the old families paid in silver coin to amuse them, taking care to separate him from the rest of the company by means of a red velvet rope. Essentially the artist is a mimic and a jester—*Buddenbrooks* began as an *imitation* of his family in order to make them laugh—and for this reason the *poète allemand* tends to feel himself out of place in decent surroundings, nonrespectable, *de trop*. Hence his sense of isolation, an estrangement from society that at times brings him close to the solitude of the criminal. (Tonio is mistaken for a swindler and finds the error quite natural.) But there is another reason for the poet's sense of alienation. Clown or rascal he may be, but he is as well an exceptional being, a special man, one who *knows*. It is the seer in him that causes good folk to shrink from the poet who stands by the wall watching the dance with love and irony. Apart from its Byronism and sentimental precedent in Theodor Storm, Mann's *Tonio*-philosophy found confirmation in Schopenhauer's belief that the presence of genius has an oppressive effect on others—a phenomenon early brought home to the young pessimist when his mother begged him not to stand around like a death's head at her Weimar parties. Schopenhauer concluded that the genius makes people uncomfortable because of his *objectivity*.

After *Tonio Kröger*, the theme of longing for "life" gradually fades from Mann's writings, although we hear its echo from time to time. In the thinly disguised family story *Disorder and Early Sorrow*, written more than twenty years after *Tonio*, we find Professor Cornelius sitting alone in his study on the night of a young people's fête at his house. He is trying to write some letters, but finds it hard to concentrate. At last he gets up, for it "occurs to him that it would be no more than friendly to contribute a box of cigarettes to the festivities next door." But in a moment he is back at his desk again. Later, to his distress, he finds his little daughter in bed crying for a merry folk singer who captured her infant heart at the party. The kindly and serious father, heretofore her beloved, can bring her no comfort. It is "Life" she wants.

Across the span of his long career, Thomas Mann lived his myth of *Bürgertum*, gravely channeling the material of experience and inner conflict into writing. He took to himself Goethe's advice to devote the freshness of the early morning hours to labor at his writing table, exploited his own Goethean compulsion *to finish things*. The formula enabled him to leave behind him at eighty years twelve thick tomes of finished work. For fifty years he played the part of husband, householder, and paterfamilias, carrying the burgher role with dignity. He dressed correctly ("Every artist is as bohemian as the devil inside! Let him at least wear proper clothes and behave outwardly like a respectable being"), his suits were conservative, their business cut countered by a faint suggestion of art in his tie knots. He liked a glass of vermouth before dinner. A slight weakness for elegance, for velvet smoking jackets and jeweled rings came doubtless from his burgher side. Still, he did not look like a merchant. He was too mobile for that. Apart from general concession that he lacked the physical stigmata the public associates with "genius," nobody could agree as to just *what* Thomas Mann looked like. More than one has described him as a Mediterranean rather than a German type. To his secretary Meisel he had the air of a retired ship's officer. An American woman visitor noticed a resemblance to the actor Clifton Webb.

The physical description of Gustave von Aschenbach in *Death in Venice* corresponds so closely to Thomas Mann's own outward appearance that it is surprising to recall the novelist's claim to have taken Gustave Mahler as the external model for the hero of that fable. The gray, bushy hair may be Mahler's, but the slender body, the large head, and the habit of cocking it on one side, belong to Thomas Mann as well as to the composer of *Das Lied von der Erde*. Aschenbach's work habits are Mann's as well. In the tale, it is a burgher-artist conflict that readies the poet for his romantic doom. But Mann is always careful to provide a naturalistic base for his high parables, and at its base *Death in Venice* is simply the story of a man who has pushed himself too far. Aschenbach is said to have written a "prose epic" on the life of Frederick the Great. Thomas Mann too wrote an essay on the Prussian—one of his most brilliant pieces of critical writing—and in that essay he warns potential Aschenbachs:

For a healthy and right human sense understands that career and accomplishment are not all of life; that life has its purely human claims and duties of happiness, to neglect which may be a greater sin than a little easygoingness toward oneself and others in the matter of one's work.

Out of pride in his craft, from a compulsive industry he traces to his bourgeois forebears, Aschenbach literally works himself to death. Here is a man who has slaved away at his career in near-solitude, for years denying himself any personal life. Now suddenly he allows himself to be dislodged, carried off at the point of exhaustion to a remote holiday place where the rule is play rather than work. In such a case it is not at all surprising that the abrupt relaxation of strain will produce odd physical or even moral effects—particularly if it is just possible that at one time in his life he had to repress vague homosexual inclinations.

Detached from their service to the art of the tale (and Mann has protested against such detachment), the "ideas" of *Death in Venice* form an unholy mixture. The key concept is Schopenhauerian, but it is Schopenhauer translated into the language of Platonic myth. Aschenbach himself is patterned on a Nietzsche-Stefan George model. His story is a fable of the revenge of Will upon Idea. The distinguished author of *Maya* (a Schopenhauerian title) has spent his years in the career of art, played himself out in the stern service of beauty. But now suddenly he *sees* it, encounters it not at one remove but directly, face to face, beauty shining in the body of the Polish boy Tadzio. Maddened ($\mu\alpha\nu\iota\kappa\dot{\eta}$), he dies of his love. Before his death he descants on the Platonic teaching that of all the intelligible Forms upon which the world is fashioned, only beauty is visible to the senses. Mythologically, Aschenbach fancies himself a dissolute Socrates trying to establish a relationship at once erotic and pedagogic with young Phaedrus-Tadzio, consoling himself for the inarticulate and distant contact with the boy by the old philosopher's assurance that the lover is more divine than the beloved. But there is no Platonic explanation for Aschenbach's death; poetic madness is not enough. Death to Socrates was an affair of hemlock or old age—not of beauty or boy-love. Aschenbach's longing for rest, his tired eyes seeking the sea, symbol of death, is none other than the Schopenhauerian longing for release from the wheel, a renunciation of individuality, a sinking back into the Absolute. As epigraph for his Venetian tale, Mann never wearied of quoting the *Tristan* sonnet of Count Platen, German romantic, humanist, and homosexual:

Wer die Schönheit angeschaut mit Augen,	He who has once looked on Beauty
Ist dem Tode schon anheimgegeben.	Is already given over unto Death.

To some critics these lines are no more than bad pre-Wagnerian metaphysics. To Thomas Mann they meant that the experience of the beautiful may awaken in the beholder a painful longing that cannot be satisfied in this life, a longing that only death can still.

Schopenhauer's Idea and Will carry over into the Nietzschean categories of the Apollonian and Dionysian. Present in nightmare at an orgiastic celebration of the Stranger God, Aschenbach is left in no doubt as to which of these two kingdoms will be the victor in his case. The sign of self-conquest in Aschenbach's character marks him as a Nietzschean hero; that he breaks down in the end simply strengthens the analogy. His artistic creed links him to Stefan George; there is a common emphasis on form and control, the hard victory of *Gestalt* over matter, the Idea hammered out of refractory stone. Both Aschenbach and Stefan George consecrated their lives to Nietzsche's Ascetic Ideal. Neither poet considered art as a simple outpouring of feeling, poetry as unpremeditated lyricism. Both shared the Greek vision—*Hellas ewig unsre liebe.* Like Aschenbach, Stefan George fell in love with a beautiful boy. Mann's hero finds pleasure in the thought that Tadzio would probably not live to grow old. George's Maximin died at sixteen, and his adorer commemorated him in verse not so far removed, after all, from simple outpoured feeling:

Du schlank und rein wie eine flamme	You like a flame, you pure and slender.
Du wie der morgen zart und licht	You like the morning calm and bright,

Du blühend reis vom edlen stamme	Of noble stem you blossom tender,
Du wie ein quell geheim und schlicht.	You like a spring concealed and slight.
Begleitest mich auf sonnigen matten	You walk with me in sunny meadows
Umschauerst mich im abend-rauch	Thrill round me in the evening haze
Erleuchtest meinen weg im schatten	Illuminate my path in shadows
Du kühler wind du heisser hauch.	You cooling wind you burning blaze.
Du bist mein wunsch und mein gedanke	You, all I wish and all I think of,
Ich atme dich mit jeder luft	With every taken breath are blent,
Ich schlürfe dich mit jedem tranke	I savour you in all I drink of
Ich küsse dich mit jedem duft	And you I kiss in every scent.
Du blühend reis vom edlen stamme	Of noble stem you blossom tender,
Du wie ein quell geheim und schlicht	You like a spring concealed and slight,
Du schlank und rein wie eine flamme	You like a flame, you pure and slender,
Du wie der morgen zart und licht.	You like the morning calm and bright.

But Mann's shadowed portrait of the artist in *Death in Venice* sets itself off from the Stefan George ideal by its pessimism, its emphasis on the pathological nature of the creative process, its fascination with the way the aesthetic sucks blood from the moral. The funerary decor of *Death in Venice,* the gondola-coffins and ubiquitous death's-heads, carries out the fable's moral: artistic production is not simply a matter of sheer joy and loveliness; it consumes. Art itself has foul-smelling roots. In his poem "Their Beginning," Constantine Cavafy wrote about a furtive homosexual episode. Shameful, of course, but

Tomorrow, the next day, years later, the vigorous verses will be composed that had their beginning here.

So Aschenbach's page-and-a-half of perfect prose, anthologized after his death in the textbooks of his native land, was written with Tadzio's body before his eyes. *Death in Venice* is the setting for a dialectical formula Mann drives almost to Gnostic extremes through his maturest work. Out of the shameful, beauty; out of darkness, light. From sickness, health; from corruption, life. Out of the pit, resurrection. In Goethe, the same rule read—die and rise. With Gide and Dostoevski, *si le grain ne meurt*. . . .

III

So Hans Castorp of *The Magic Mountain* takes his place in the line of alienated merchant- and artist-heroes who precede him: Thomas Buddenbrook and his *Sorgenkind* Hanno; Tonio Kröger; Gustave von Aschenbach; even Klaus Heinrich of *Royal Highness*, Mann's nuptial novel of 1909 that so amusingly anticipates the Rainier-Kelly match. What is the nature of Castorp's alienation? Does it differ at all from that of the types that go before? Aschenbach and Tonio are poets; Klaus Heinrich is a prince standing in for a poet. But Hans Castorp, like Thomas Buddenbrook, has been trained for the practical world of business and technology. It is from the commercial and industrial sphere, rather than from "life" or the "blue-eyed" that Hans Castorp (who *has* blue eyes) seems to be estranged. That *The Magic Mountain* is a parable of sick Europe, of modern liberalism's febrile decline, an indictment of Western civilization, are critical commonplaces to which Mann himself has nodded benign approval. Some critics have taken the novel as standing "against capitalism." Son of a merchant family, Thomas Mann throughout his career showed a certain suspicion of "business." Christian Buddenbrook's claim that every businessman is a crook is not unlike Brecht's statement via Macheath that it is more honest to rob a bank than to found one. Throughout the second half of *Zauberberg* there is more than one nod of approval for Naphta's anticapitalist fire-breathing. Mann himself became restless under the "capitalism" of post-F.D.R. United States, and went home to Europe to die. So it is easy to interpret Castorp's sickness as part of that estrangement which, according to Marx, comes into being when society confronts man as an alien thing, as a hostile power. This line of interpretation can be reinforced by citing Castorp's poet predecessors as typical "artists under capitalism," their values standing in contradiction to the values of the society which bears them, pays them, "keeps" them. Mann gained his first success by writing stories featuring descriptions of the artist in bourgeois society as a clown, a gipsy, a disreputable entertainer, a swindler. One of Mann's first masked artist-heroes, Felix Krull, was a confidence man. Mann's last work was an attempt to finish that story of the charming little crook who enjoyed robbing the rich.

But we know that the genesis of the alienated artist-type antedates "capitalism" in European literature. True, the frequency with which the estranged poet appears in literature can be made to parallel the course of the Industrial Revolution and its triumphant progress through the second half of the nineteenth century and *la belle époque*. But alienated genius was already familiar in preindustrial Western society, and may be traced back as far as various wandering rogue types and mad troubadour heroes, or (more respectably) to Hamlet and Don Quixote. In his *Decline of the West,* Spengler points out that the Renaissance artist, who accomplished his life in the light of a courtly existence, was the one single type of Western man for whom the word "loneliness" had no meaning. When America was still a set of British colonies, Rousseau, wandering in England as Hume's guest, thanked God he was "different." *Werther* appeared in 1774; *René* in 1802; *Childe Harold* in 1812. When their land was still a semifeudal patchwork of agrarian states, the German literary romantics were already loud in their complaints of homelessness and estrangement; already they were seeking blue flowers as Tonio Kröger would yearn for blue eyes. In Germany, Byron's isolated Cain blended easily with the Werther ideal, and Schopenhauer's Manfred-inspired metaphysics of "genius" helped fix the lineaments of the lonely poet-hero. But those solitary talents felt themselves estranged from "life" and from "the world of men" rather than from capitalistic industrial society. It is true that in the heavily commercialized European society of the late nineteenth and early twentieth centuries we find the song of the artist and his *Abgelöstheit von der Gesellschaft* played in all registers of every instrument in the hands of German poets, dramatists, and novelists. But it is not until we come to the post-1918 critics that we find any pressing awareness of need for a critique of bourgeois capitalism in order to understand the alienation of the artist. By this time the revolution in Russia had been accomplished.

Hans Castorp is a German romantic hero who rejects the values, not of "capitalism," but of the normal humdrum workaday world, just as Wilhelm Meister, his forebear, knew that *his* destiny would "tear him out of the dull and stupid bourgeois life, out of which he had long wished to rescue himself." The restlessness that brought Mann's young engineering student to the sanatorium is a standard romantic symptom; so is his disease itself, his *Sympathie mit dem Tode*, his love, his music, metaphysics, dream, and magic. Of the German Romantic hero, Santayana says that "He would take life arrogantly and egotistically, as if it were an absolute personal experiment"; the date of the philosopher's lecture is 1910, but how well it all fits Hans Castorp:

Like Faust, he flouts science, and is minded to make trial of magic, which renders a man's will master of the universe in which he seems to live. He disowns all authority, save that mysteriously exercised over him by his deep faith in himself. He is always honest and brave; but he is always different, and absolves himself from his past as soon as he has outgrown or forgotten it. He is inclined to be wayward and foolhardy, justifying himself on the ground that all experience is interesting, that the springs of it are inexhaustible and always pure, and that the future of his soul is infinite.

Castorp's story would be no more than a *caricature* of German Romanticism if the elements composing it were not woven into the total fabric with sympathy as well as art. As the novel goes on, Hans and his awakening are treated more with love than irony. At the end the narrator-author confesses to real tears at the thought that he will see his delicate child no more. (How different from Thackeray who, at the close of *Vanity Fair*, smirks, "Come, children let us shut up the box and the puppets, for our play is played out.") It is true that Mann intended *The Magic Mountain* to convey criticism of certain factors in German culture he believed responsible for Germany's prewar isolation as well as to point out some deficiencies in the camp of the democracies. He makes every attempt to get across to the reader that the sanatorium may be construed as an analogue of Europe before 1914, that Castorp is an ambassador of Germany and his tutor, the liberal Settembrini, a representative of the Triple Entente. Nevertheless, the politics of *Zauberberg* is romantic politics, Thomas Mann-politics, and as such far less descriptive of the actual political and cultural situation in 1907-1914 than the sympathetic reader, overborne by the novel's tone of authority, dazzled by its pyrotechnics, may care to think. *The Magic Mountain* lies at least as close to Utopia as it does to prewar Europe. Naphta (who is "nearly always right") has no more political reality than a dragon. Tempting as it may be to make sociological observations about the German *Bürger* on the basis of all the self-conscious material Mann piles up in his writings, it is a good idea to remember that his art is so highly individual, his genius such a powerful solvent, that concepts such as art, life, disease, psychology, and the like, take on exalted meanings under his pen—meanings that are, while still quite German, peculiar to Thomas Mann. This holds true especially in the case of the *Bürgertum* motif which may in Mann's hands begin simply enough with a North German afternoon tea party, but before three paragraphs have elapsed will leap up to combine with high cultural categories like music, pessimism, "the Dream," "*Kultur*," and the rest. Such practice is flagrant in the set of variations on the burgher theme in Mann's only work untranslated into English, the 1917 *Reflections of a Non-Political Man*—his bulky collection of wartime essays written while the first volume of the Davos novel was well under way. But *The Magic Mountain* does not captivate its readers because it is another cunning artist-burgher parable or even a towering political allegory. A great part of its charm flows from the fact that it is a *Tristan* story.

Mann often reminds his readers that he first thought of the Davos novel as a comic counterweight to *Death in Venice,* how he planned it as a piece of about the same length concerning a naïve young man in a tuberculosis sanatorium caught in conflict between bourgeois duty and bizarre temptation. Just after the Buddenbrooks saga, he had published a sardonic rest-cure tale called *Tristan* in which the legendary romance is parodied by two patients who celebrate their ungainly awakening over a piano transcription of Wagner's masterpiece. *Zauberberg* turned out differently, but it has its *Tristan* motif all the same. Here Castorp is an ingenuous Tristan, Clavdia the Isolde with Kirghiz eyes. Their disease is the love potion. To the love-music of the second act corresponds the salon dialogue on Carnival night, its *Vorspiel* Clavdia's lecture on the morality of abandonment, that is to say, Tristan-morality. In Mann's novel it is Tristan not Isolde who sings the *Liebestod,* that Novalis-keyed, scientific-lyric love address so wisely left in French, the language of Hans's dream. "Let me die, my lips to yours," Hans cries to his hyperborean *femme fatale.* In that supreme moment before the satisfaction of his heart's deepest desire, for Hans as for Tristan, his beloved's body, love, and death are one. Passionately the ex-engineer affirms the unity of his disease and love:

The fever of my body, the beating of my tormented heart, the shivering of my limbs—this is no incident, it is none other than my love for you . . . my ancient love . . . I love you . . . I have always loved you . . . my dream . . . my eternal desire.

Somewhat belatedly, the royal Peeperkorn shambles on the scene as King Mark to part the lovers by his suicide. His death is the end of the affair; there would be no point going on. "Death is the salt of love," says François Mauriac. "It is life that brings corruption." Castorp's passion, like Tristan's, is a fatal love, one that can be

preserved only in death. By definition, Tristan-lovers cannot marry.
A Frau Castorp would be nearly as absurd as a Madame Tristan.
Holding aloft the romance of Cornish knight and Irish princess as
the great European myth of adultery, Denis de Rougemont says,
"What stirs lyrical poets to their finest flights is not the satisfaction
of love, but its passion." All the same, Hans is a German Tristan, not
a Celtic one. Even his passions have inner polarity. Madame Chauchat
reminds her gallant that passion is self-forgetfulness, not self-enrich-
ment. He gently defends himself; he has his passions, phlegmatic
ones. In art, as in thought, Thomas Mann tries to bring about the
fusion of every concept with its opposite.

Back of *The Magic Mountain*'s Tristan-philosophy moves a dialectical elaboration of the old Schopenhauerian dualism, impulse
versus reason, Will against Idea—as well as effort to mediate between them. "You see, gentlemen, reason is an excellent thing," says
Dostoevski's Underground Man, "there's no disputing that. But
reason is nothing but reason and satisfies only the rational side of
man's nature, while will is a manifestation of the whole life, including reason and all the impulses." Much of *Zauberberg*'s ironic
effect derives from the fact that Castorp learns more from his
irrational and magic experiences than from the humane enlighten-
ment of his tutor Settembrini. Hans prefers love to politics, dream
to action; he finds Krokowski's concept of disease as something born
in unconscious will far more interesting than Behren's rational concern with X-rays and bacilli. Yet Settembrini, the only one of
Castorp's teachers to remain with him to the end, never tires in his
efforts to redress the ideological balance in favor of reason. To Mann,
"psychology" is knowledge of the ways Will has of subverting Idea;
he gives the name "criticism" to the support ethics and logic give
to Idea to prevent its succumbing entirely to the greater power and
cunning of Will. Settembrini is the critic of *The Magic Mountain*.
As a person, he is charming, although ideologically he is an improbable paste-up of doctrines Mann associated with nineteenth century
bourgeois humanism, anticlerical rationalism, and militant democracy.
He is an epigone of the Italian patriot Mazzini, also noted for his

fine literary style. That republican, Freemason, and humanist declared to his laggard countrymen, "I am but a voice crying *Action!*" As critic, Settembrini is sensitive to the danger present in the irrational forces at work on the soul of Hans Castorp, and many of Nietzsche's anti-romantic and anti-German quips issue from his fine mouth barely paraphrased. Yet the humanist's wordy speeches in behalf of Reason avail nothing when Clavdia Chauchat—she who in the first seven months of Hans's stay at the sanatorium had not said one word to him beyond a casual *"merci"*—turns her Steppenwolf eyes in the young engineer's direction. The progress of Castorp's love is neither a political nor a literary affair; it is wordless, musical.

The Idea-Will dualism is made concrete in the first half of *The Magic Mountain* by this Settembrini-Clavdia polarity. (Though they never meet, they detest each other.) In the novel's second part, the side of Will is doubled by Peeperkorn, Dionysian disciple of feeling who joins Clavdia on her return to the Berghof, while the side of Idea is in turn reinforced by Leo Naphta, the Marxist-Jesuit. Peeperkorn is represented as companion and ally of Clavdia, but the Jesuit, though an intellectual man, goes head-down for Settembrini every chance he gets. Although his clichés are tattered, the Italian pedagogue's ideas do hang together after a fashion; his rationalism possesses at least a surface consistency. But Naphta is a monster, an ideological centaur; he wears his contradictions on his sleeve. It is hard enough to be a Jew and a Jesuit (the Society requires a special dispensation in such cases), but to be at one and the same time a militant Catholic and an ardent Marxist is quite impermissible. That Mann felt Naphta's chimerical inconsistencies needed more than a philosophical explanation is shown by the trouble he takes to give a naturalistic account of this stage-Jesuit's background. Castorp apart, Naphta is the only personage in the novel who rates an excursus into his childhood and youth. The narrator takes pains to inform the reader that Naphta was the son of a Jewish ritual slaughterer, that his father's bloody work bound together for the boy the ideas of piety and terror. Why then is Naphta both a Catholic and a Marxist? Communism and Catholicism contradict each other (we can put aside the cheap and easy charge of twin authoritarianism), but they agree on one point—their opposition to bourgeois humanism. The fact that the Vatican today has less trouble coexisting with the forces of liberalism than with the Kremlin should not make us forget that the war cry of the nineteenth century militant democrats in Europe was *"Écrasez l'infame!"* With a magnificent rearguard gesture in his "Syllabus of Errors," Pius IX denied that "The Roman pontiff can and ought to reconcile himself and come to terms with progress, liberalism, and modern civilization." That is to say—Settembrini. Naphta, who denounces Freemasonry as "a god-forsaken bourgeoisiedom in the form of a club," makes tougher talk than Pio Nono; we smell the faggots whenever he is around. He is like Léon Bloy who would welcome a theater fire so long as it was the bourgeoisie who burned. In the wake of Mann's schizoid Jesuit a train of contradictions sputters—his decor carries it out: the stark *Pietà* and rich cake, his humble room and silken hangings—and it is not surprising to learn that shortly before his sticky end he suffered outright psychotic spells.

Peeperkorn's place on the voluntaristic side of things in *Zauberberg* is pretty obvious: the Dutch East Indian coffee king constantly *overpowers* the "cerebral" Naphta and Settembrini by the strength of his inarticulate presence. The ailing Hollander's connection with the Dionysian principle is made plain by his state of constant drunkenness, although it is as much intoxication with feeling as it is tipsiness from gin that causes him to founder. But Peeperkorn drunk towers over lesser men sober. As Castorp realizes at the Dutchman's first all-night supper party, it all depends upon *who* is drunk —just as what matters in art is *whose* feelings are expressed and (in the case of disease) *who* is sick. A mean man drunk is meaner still. The drunkenness of a king is—or should be—royal; that of a god, divine. (Gide says, "Verlaine drunk was *tremendous*.") Mann's fevered King in Thule is the first of two of Hans Castorp's principal teachers to meet a violent end in the course of the novel. As in Naphta's case, Peeperkorn's death has both ideological and naturalistic explanations. Obscurely hinted at, the Dutchman's sexual im-

knight rides past Death and the Devil, his courage shaken by the presence of neither, his blue eyes obstinately fixed straight ahead.

IV

The Western world knows *The Magic Mountain* for a time-novel. It is commonplace to point to the concern of twentieth century European and American literature with time, and to claim that this concern is deducible from a more general interest in time that marks the age in which we live. Our century's anxiety about time is probably a function of the rapidly accelerating technological and social change that has been snowballing since the Industrial Revolution. A hundred and fifty years ago, a man could grow old and die without having witnessed appreciable change in his surroundings or in the way of life of his people. But such a man's grandchildren would have a different story to tell. Hans Lorenz Castorp died unreconciled to change in Hamburg, but before his grandson left for Davos the citizens of the old Hanseatic city were planning large-scale regulation of the Elbe. ("Epoch-making for the development of our shipping.") Generation of power from steam and electricity brought a new way of looking at locks and calendars. In *A la recherche du temps perdu,* Proust noted the effect of timetables:

Since railways came into existence, the necessity of not missing the train has taught us to take account of minutes, whereas among the ancient Romans, who not only had a more cursory science of astronomy but led less hurried lives, the notion not of minutes but even of fixed hours barely existed.

Demoting Being and permanence to second-class ontological citizenship, nineteenth century philosophers contributed to the new importance of "Time" by making change, process, and development primordial characteristics of Reality. German metaphysicians took the lead in exalting the ever-changing. (Goethe's concern with time and becoming was well known.) Fichte rejoiced that "the dead Substance of the Latins" had been replaced by "Teutonic Becoming," while from his pocket Hegel produced a system of universal knowledge based on the metaphysical postulate of dialectical progress. Implications of the Darwinian theory of evolution poured in to swell the tide, and as the new century dawned, English philosophers were constructing theories of Emergent Evolution. In 1907, the very year Hans Castorp set out for Switzerland, Henri Bergson published in France his *Creative Evolution,* a new cosmology based on a first principle of creative flux and novelty. From his voluntary exile in America two decades later, Whitehead summed it up: *"One all-pervasive fact, inherent in the very character of what is real is the transition of things, the passage one to another."*

Hans Castorp's time-philosophy is based on a distinction similar to but not identical with Bergson's differentiation between "real" time (duration) and mathematical or abstract ("clock") time. To the French philosopher, abstract, or "clock" time is a product of human intelligence made for the necessary practical purpose of measuring quantities. "Real" time or duration, on the other hand, is inseparable from the basic changefulness of things. This changefulness has none of the random character of colliding Epicurean atoms; analogous to growth or creative process, it is the fundamental fact of reality. Now for convenience in handling material bodies, intelligence lays hold of this "real" time, which is inseparable from the constant flow of things into newness, cuts it up conceptually into even bits, then pastes the bits back around the face of a clock dial in regularly spaced intervals. But the abstract nature of this "clock" time is proved by the fact that we never *experience* it as an immediate fact of consciousness. "True duration," says Bergson, "that which consciousness perceives . . . is not a quantity, and so soon as we try to measure it, we substitute space for it unconsciously." Castorp's first experience with the thermometer suggests to him a remarkably similar distinction:

"You say 'actually.' . . . But after all, time isn't 'actual.' When it seems long to you, then it *is* long; when it seems short, why, then it is short. But how long, or how short it actually is, that nobody knows." He was unaccustomed to philosophize, yet somehow felt an

impulse to do so. . . . "But it takes such a varied length of time—
to our senses! And as a matter of fact . . . it is motion, isn't it,
motion in space? Wait a minute! That means that we measure time
by space. But that is not better than measuring space by time, a
thing only very unscientific people do. From Hamburg to Davos is
twenty-two hours—that is, by train. But on foot how long is it?
And in the mind, how long? Not a second!

Bergsonian time—in the sense of duration—is *real;* in no sense
has the future happened yet. Although we reach it in consciousness,
duration is not merely a matter of subjective impression. The question
rises: does Hans Castorp's conscious experience, as he sits there
with the thermometer in his mouth, bring him in touch with "real"
time, that is, with an objective process existing independently of
him—or is the time he experiences subjective or psychological only?
It would seem to be the latter, for Hans emphasizes that the longness
or shortness of experienced time appears to be completely relative
to the person experiencing it and to his particular context. As experienced, time expands and contracts concertina-fashion. Empty of
content or novelty, time seems long living through it ("drags"),
short looking back on it; but time full of content seems short living
through it ("flies"), long looking back on it. Thus Hans is not for
a moment bored with his long day full of novel experiences on arrival at the sanatorium; yet toward evening he exclaims, *"Gott, ist
noch immer der erste Tag?"* It seems to him that he has been up
there ages. Later, as he gets used to his bizarre setting, months and
even years slip by hardly noticed; looking back, he finds they have
shrunk almost to nothing in his conscious memory. From the first,
Hans noticed that the long-term patients at Davos did not have the
same time-consciousness as Flatland people. To veterans of the cure,
the smallest unit of time is a month; for Joachim, three weeks is a
day. As his own stay lengthens, Hans's time-sense too becomes en-
feebled, weakening progressively until it fades almost entirely away.
What causes this decay of time-sense in the patients? First, there is
the effect of institutional routine, the eternal round of temperature-
taking, rests, meals, *Ewigkeitssuppe*—"Soup Everlasting." Endless

recurrence, even of meals, destroys time. Second, the fact that the sanatorium is cut off from the active life of the world lends to it a "hermetic" character. Hans compares the Berghof to his house-keeper Schalleen's preserves; sealed in a jar, and thus placed beyond the corrupting effects of outside air, they are in a sense set outside time. *His* existence too is hermetic, Hans thinks, not only because he stays in a place sealed off from time, but also in the magical con-notation of the word. The sanatorium is analogous to the sealed crystal retort in which the old alchemists directed occult forces on a substance to bring about its metamorphosis. To live in the sanatorium means to subsist in a kind of deathlike sleep; cut off from time, one inhabits a kind of Alpine eternity. "Eternal snow!" was the first un-flatlandish expression Hans permitted himself, barely off the train. And when he moves to the borderline of life and death in his snow-dream, time seems to stop while the near-frozen ex-engineer enjoys his vision of humanity, his ecstasy of rebirth. When finally he wakes up, his watch tells him the whole thing took only a quarter-hour of clock time. "The time which flows for the sleeper," says Proust, "is absolutely different from the time in which the life of a waking man is accomplished. Sometimes its course is much more rapid, a quarter of an hour seems a day, sometimes much longer. . . ." Proust goes on to say that perhaps waking time is after all the only time, since the life in which a man sleeps is not included in the category of time. In the last years of his stay at the cure, Hans sinks into a torpor, an unbroken sleep, a suspension in eternity. For the engineer who has lost his watch and let his little Russian beard grow, "There is no time up here to speak of, either long or short." From the start, Settembrini constantly warns his dreaming pupil about the dangers of a decaying time sense. He accuses him of weakness for "Asia"— which to Hans means the Kirghiz-eyed Clavdia, meditation, allowing things to take their course, renunciation even to the point of letting oneself perish. But the democrat Settembrini, Hans's conscience, never fails to remind the former Flatlander that outside the sanatorium in the world of actuality down below, real happenings, important historical changes are taking place. With the international situation worsening, the Central Powers are headed on collision course with the Triple Entente; events are moving forward with undreamed-of rapidity. As reader of newspapers, as politician and partisan of action, it is Settembrini's duty to remind his nonpolitical pupil of the *objectivity* of time. While Castorp lies dreaming away in his deck chair, real time—not just clock time—gnaws away at the world. At this point the narrator of *Der Zauberberg* allows his opinion to coincide with Settembrini's:

Time, however weakened the subjective perception of it has become, has objective reality in that it brings things to pass. It is a question for professional thinkers—Hans Castorp in his youthful arrogance had at one time been led to consider it—whether the hermetically sealed conserve upon its shelf is outside of time. We know that time does its work, even upon Seven-Sleepers. A physician cites a case of a twelve-year-old girl, who fell asleep and slept thirteen years but bloomed into ripe womanhood while she slept. How could it be otherwise? The dead man—is dead; he has closed his eyes on time. He has plenty of time, or personally speaking he is timeless. Which does not prevent his hair and nails from growing. . . .

Thus, four basic time-categories in *The Magic Mountain* may be distinguished: clock time ("seven minutes"); subjective or psychological time ("seems long"); objective time or duration (nails grow; the world situation deteriorates); and eternity, the realm of death, which is entirely untouched by time. These categories do not include the "historical" time of the novel (1907-1914), or the years it took for the novelist to write the book (1912-1924), the year of Our Lord in which the reader peruses the work, or the time it takes him to complete his reading. Forced by her husband of the time to acquire culture, motion-picture actress Ava Gardner filed suit for divorce, "He made me read *The Magic Mountain*," she complained. "I thought I'd never finish that damn book."

Mann's playing off of "time" against "eternity" in his *Zauberberg* is, of course, quite anti-Bergsonian. When to the tune of "Valentine's Prayer" from Gounod's *Faust* Hans Castorp raises the ghost of his cousin Joachim, the laws of time are abrogated so that the dead lieutenant may appear at Krokowski's séance in the uniform of a German soldier of the 1914 war—which at the time of the occult experiment had not yet happened. Bergson's *élan vital* is a continuous creative flow in which cycles, repetitions, and recurrences play no part. Since time is real, the future is really future, and cannot be a *fait accompli* even on the supernatural level. Nothing— not even God—can be outside time, for there *is* no outside. God himself, as Sartre says, must wait for the coffee to cool. But in Hans Castorp's story, Mann *stops* time, solemnly invoking an "All-soul" to give metaphysical backing to the dramatic violation of chronology by Ziemssen's ghost. The services of the All-soul had been required in an earlier crisis in the novel when Hans, lost on his snowy mountain-peak, had felt himself the instrument of a dream dreamed by "the great soul of which we are a part." Now the reader is told of Dr. Krokowski that:

The field of his study had always been those wide, dark tracts of the human soul, which one had been used to call the subconsciousness, since from them sometimes emanates a knowingness beyond anything of which the conscious intelligence is capable, and giving rise to the hypothesis that there may subsist connexions and associations between the lowest and least illumined regions of the individual soul and a wholly knowing All-soul.

Belief in a world soul or universal consciousness related to our minds as general to particular is a basic element of the Gnostic-hermetic tradition. In Indian metaphysics, the parallel doctrine is the Brahma-atman relation. In the West many orthodox philosophers from Plato to Bergson's colleague William James have made use of one or another version of the hypothesis. Giordano Bruno taught the existence of a world soul. Philosophical idealism has been particularly friendly to the idea; its analogue in Hegel is "Spirit," in Royce, "the larger self." It is, as well, one of those large quasi-philosophical notions that appeal to the poetic and literary mind. Mann's introduction of the All-soul in *Zauberberg* is consistent with the novel's depth-psychology. On Castorp's mountain height love and death transcend time as well as politics.

Thomas Mann, as well as James Joyce, employs *recurrence* to suggest timelessness. While Mann's use of the device is most obvious in the Joseph story where the subject matter calls for an elaborate array of cycles and repetitions, the use of patterns that repeat themselves, suggesting endless return, marks Mann's writings from *Buddenbrooks* on. In his Schopenhauer revelation Thomas Buddenbrook saw that "Nothing began, nothing left off." There was only an "endless present." Weinschenk's swindle recapitulates Grünlich's diddling of old Johann Buddenbrook, and Toni's words to her daughter Erica are the same as her father's to her at the time of her own unhappy marriage, "My child, do you still love your husband? . . ." The action of Mann's *Tristan* is a bizarre variation of that eternal love theme. Aschenbach of *Death in Venice* gloomily participates in a Socrates-Phaedrus pattern while four look-alike strangers with bared gums successively appear and vanish before him. Mann's wartime essay on Frederick the Great is premised on the assumption that the Western Allies' "encirclement" of Germany in 1914 repeats the pattern of the Grand Coalition against Prussia in 1756. *The Magic Mountain* itself is packed with multiple repetitions and simultaneities. On the psychological dimension, the parallel between Hippe and Clavdia is crucial, and it is pushed to the detail of doubling moist spots and pencil-borrowing. On Carnival night Hans makes clear to his beloved that his schoolboy *Schwärm'* for Hippe and his present exalted passion are the *same* love affair. The Carnival scene itself is doubled in subdued tones in the second part of the novel; after her return to the sanatorium with Peeperkorn, Clavdia seeks an interview with Hans on the pretext of needing, not a pencil, but a postage stamp. Hans's love for Madame Chauchat is doubled by Joachim's fatal infatuation for the giggling Marusja. Both ladies are Russian, although unlike Marusja Clavdia is a serious person, Hans's boning-up of his French doubles Joachim's conning his Russian grammar; both have an amorous end in view. The red lamp at the *Nachtspuk* séance where Joachim's ghost appears, is anticipated by the red light of the X-ray room where Castorp first saw his cousin's skeleton through the fluoroscope. Tienappel's visit to the sanatorium is a crude repetition of Hans's first week there;

the Hamburg *Pfahlbürger* develops early symptoms of malaise and
eros until he is scared off by Behren's talk on putrefaction. Even the
grand duel between Settembrini and Naphta has its comic rehearsal
in the affair of honor between the Polish gentlemen with the un-
pronounceable names.

But a good part of Mann's simultaneities and recurrences have
more musical-poetic import than philosophical significance. As a
true son of the romantic movement, the novelist encourages his art
to aspire to the condition of music. Since both music and storytelling
are time arts—that is, they "take time" to perform—the production
of any effect of *simultaneity* in them must rely on repetition, variation, evocation. Mann's use of the literary *leitmotiv* to help achieve
the impression of simultaneity has been the object of much commentary, his own not excluded. In *The Magic Mountain* or the *Joseph*
story, he would have it that the leitmotiv is the "magic formula which
points forward and backward, a means of calling its totality up to
the present at any time." Although we need some familiarity with the
German language to appreciate the subtlety and thoroughness with
which Mann works his "Book of Kells" device, there are many
obvious examples. As in *Tonio Kröger* where the phrase "blond and
blue-eyed" (*die Blonden und Blauäugigen*) is used to suggest the good
looks of Hans Hansen and Ingeborg Holm, then repeated reprise-
fashion to recall the world of the normal and warmhearted to which
they belong, so in *The Magic Mountain* Clavdia's theme "Kirghiz
eyes (*Kirgisenaugen*) evokes not only memories of Hans's schoolboy
idol Hippe, but calls up as well the entire "Asiatic" complex Hans
has come to associate with those eyes—love, compassion, renunciation, death. The words "anonymous and communal" (*anonym und
gemeinsam*) attributed in Hans's dream in the snow to the All-soul,
recall the sanguinary painting on Naphta's wall as well as (by association) the ways and values of the whole late-medieval world. For
Joachim Ziemssen, and for the military categorical imperative to
which he has dedicated himself, the leitmotiv "fanatical" (*fanatisch,
schwärmerisch*) is allowed to cross over from its association with
the Catholic-Loyolan realm of Spanish punctilio to blend with the

warmest personal affection. Tender overtones in the word sound in the lines describing the young officer's burial with military honors, as the narrator asks his readers to:

... take our stand in spirit with Hans Castorp on his lonely height, and gaze down with him upon a damp burial-ground in the flat-land; see the flash of a sword as it rises and falls, hear the word of command rapped out, and three salvoes, three fanatical salutes reverberating over Joachim Ziemssen's root-pierced grave.

V

The Magic Mountain was a hard act to follow. Although thirty years remained to him after the publication of his Davos chronicle— years in which he produced two major novels, five minor ones, as well as a shelfful of critical writing—the balance between charm and idea so long sustained in the hermetic fable that crowned his mid-career is achieved only intermittently in his later work. Not that the Nobel laureate in full maturity backed down from his ideal of art as equilibrium between jest and high seriousness. On the contrary—after *Zauberberg* he redoubled his efforts in precisely that direction, changing his pace just enough to accommodate emphasis on myth-psychology, and a renewed concern with Goethe. Yet it seemed that the more self-consciously he strove for the Goethean norm of "Entertainment for the people; for the initiate the mystery behind," the harder it was to prevent evaporation of the magic of his earlier tales. *The Beloved Returns* (Lotte in Weimar) is delightful, of course, but that series of "high conversations" on the subject of Goethe is hardly a novel at all. *The Transposed Heads* (*Die vertauschten Köpfe*) is a metaphysical joke on the old theme of the polarity of Nature (Will) and Spirit (Idea) by way of an Indian legend of two youths who come to grief over a girl with beautiful hips. Not only is this little work overborne by the faintly elephantine humor increasingly noticeable in Mann's post-*Zauberberg* work (the *Joseph* story is not free of it), but it also shows a parallel tendency to heavy-handed erotic description, a mannerism particularly regrettable in an artist who achieved such effects of high irony in his earlier career by tactful handling of sexual encounters. *The Holy Sinner* (*Der Erwählte*) has a certain winsomeness. This story of the shameful birth and miraculous "choosing" of old Pope Gregory is still another variation on the "die to live" tune earlier mounted on Wagnerian scale in the *Joseph* story. Just as "I can read tablets and write cuneiform," were Joseph's first words to the Chaldeans who hauled him out of his pit, so Gregory, more hedgehog than human after twenty years' exposure on his lacustrine rock, croaks to the Cardinals who rescue him, "I can read Latin." In his last work, an extension of the *Felix Krull* fragment of 1911, Mann comes back to his old obsession with the relationship of artist to criminal: the picaresque hero becomes a Shandyian Don Juan, his fun interrupted from time to time by Mannian encyclopedics (Dr. Kuckuck's excursus on the dinosaurs, for example) that now seem so oddly out of place. As for *The Black Swan* (*Die Betrogene*) in which Mann returns for the last time to the theme of disease and glory, the best comment is Goethe's remark about the cool reception of one of his works (*Clarigo*, perhaps), "Well, who is there who writes nothing but masterpieces?"

If only because of its monumental scope, the *Joseph* saga deserves far more respectful attention. Mann's four-volumed historical novel about the Biblical youth who rose from the pit took him seventeen years to complete—exactly the number needed by James Joyce to finish the dream-drama of Tim Finnegan whose resurrection from his own bed is just as mytho-psychological (though much less sober) than Joseph's ascent from his well. Of the two novelists, line for printed line, Mann comes out considerably ahead of the Irishman. Not only is the *Joseph* epic the longer of the two works by three thousand pages or so, but also the industrious German was able to toss off two smaller novels as "finger-exercises" during the construction of his monster tale, at the same time dispatching to the world shoals of antifascist and wartime tracts. Of course, Mann spared himself Joyce's task of constructing a new language for his chronicle.

That Mann should have embarked on his massive legend of

the Jews in the decade before that people's near-total destruction in modern Europe induces respect for his prophetic powers. Those powers had been exercised at least once before; the exalted gloom of *Death in Venice* foreshadowed the darkness to come down on Europe in 1914, closing an epoch. Mann's own account of the inspiration of his *Joseph* is well known—the portfolio of the Munich artist, the family Bible, the recollection of Goethe's saying that the old narrative was charming but indeed filling-in of details. André Gide once had a dream on the subject, a dream of "A wonderful drama of Joseph; and particularly of the prison scene: Joseph between the chief baker and the chief butler." Gide let his dream go, but Mann seized the chance to explore human nature in depth, to play off "myth," the universality of the type, against "psychology" —the singularity of the individual.

Mann's Joseph is an Everyman; through him history repeats itself with a difference. In the *Prelude* we are told outright that the long narrative to follow seeks to throw light on the "first and last of all our questioning . . . the nature of man." Just as the novelist's earlier "homogenius man" Hans Castorp discovered himself in his snow-dream to be the delicate child of the universe and lord of the counterpositions, so too his successor Joseph is *tâm,* composed of light and dark elements, "blessed with blessings from heaven above and from the earth beneath." In *Dichtung und Wahrheit,* Goethe mentioned the Joseph story in passing; but in the same book he descants at greater length on the hermetic cosmology of the ancient alchemists: how the primal spirit Elohim ruled at first unrivaled in the heavens, how Lucifer revolted and was deposed, becoming by this Fall the prince of matter, and how the gulf between the lord of spirit and the demon of nature was finally bridged by the creation of man, through whom the original connection with the Godhead was restored. Thomas Mann's *Joseph*-cosmogony is hermetic-Gnostic too, with a pinch of Bergsonian *élan* thrown in. Behind Abraham, the Tower of Babel, the Flood, the Lost Continent, and older, vaguer shapes from the "time-coulisses" of the past, stands the story of the Creation and the sacred drama of the Fall. In the beginning were three things—God, soul, matter. Soul dwelled with God. Now soul, moved by a high curiosity, went adventuring. Encountering matter, soul plunged into the refractory stuff, impelled by a guilty desire to mingle itself with the formless and to bring forth forms. But matter, sluggish and inert, resisted soul and would have defeated its creative purpose had not God lent a hand, helping soul to press out forms from the matrix of matter. In this way the world was made and living nature came into being—a mixture of soul and matter. Then out of his own being God sent an emissary, spirit, to break up this sinful union of soul and matter, to recall soul to its high place in the upper world. But soul would not be won away, and to this day the ancient tensions hold between nature (that is, soul-informed matter) and spirit. Soul resists spirit, "the second emissary," yet soul and spirit are one. Or rather they will be one when the final interpenetration of spirit and nature has been accomplished, the equilibrium of Idea and Will. The breakthrough is achieved in man, that future-heavy creature signed with blessings from above and below. Like Castorp, Mann's Biblical Everyman is a bridging genius, *homo humanus* and *homo dei*.

All this is a rather heavy load to place on poor Joseph's not very muscular shoulders. In addition, the lad must bear the archetypal weight of millenia. He is Osiris who went down to the Egyptian underworld; Hermes-Thoth, letter writer to the gods; Tammuz-Adonis, rent by the boar and laid away amid lamentations in the fruitful earth. With Potiphar's wife he is Gilgamesh refusing Ishtar's present, a sterner Adam who tells his temptress, "I may not set my teeth in the lovely apple which you offer me, that we should eat transgression and lose all." In Mann's chronicle it is no slouching beast but a young man in a gay coat who travels the road to Bethlehem. Joseph prefigures the Saviour with differences: he *saves* in that he supplies the hungry of his world with stored corn. His mother was afraid there would be no room at the inn, although it was Benjamin, not Joseph, she was carrying in her womb at the time. Joseph styles himself "born of a virgin," because Rachel was so young and beautiful you might as well call her that. As a boy, he stands forth among the learned and amazes them. After the assault, his brothers propose to sell Joseph for thirty pieces of silver, but they settle for twenty. An angel (temporarily wingless) guards the dry well from which the bruised lad has been lifted out, and tells Reuben, who has come to ask who rolled the stone away, that what has happened is only a play and a feast, that the story is still growing. God has a long biography. Before his Egyptian jailer Mai-Sachme, Joseph announces himself with the Christ-formula, "I am he." And at the end of his part in the ageless story, Joseph stands blessed from heights and depths; yet his father Jacob's formal blessing eludes him, going instead to Judah of whose tribe Jesus will be born.

"Let us therefore die and enter into darkness," says St. Bonaventure. Joseph "dies" three times, and the theme of the pit is sounded with every possible variation in the course of his story. The very telling of the tale, the narrator reminds us, is a descent into hell, for it means sounding the well of the past which, since it *is* past, is timeless and dead. Jacob remembers Laban's country as pit and underworld, his return from it as a resurrection. The night he discovers Joseph sitting out under the moon beside a well, Jacob fears lest the boy fall into it. Later, the doting father's premonition is confirmed when his brothers throw the lad into the dry well. But Joseph dies only to be born again. Hauled from the pit by the Chaldean traders ("Father," he calls their chief), he is soiled like a newborn child and dribbles the milk they give him. Going down into Egypt is, for a Jew, to descend into darkness, the land of the dead; but once there, Joseph rises to eminence in Potiphar's house ("Father," he calls Mont-Kaw, the steward who bought him from the traders). Denounced by the high courtier's wife, the handsome scribe descends into a second pit. The Egyptian prison is like the state of death; here, says its warden, there is nothing but nothingness, "Here, utter boredom reigns." Sowing time is mourning time, the Corn King is buried, Usir goes down to the dark underworld. But— *si le grain ne meurt*—"I remind you of the grain of corn when it is lying in the grave," says the angel to Reuben who believes his brother dead. "For it is so that the corn falling into the earth and dying brings forth much fruit." In the endless recurrence of nature's seasons, in the cycles of sowing and harvesttime, myth and the timeless have their natural base. In God's world, in eternity, they find their ideal fulfillment.

Seemingly aware that his young Bible hero might not have the strength to carry all this mythological apparatus unaided, Thomas Mann distributes the weight of his symbols so that Father Jacob shares the burden as well as the glory. Jacob is Abel pursued though not killed by the cheated Esau-Cain, who in his turn is also the Mesopotamian Nergal and Edom the Red. Laban's substitution of Leah for Rachel in Jacob's marriage bed brings the hoax theme forward in the time-dimension, just as the Egyptian sequences carry it back. In a dream, Jacob learns from Anubis that Hathor was entered by "the wrong one." Later his son Joseph hears from the gossip of Potiphar's aged parents something about a wrong brother-sister pair embracing, and of other "mistakes" as well, not forgetting the rather serious one of having made their son a eunuch. In his turn Jacob treads the path of his father Isaac. When Joseph presents his Egyptian children to the patriarch, the old man exaggerates his blindness so that he may bless "the wrong one"; although Joseph had gone to the trouble of placing his sons in the right order for blessing, Jacob fools him by crossing his hands in the act of benediction. Like Abraham his grandfather (though "grandfather" must not be taken quite literally), Jacob is called on by God to sacrifice his son, who is then restored to him. Like Abraham, Jacob too is served by a man named Eliezer, a person who in his turn fancies himself the "same" Eliezer who attended the man from Ur.

Modern men consider themselves separate and isolated beings. Mann's Bible characters, although presented as real men, blur into their mythical forebears and models—a process quite consistent with much contemporary theorizing about the behavior of early "pre-philosophical" men who believed (it is said) time was cyclical, felt insecure unless they acted "archetypally" and in conformity to a pattern previously laid down. To accommodate this "archetypal" behavior, Mann postulates a collective unconscious, a development of his earlier concept of the All-soul. Myth is the presentation of a truth in story form. Now is this truth a dimly remembered historical fact? Or does the event celebrated in the tale "really" take place in the unconscious psyche? With his old love for simultaneities and polarities, Mann replies in effect—"Outside-Inside." Myth is the externalization of the drama of the human soul; psychology is history "from the inside." Mann found confirmation of these ideas in Jung, heresiarch of the psychoanalytic movement. Freud detested anything smacking of "mysticism," and arrived at a point where he dismissed Jung quite frankly as "a bit of a mystic himself who hasn't belonged to us for years." Thomas Mann was well aware of Freud's low opinion of his former colleague; yet in his Vienna speech in honor of Freud's seventieth birthday the novelist could not refrain from improving the occasion to pay tribute to that "able but somewhat ungrateful scion of the Freudian school." Jung's treatment of the relation of character and fate in his commentary on the Tibetan *Book of the Dead* gave Mann a proof-text which he used on the spot in an excursus of his own on the unity of doing and happening in the *Joseph* novels. It is touching to read Mann's words apologizing for the digression, reassuring his audience that despite his comments on the similarity of Jung's insights to his own, he, Thomas Mann, really had Freud in mind all the time.

Mann's relation to Sigmund Freud's doctrine is a curious problem, the simplest solution to which seems to be that the novelist worked out his "Freudianism" without any direct help from the Vienna school, indeed without any firsthand knowledge of Freud's writings until he finished *The Magic Mountain*. Enough of psychoanalysis was already in the pre-1914 air to enable Mann to construct the convenient Krokowski, spokesman for the peculiar psychosomatic theory of illness advanced in the Davos novel. But Mann had a long time back established his own metaphysical psychology on independent grounds, a set of ideas growing out of his interest in the way Life gets around Mind, the tricking of Idea by Will. This Mann-psychology derives from notions the novelist found in Goethe, as well as in Schopenhauer and Nietzsche—notions that blended quickly with his native poetic talent to produce his carefully woven tales. No Freudian influence is needed to account for this statement near the close of the *Joseph* story; it might have come from *Buddenbrooks:*

Whatever we do in life is determined by fundamental tastes and sympathies, by deep-lying private destinies which color our whole existence and dye all our doing. These are responsible for our acts— these and not any of the reasonable grounds we are likely to adduce to others and to ourselves.

Goethe's play on the essential unity of "what I do" and "what happens to me" had already caught his eye, as a young writer:

How closely linked are Luck and Merit
Doth never to these fools occur.

Schopenhauer's interpretation of this "aristocratic" theory of merit— the belief that in this life each one of us gets exactly what he deserves—had been blended into the high pessimism of *Buddenbrooks:* What a man does (*operare*) and what befalls him is a function of what he is (*esse*). Mann could never quite understand how Freud managed to arrive at his formulation of the conflict of ego and id without ever having read Schopenhauer on the eternal struggle of Idea against overmastering Will, or Nietzsche's sly demonstrations of Life's power over Truth, his proofs that the will is not a simple fact, but a very complicated business. Did not Nietzsche point out that a thought comes to us when "it" wishes, not when "I" wish?

"I did that," says my memory, "I could not have done that," says my pride, and remains inexorable. Eventually—memory yields.

To Thomas Mann, Sigmund Freud is but one of a series of giant figures rising from the nineteenth century, all of whom played their part in the exploration of the realm of the dynamic and instinctive. In this sequence of *Kulturmenschen,* Mann includes—in addition to Schopenhauer and Nietzsche—Richard Wagner, Freud, and himself. If Freud ever demurred at this grouping, he did so privately.

Although his understanding of Mann's writings remained this side of profundity, the old physician's respect for the novelist was great. Freud read the early volumes of the *Joseph* story and offered to the author *sine pecunia* the advice that Napolean Bonaparte was a Joseph-figure. Did not the Corsican fight with his brothers in his youth, and did he not afterward go down into Egypt to conquer?

Gently Mann disassociated himself from Freud's positivism, his rejection of philosophy, his critique of religion as illusion, his reduction of God to a father-image. His reply to Freud's skepticism on the value of philosophy is well known. *"I believe that in actual fact philosophy ranks before and above the natural sciences and that all method and exactness serve its intuitions and its intellectual and historical will."* Hegel would have said amen to that. Later Mann reinforced his sturdy defense of the Queen of the Sciences in *Doctor Faustus,* encouraging his narrator Zeitblom to enlarge on the justice of philosophy's claim to priority among the humane studies. As crown of the humanities, says Leverkühn's biographer, philosophy is subordinate only to theology, the study of God and His Word. To Thomas Mann, "religion" meant *care,* paying serious attention to those things reminding us we are subject to time and death. Long ago in his 1917 war meditations he wrote: "I dare not say I believe in God. And even if I did, it would be a long time, I think, before I would say so." Forty years later, in the year of his death, he stated as a maxim that we must behave "as if" (*als ob*) the world were created for man. All through the writing of the *Joseph* story he found himself compelled to write "as if" God existed. In the theology of his Biblical chronicle, particularly in the hypothesis that God is in part, but only in part, a creation of Abraham's consciousness—Mann touches an idea familiar to readers of the emergent evolutionists, Whitehead and William James. God and man are *interdependent,* each needing the other in order to survive. Mann associated this concept of the mutual sustainment of God and man with the tradition of Angelus Silesius:

I know that without me God cannot live a moment;
If I am destroyed He must give up the ghost.

But all this is "mysticism" to Freud, to whom philosophy and religion were but related forms of illusion.

By the time he had got well along with the Joseph story, Mann had acquired more direct acquaintance with Freudian psychology. To questions about his own personal experience with analysis, Mann always replied with noncommittal dignity. He tells a correspondent that he read Freud's main works in the second half of the twenties, mentioning as the master's greatest work, *Totem and Taboo*—an odd preference for a book containing so much secondary material, rehashes of nineteenth century anthropological surveys of the Frazer-Tylor sort. In any case, Mann fits out the *Joseph* story with some recognizably Freudian apparatus—which is, after all, no more than suitable for a twentieth century chronicle of an ancient interpreter of dreams. The rather obvious Viennese arabesques in *Joseph* have been well noted by the commentators as well as by Mann himself—the purposeful slips of the tongue, the intended forgettings, the sexual emblems, and the rest. The most dramatic "Freudian" moment of the entire saga occurs in the midst of the *Salammbô*-like splendors of the Egyptian volumes when the lady Mut, Potiphar's wife, sounds the Oedipus theme *fortissimo*. Wagner-fashion the motif had been intoned earlier in the story when Reuben had been caught sporting with his father's concubine Bilhah and had suffered the wrath of Jacob for this usurpation of the father-right. In his denunciation of his errant son, Jacob calls him "shameless hippopotamus" for this animal was reputed to kill its father and mate with its mother by violence. Now in the grand seduction scene in *Joseph in Egypt,* the young Jewish steward draws back in horror from the hint of the unhappy noblewoman that he murder her husband and live with her. "Potiphar, my lord," says Joseph, "is to me like a father; were I to live with you in the house of murder it would be as though I lived with my mother." But the lady Mut has a prepared answer:

With his mother each man sleeps—the woman is the mother of the world, her son is her husband, and every man begets upon his mother—do you not know, must I teach you these simple things? Isis am I, the Great Mother, and wear the vulture hood, and you shall name me your name, sweet son, in the sacred sweetness of the begetting night—

Neither Freudian panache nor mythological luggage can conceal the fact that Joseph is an old-line Thomas Mann artist-hero and exceptional man—a Hans Castorp in a coat of many colors. Joseph is "late," a little spoiled, somewhat delicate. His gift of prophecy is inseparable from a boyhood tendency to fits—Krull-like epileptic seizures. He is a special man, a dreamer, an artist-in-words. We are told that his learning "sets him apart." Everybody takes notice of him. Even Khamat the scribe exclaims, "By the aardvark!" blushing to find himself compelled by the young slave's mere presence to "utter some uncommon truth." Like his German cousin Hans, Joseph is garrulous, good-natured and cheerful, adept at consoling the moribund—although his consolations may be less innocent than Castorp's in that his soothing of the sick Mont-kaw hurries that poor Egyptian to his death so that Joseph can take his place. Like Hans's, Joseph's elevation begins with a *dépaysement*. Thrown out of his native surroundings, he descends to the kingdom of the dead, a fall followed by a rise from the grave, resurrection and ascent, *Steigerung*, hermetic metamorphosis. For all the richness of their respective self-realizations, the careers of both Hans and Joseph end in partial failure. At the close of his sanatorium stay, Castorp has sunk into Asiatic torpor, and the reader suspects that he will die for that fault. The end of Joseph's saga is anticlimactic; it is Judah, not Joseph, who receives the official blessing from Jacob. Tardy revelation of the brothers' assault confirms the old mute sign of the torn *ketonet;* the patriarch knows that God has *disapproved* of his having marked Joseph off from his brethren by exclusive and extraordinary favor.

Joseph does differ from Mann's earlier artist-heroes in at least one respect—his personal beauty. Of course, the comeliness of Jacob's favorite son is a requirement of documentary fidelity. Old Testament, the Koran, Flavius Josephus, the Persian and Arabian commentaries (Mann's *Joseph* story is "researched" with Teutonic thoroughness) all make a point of Joseph's perilous good looks. But there is more to the fair brow of Mann's Joseph than scholarly correspondence to the sources. Through the beauty of Jacob's son, ambiguous and epicene, we may trace a line back to those strange *anima*-like characters that appear so frequently in Mann's pages—the handsome youths, the beautiful boys who touch the artist's soul with desire— Hans Hansen, Tadzio, Pribslav Hippe, and the lovely boy of Castorp's snow-dream. Regretfully, Mann concedes the transiency of Joseph's beauty. His task accomplished, the middle-aged Mouth of Pharaoh allows himself to get a little fat. Jacob's first words upon catching sight of his long-lost son come to meet him in Egypt are, "Who is the fairly thickset man, arrayed in all the splendor of this world? . . ."

As if one exceptional man were not enough for his Biblical chronicle, Mann surrounds Joseph with an array of personages whose "special" natures are signaled by some wound, mark, moist spot or other. Potiphar, courtier of the Sun, is mutilated, solitary, remote; like the angels, God's eunuchs, his existence is purely formal—much as Klaus Heinrich of *Royal Highness* feared his own princely existence would be. In a superb "high conversation" with his wife, Potiphar reminds the lady Mut that she should remember that she is an exceptional woman (*die besondere Frau*) and not an ordinary one. The youthful Pharaoh of the final volume is a Hanno Buddenbrook type, drawn to the peaks, yet too weak and sickly to be successful in conquering them. This young Ikhnaton, tortured by migraine, foreshadows Adrian Leverkühn. Even the foursquare Jacob, healthy enough despite his extreme age to make the long journey down into Egypt for reunion with his son, confesses to an exceptional nature in a rather Tonio-Krögerish way. Why was he drawn to the tender Rachel? "Serious was my heart but soft, therefore was it soft before beauty. Called to the heights and to the sight of diamond-sharp steeps, secretly I loved the gentle hills."

VI

Everyone knows that *Doctor Faustus* is a novel in the form of a biography of a fictitious German composer Adrian Leverkühn who sells his soul to the devil in return for the power to create musical masterpieces. Built on the ground plan of the old Spies version of the Faust legend, the superstructure of Leverkühn's story contains a prophecy of the death of Western art—*parody* being the symptom of her last extremity—as well as a double allegory where the hero is concerned: Leverkühn is both Nietzsche-artist and Germany. For Thomas Mann, Friedrich Nietzsche remained to the last the very *Gestalt* of the genius with an incurable wound. Accordingly, Adrian is infected with a cerebrally-oriented syphilis which drives him mad before killing him. Elements of Leverkühn are borrowed from the composer Hugo Wolf, another Wagnerite and brain-diseased artist, of whom his friend Haberlandt said that when he was composing he always seemed possessed by a demon. By incorporating the Nietzsche-Wolf life pattern into the biography of his tragic hero, Mann builds a third term, a bridge between Leverkühn and the Germany he is meant to represent. In this way he tries to avoid a thinness in the narrative and at the same time to increase the density of the allegorical structure so that the novel as a whole gains in solidity.

For all its structural elaboration, *Doctor Faustus* is a cry from the heart. Written by Mann in exile in the United States during the Second World War, the novel's most moving effect upon its first appearance was produced by its heartfelt, passionate lament over Germany, a Germany considered by its narrator to be irretrievably done for, finished, *kaputt*. "It is all up with Germany," groans Serenus Zeitblom, the humanist-narrator whose style Mann frequently allows to parody his own, "it will be all up with her. She is marked down for collapse, economic, political, moral, spiritual, in short, all-embracing, unparalleled, final collapse." In the sob of the novel's closing line, the narrator announces the identity of the dead composer with Germany—"God be merciful to thy poor soul, my friend, my Fatherland." But it is precisely this strong lament for Germany, so touching on first reading, that was ignored by the course of post-war events. It fell out that it was by no means all up with Germany, even though the victorious powers had pulled her in two. Like the revitalized pieces of the water-carrying broom cut by the sorcerer's apprentice of Goethe's tale, the halves of severed Germany speedily took separate life—the Western federation feverish with Volkswagen-Mercedes prosperity, the Eastern "people's democracy" a sullen captive, but growling and dangerous nonetheless. That history should have made just this ironic turn is not Thomas Mann's fault; it is a circumstance external to his art that Germany escaped, after all, that "all-embracing, final collapse," because two superpowers had to rush into the vacuum left by the destruction of the Third Reich. But on that account the impact of *Doctor Faustus* is today somewhat diminished. Heinrich Mann, ancient foe of chauvinistic Germanism, said that the speed and thoroughness with which Germany accepted the Nazis took his brother Thomas by surprise, and hence his wrath was absolute in his damning of the German nation:

He who was taken by surprise must be on his guard that in his wrath he does not condemn the whole nation with a few scoundrels or with a generation of the vicious. When we now talk—we talk little and rarely—about what our epoch has accomplished, the whole beautiful mess, it is I rather than my brother who does not see a unique monster in the unfortunate country of our birth.

There are difficulties internal to the novel as well. As a character the hero Leverkühn has no thickness. Despite the absorbing account of his boyhood linden-tree days and his theological studies at Halle, Zeitblom's friend remains two-dimensional throughout the long story of his life, a construct rather than a personality. *Doctor Faustus* is an artwork whose meaning has more weight than the line that draws it. For the reader it is not easy to sympathize with Leverkühn, either in his agonies of suffering creation or in his personal losses touching Marie Godeau or little Nepomuk, Professor Zeitblom's pedantry is a little hard to swallow—Settembrini's never lacked a certain charm. Encyclopedics stopping the narrative flow seem overobvious (as in the case of the musical instrument catalogue of the seventh chapter) or dragged in (like chapter twenty-seven's excursus on cosmology). A more serious obstacle to the passionate central impulse of the novel is the subplot dealing with the dismal fates of the

Rodde girls. It is true that the Clarissa-Inez sections have deep and painful roots in Mann's personal life; not one word of Carla Mann's suicide note is changed in its transposition to the pages of *Doctor Faustus* where it does identical service for Clarissa Rodde. Still, the sad destinies of the Frau Senator's daughters have little intrinsic relation to Leverkühn who watches the approaching catastrophes (one of which will kill off his young violinist friend Rudi) with an air of detachment. It is Zeitblom-Mann who is distressed by them. Perhaps the only defense of the claim that the Rodde episodes form an integral part of the novel lies in George Lukács' observation that in *Doctor Faustus* hell is just a continuation of our feverish and extravagant life, that the Devil is a critic of the entire bourgeois culture—the anxious febrile lives of the members of the Rodde circle illustrating this general condition.

Coming as it does after the Joseph cycle in which Mann explored somewhat different frontiers with a certain success, Leverkühn's story marks a regression to earlier themes. The controlling idea of the novel stems from Mann's old concern with the pathology of genius, with art as a *consuming* power—a notion Gottfried Benn in his old age labeled "bourgeois-romantic ideology," dismissing it as an obsolete heritage from the nineteenth century *poétes maudits*. What is new in *Faustus* is the extreme to which the idea is pushed. In the novel Mann assimilates the concept of the German musical-romantic to the political order, and recoils in horror at the result—although he had arrived at the same conclusion several years before:

What we call National Socialism is the virulent perversion of ideas that always bore within themselves the seeds of murderous degeneracy and that were very much at home in the old Germany of culture and learning. There these ideas eked out a life in the grand style—they were labelled "Romanticism" and exerted a good deal of fascination on the entire civilized world. It is not too much to say that they have now gone to the dogs, and that they were destined to go to the dogs, since they were to go to Hitler.

The musical aspect of *Faustus,* Schönbergian twelve-tone scales and the rest, is more interesting as *writing* than as poetry. It is hard for the reader to associate Leverkühn personally with the compositions he is said to produce, although ideologically they are suitable enough. As a true German genius, Adrian must express himself through what the Romantics considered *ars artium*. Metaphysics, music, and the dream—that is Germany. At least so Thomas Mann said in his 1917 *Reflections,* sections of which are cannibalized for the benefit of the "What is German?" discussions in *Doctor Faustus.* But Leverkühn's musical compositions, as Mann represents them, are afflicted to the point of embarrassment with Romantic gigantism, a Strauss-Mahler bombast, that ends by conveying a distinctly nonmusical impression. The primitive howling and thundering of Leverkühn's masterwork *Apocalypse,* its "hellish laughter," the "yelling, screeching, bawling, bleating . . . piping, whinnying"—all that is far more *literary* than musical. Something of the same sort (though far more restrained) had already occurred in *Zauberberg* where the five musical favorites of Hans Castorp are chosen not so much for their musical value as for their ideological significance. For all his passion for the art, genuine and deeply felt as it was, Mann remained an *amateur* of music. Like Nietzsche, a remarkably similar musical devotee, Mann never got over his youthful encounter with Wagner, an experience so violent and ineradicable that in the case of a victim of lesser stature we could compare it only to a rape. Consider how Mann's growing children were struck by their distinguished father's habit of shutting himself away to play the piano. "He doesn't know how to play, really," said their governess. "He just improvises a little." But said his son Klaus, remembering:

What he played in the solitude of the dusky salon could hardly be called an improvisation. It always was the same rhythm, at once drawling and violent: always the same desperate tenderness: always that swelling, weeping, jubilating song: it was always *Tristan.*

Or his secretary Meisel, in Princeton:

It is an experience to see him listening to phonograph records of *Tristan* or *The Twilight of the Gods.* A strange abandon slowly invades the disciplined face. It is that of a man who has taken off his spectacles: limp, mellow, suffering, and enthusiastic.

Or Mann himself, conceding the "Nazism" in Wagner's music, yet at the same time confessing:

> I have so loved that work that even today I am deeply stirred when a few bars of music from this world impinges upon my ear. The enthusiasm it engenders, the sense of grandeur that so often seizes us in its presence can be compared only to the feelings excited in us by Nature at her noblest, by evening sunshine on mountain peaks, by the turmoil of the sea.

Mann was shocked to find that Adolf Hitler had experienced a Wagnerian trauma much like his own, had heard *Meistersinger* two hundred times, had had himself painted as Lohengrin in white armor. A performance of *Walküre* had made the Führer receptive to Spanish proposals for German military aid to Franco; the operation was dubbed "Magic Fire." On the day of Poland's invasion, and again when France fell, Hitler ordered *Götterdämmerung* performed in Berlin. The more reason then for the author of *Doctor Faustus* to see in the German dictator a terrifying parody of German genius. "Mortifyingly enough, it is all there: the difficulty, the laziness, the pathetic formlessness in youth, the round peg in the square hole. . . ." He was a genius after all, that awful freak was a brother-artist, another German misfit with a touch of hellfire lighted under him.

VII

Doctor Faustus brings to a close that period of Thomas Mann's political development which is marked by the antifascist polemics and prodemocracy pamphlets of the years leading up to and through the Second World War. It can be argued that Mann never had more than one basic political position—that is, politics is a dirty business—and that his various "stands" from 1914 to 1953 were one and all responses to the challenge of various kinds of "politics." But if this seems oversimplifying, we may distinguish four periods in the novelist's ideological career, of which the fourth may be considered a kind of dispirited return to the "third-force" neutralism of the second. In the years before the Kaiser's war, Thomas Mann was convinced that politics and democracy were "un-German" concepts, that the German spirit was fundamentally alien toward the realm of politics and democracy—these two being one and the same thing. Politics and democracy, Mann said in those days, were necessary to the West, most of all to France whose ideal was Civilization. But the heritage of Germany was metaphysics, music, and the dream; this ideal was comprehended by the concept of Culture. For the West, the highest social category is the *Nation*, but for Germany it is the *Volk*. This notion of German culture as essentially nonpolitical Mann held to be a legacy from his burgher forebears. He saw the 1914 war as Germany's defense of her high world-destiny against the shallow rationalism of the democracies, and he took upon himself the defense of his dear *unliterarische Land,* fumbling, inarticulate, awkward before the moralistic abuse of the *Zivilisationsliterat.* Rejected for military service because of a bad ankle, Mann threw himself into the cultural service of Germany's cause:

Denn der Mensch verkümmert im Frieden,	For man pines away in peace,
Müssige Ruh'ist das Grab des Muts.	Idle rest is the grave of courage.
Das Gesetz ist der Freund des Schwachen,	Law is the friend of weakness,
Alles will es nür eben machen,	It would only make all equal,
Möchte gern die Welt verflachen,	Would like to level the world,
Aber der Krieg lässt die Kraft erscheinen.	But war lets strength shine forth.

But the Kaiser's war had not yet ended when Mann began to revaluate the concept of the "nonpolitical," to move to the conclusion that the German burgher's traditional aloofness from politics was a fault and not a virtue. Precisely this nonpolitical quality in the German spirit, he admitted, contributed most heavily to the catastrophe.

Germany's weakness was that she had not "read the newspapers." She had been drowsing like one of the Seven Sleepers, a political Rip Van Winkle. She should wake up! After the war Mann edged forward the Goethean idea that Germany's mission was to mediate between the Western democracies and the East (Russia, Asia), receiving from all, teaching all. Mann composed the second half of *The Magic Mountain* during this transition from the romantic "nonpolitical" pre-1914 period to his stand against fascism in the thirties and forties backed by his passionate advocacy of democracy. Thus Hans Castorp, dreaming of himself as "lord of the counterpositions," stands thoughtfully in the middle between Naphta, the antibourgeois Jesuit Marxist and Settembrini. The noisy *Zivilisationsliterats* cry of "Infamous!" to Naphta echoed pro-Allied Heinrich Mann's *"Infamie!"* to his brother Thomas. By 1924, the year of *The Magic Mountain*'s publication, Mann had already committed himself to the side of the democracies in the coming struggle by joining the defense of the Weimar Republic and open warnings against German fascism. But Thomas Mann, antifascist and prodemocrat, is most clearly seen in the period between 1933, date of his exile from Germany, and the publication of *Doctor Faustus* in 1947. These years included the editorship of *Mass und Wert* in Switzerland, the removal of himself and family to the United States, the anti-Nazi polemics, official radio broadcasts, the Library of Congress post, and the attempt to settle down as an American citizen amid other distinguished German émigrés in Pacific Palisades, California. But America had begun to go sour on him before *Doctor Faustus* appeared in English translation. The postwar polarization of the two world superpowers, each seemingly bent on the other's destruction, made him turn in bewilderment to "liberalism." In 1948 before a gathering of Hollywood notables, Mann declared "America's most loyal son," to be Henry Wallace:

In the eyes of the whole world, the millions who will give him their votes will represent the moral and intellectual elite of America . . . we cannot but recognize in the Russian-American conflict the one appalling obstacle for all human progress. The future of mankind depends on its solution, and Wallace means to help solve it. . . .

By the time the McCarthy Senate committee had turned its attention to some of his California friends, he had had enough. Shaking the dust of the United States from his feet—that country which "had never had a history; only a success story"—he retreated once more to neutral Switzerland. There he drew up a final plan—to enlist a few of the world's intellectual leaders to issue a World Peace appeal to all the nations of the earth. Not only was the continuation of human life at stake but also the honor of mankind. If the superpowers went to war, all the victories the human race had won so painfully over so many thousands of years would be rubbed out; all would turn to dust and ashes. The appeal plan came to nothing. Years before, a poet of the "old" Germany had given his opinion of such gestures: "War," said Stefan George, "is only the final result of senseless activities which for years have been recklessly directed towards it. The attempt of a few individuals to plaster over the breach seems to me to have no effect."

In his old Schopenhauer days Thomas Mann believed that the poet's soul was longing and that longing was for death—death as deliverance from the painful constriction of individual personality, death as the end of an illusion. In later years he felt less sure about the object of that poetic longing; what the poet wants is life, not death. In a post-*Zauberberg* essay on Theodor Storm, he touches on the aging master's dread of the night of being forgotten, extinguished, annihilated, of that long night from which he can never emerge, not even to help his children who survive him—"That I shall no longer know about you, can do nothing more for you, that is frightful!" Mann says gently that these are a poet's fears, adding the consoling note that it is, after all, the *idea* of death rather than death itself we dread. As far as the actual event is concerned, for simple and complicated personalities alike, "the dread and horror pass, and in peaceful, half-dreamy bewilderment we mostly murmur, 'Now I will go to sleep.'" Knowledge that his own works would survive comforted him. Finding a vacationing American college girl poring over *The Magic Mountain* filled the aging novelist with delight. There was a moment with her, all kindliness and dignity, yet faintly reminiscent of that poignant scene in his own novel where Joachim Ziemssen, already given over to death, bids farewell to young Marusja. Youth held his heart to the end. It was, after all, the young who fell in love with *Tonio Kröger;* it would be the young who would keep his work alive. Before leaving the United States for good, he wrote to an American teacher who had told him of the love of students for his books:

Of course the most eloquent tongue would be of no avail if there weren't warm young hearts, thirsting for the good and the spiritual, to respond to it. That they are there . . . is a beautiful comforting sign. I personally am, naturally, quite moved by the news that these striving and receptive young people like to hear about my books and take pleasure in reading them. After all, we poets are all longing for a little immortality, the sympathy of the young generation for our work is a guarantee that it will survive us for a little while. Please give my kindest regards to your pupils, together with my best wishes for the success of their studies. By that I do not mean just the outward success, but I hope that the devoted study of what great minds, through their suffering have contributed to the world, may form them into human beings which are able to cope with the difficulties of this confused period of transition.

He had always been apprehensive about death. As a young man he thought he would die at 45. Like the good bourgeois he was, he believed that hard work alone kept him alive. Without *Faustus,* he said, he would have faded out at 70, the terminal age he predicted for himself in 1930. His family remembered moments of anxiety and gloom in California; he would quote Prospero's words, "And my ending is despair" when his thoughts turned to his own death. But when it came, it was peaceful enough, and the manner of it was fitting too. The final year was one of jubilee—the Schiller festival, his own golden wedding anniversary and eightieth birthday, the official visit to the Netherlands and his reception by the Queen. Like his own Aschenbach, he was stricken on holiday at the seashore. The thrombosis stole on him as he sat in his beach chair at Noordwijk, solitary, diligently writing, pausing from time to time for a restful glance at the sea. We are told that when young Hans Castorp in his Flatland days looked out on the ocean, he felt an overpowering desire to shut his eyes safe in eternity—until he saw a sail on the horizon. On that last day in his beach chair, Thomas Mann saw no sail. Yet in the Zurich hospital bed where he lay some days later, comforted by his loving family, he did not seem to know what was happening to him. He died in his sleep. His daughter Erika records that it was his "music face" he turned to his wife at the moment of death, "the expression absorbed and deeply attentive, with which he used to listen to his most familiar and beloved pieces,"—the face secretary Meisel once described as that of a man who has taken off his spectacles.

His humanism was noble. It is the idea of the human being, he believed, that survives that "inoculation with death," which Novalis prophesied. In 1919, he claimed the right to say with Adalbert Stifter, "My books are not just literature: as ethical revelations, as human dignity upheld with rigorous seriousness, they have a value which will survive longer than their poetic value." Until his death he clung to a hope in the redemptive power of art. In the essay on Chekhov—one of his two final pieces of writing—he talks of the poet's task as one of work, of giving form to truth, hoping "sometimes almost confidently" that truth and serene form may one day avail to set the human spirit free and prepare mankind for a better life. But Thomas Mann's humanism *as* humanism has no offspring; it is not a doctrine; it contains no germ of action. We would be wrong in saying that this humanism was nothing outside his creative work, for before, during, and after Hitler, he was acutely sensitive to the need of defending humane values, and out of that sensitivity he acted like the strong serious man he was. But now there remains nothing but the work and the memory. It is as if that work were so great that it drew all to itself.

Notes

To AVOID PUTTING note numbers or reference symbols into the pages of the text, I have given below the page and line numbers, as well as cue phrases—usually the last words of the sentence annotated.

PREFACE

iii: 2   . . . *Three Philosophical Poets.* (Cambridge, Mass., Harvard University Press, 1910.)

iv: 8   . . . occasion to Bergson's. For example, by Wyndham Lewis in *Time and Western Man* [1927] (Boston, Mass., Beacon Press, 1957), p. 198.

INTRODUCTION

vi: 11   . . . *The Intellectual Hero* . . . (New York, J. B. Lippincott, 1961), p. 11.

vi: 12   . . . *The Novelist as Philosopher* . . . (New York, Oxford University Press, 1962).

vi: 18   . . . tragic element in man." Malraux quoted by Cruickshank in *ibid.,* pp. 6-7.

vii: 6   . . . form of a *romance* . . . Notably by Richard Chase in *The American Novel and Its Tradition* (Garden City, N.Y., Doubleday & Co., 1957), pp. 21 *et seq.*

vii: 33   . . . daughter of Wonder." "Poésie," in *Nouvelle Revue Française* (Paris, 1 Jan., 1961), p. 79.

viii: 5   . . . density of our lives." "Against Dryness," in *Encounter* (London, Jan., 1961), p. 20.

viii: 16   . . . the Communist Party." *Sartre: Romantic Rationalist* (Cambridge, England, Bowes & Bowes, 1953), p. 35. *The Concept of Mind* (1949) by Oxford philosopher Gilbert Ryle denies a commonly assumed dualism between actions and mental events.

viii: 21   . . . *The Mystery of Being.* Marcel's Gifford lectures. (London, Harvill Press, 1950-1951).

viii: 24   . . . criminal playwright Genet . . . *Saint-Genet, comédien et martyr* (Paris, Gallimard, 1952); *Genet* (New York, George Braziller, 1963).

ix: 5   . . . a certain tranquil convention. Nicolson is cited by Harvey Breit in *The New York Sunday Times Book Review,* April 19, 1952.

ix: 13   . . . as a *philosopher.* . . . As a theologian too! See *Religion from Tolstoy to Camus,* ed. Walter Kaufmann (New York, Harper & Row, 1961).

ix: 36   . . . the ontological argument." *The Myth of Sisyphus and Other Essays,* trans. Justin O'Brien (New York, Alfred A. Knopf,

Inc. 1955), p. 15. "The great novelists are philosophical novelists," Camus writes in *Sisyphus,* citing Balzac, Melville, Stendhal, Dostoevski, Malraux, and Kafka. By "philosophical novelist" Camus means one who does more than simply tell a story or urge a thesis—one who creates his own universe.

x: 31   . . . rank and status." *The Ironic German: A Study of Thomas Mann* (Boston, Little, Brown & Co., 1958), p. 57

xi: 17   . . . service of beauty. See note to epigraph of Gide chapter.

xi: 32   . . . the novel copies reality . . . See Richard Chase, *op. cit.*, pp. 21, 24

xii: 9   . . . *Surface and Symbol* . . . (New York, Oxford University Press, 1962).

xii: 1   . . . in his superstructure." To Arland Ussher, Joyce is "a genuinely philosophical novelist." *Three Great Irishmen* (London, Gollancz, 1952), p. 148.

xiii: 7   . . . usually bored Gide. An exception was Schopenhauer's *The World as Will and Idea* which young Gide read with enthusiasm while preparing for his baccalaureate. ". . . I freed myself from Schopenhauer's influence pretty soon," he says, "but it is to him I owe my initiation into philosophy and to him alone." (See note to 123: 12.)

xiii: 24   . . . and their venom." *Scepticism and Animal Faith* (New York, Charles Scribner's Sons, 1923), p. 76.

xiv: 13   . . . about my 'intellectualism.' " Letter to Gerhart Hauptmann, April 11, 1925, trans. Ralph Mannheim in *Encounter* (London, Dec., 1962), p. 7. *Briefe, 1889-1936* (Frankfurt, S. Fischer Verlag), 1961, p. 234.

I. JAMES JOYCE

Most of the references to Joyce's books are to the following texts:
Portrait of the Artist as a Young Man (P)
New York, The Viking Press, Inc., 1956.
Ulysses (U)
New York, Random House, 1934. (Page numbers of the Modern Library edition are the same.)
Finnegans Wake (FW)
New York, The Viking Press, Inc., 1947.
References to other Joyce writings have bibliographical information appended. The same is true of writings mentioned other than Joyce's. Where more than one reference is made to the same item, the bibliographical information is found in the first reference only.

Epigraph 1.   From a letter of August 20, 1931, to Louis Gillet quoted in full in Richard Ellmann, *James Joyce* (New York, Oxford University Press, 1959), p. 631.

Epigraph 2.   *Ulysses* 682.

Epigraph 3.   *When We Dead Awaken,* Act II. *The Collected Works of Hendrik Ibsen,* trans. William Archer (New York, Charles Scribner's Sons, 1907), p. 396.

3: 14   . . . can be explained." Oliver St. John Gogarty, "James Augustine Joyce," *The Times Herald,* Dallas, Sept. 15, 1949.

3: 25	. . . frivolous profundities." *The Classical Temper: A Study of James Joyce* (New York, Barnes & Noble, Inc., 1961), p. 24. Mr. Goldberg, now thirty-seven, holds the chair of English in the University of Sidney, Australia.
5: 11	. . . the universal language." U 585.
5: 17	. . . as none perceived." U 652.
5: 28	. . . whatness of allhorse." U 184.
5: 33	. . . of meltwhile horse." FW 111.
6: 11	. . . in the original." U 203. According to Father Noon, who has looked into the matter, there is no evidence that Joyce ever took any formal courses in philosophy as an undergraduate at University College. See William T. Noon, S.J., *Joyce and Aquinas* (New Haven, Yale University Press, 1957), p. 3. In the *Portrait,* Stephen Dedalus claims only to have read Aristotle's *De Anima* and *Poetics,* and a *Synopsis Philosophiae Scholasticae ad mentem divi Thomae,* p. 176.
6: 24	. . . *catharsis* or purgation. *Poetics* 1449b28.
7: 5	. . . desire and loathing." P 205.
7: 13	. . . of the feelings. I. A. Richards, C. K. Ogden, and J. Wood, *The Foundations of Aesthetics* (New York, Lear Publishers, 1925), p. 14.
7: 22	. . . *quae visa placent* . . . P 186. The text of Aquinas reads "pulchra enim dicuntur quae visa placent." *Summa Theologica,* Part I, Question 5, Article 4. See Maurice Beebe, "Joyce and Aquinas: the Theory of Aesthetics," in *Joyce's Portrait: Criticisms and Critiques,* Thomas E. Connolly, ed. (New York, Appleton-Century-Crofts, 1962), pp. 275-276.
7: 25	. . . *(interesseloses Wohlgefallen). Critique of Judgment* trans. J. H. Bernard (New York, The Macmillan Company, 1951), p. 45.
7: 32	. . . art with eugenics. P 208-209.
8: 2	. . . World Will within us. *The World as Will and Idea,* trans. R. B. Haldane and J. Kemp (London, Routledge & Kegan Paul, Ltd., 1833), p. 254. Both Kant and Schopenhauer describe the aesthetic judgment as "without personal interest."
8: 7	. . . nude female body. *The Philosophy of Nietzsche* (New York, The Modern Library, n.d.), "The Genealogy of Morals" 103.
8: 29	. . . *wholeness, harmony and radiance.*" P 211. Aquinas's text is *Summa Theologica,* Part 1, Question 29, Article 8. An interpretation of the text along neo-Platonic lines is offered by E. F. Carritt in his *Philosophies of Beauty* (London, Oxford University Press, 1931), p. 50.
9: 3	. . . *quidditas,* the whatness . . . Schopenhauer says that in the aesthetic experience the subject "looks simply and solely at the *what*" of the object. *The World as Will and Idea,* Vol. I, p. 231.
9: 11	. . . *haecceitas* or *this-ness* . . . There is a discussion of "haecceitas" in Noon, p. 51.
9: 13	. . . Hopkins's *inscape* . . . Alan Heuser compares 'claritas' and 'inscape' in *The Shaping Vision of Gerard Manley Hopkins* (New York, Oxford University Press, 1958), p. 106 n.
9: 27	. . . of the mind itself." *Stephen Hero* (New York, New Directions, 1944), p. 211.

9: 29   . . . achieves its epiphany." *Ibid.*, p. 213.

10: 2   . . . with extreme care . . ." *Ibid*, p. 211.

10: 16   . . . and could bless." "Vacillation IV" in *The Collected Poems of W. B. Yeats* (New York, The Macmillan Company, 1954), p. 246.

10: 31   . . . brute natural fact. A clear statement of the Platonic interpretation of Symbolism was given by young André Gide, still under the spell of Mallarmé, in his *Treatise of the Narcissus:* "Appearances are imperfect, they only half reveal the truth which they conceal; the poet must be able, at a hint, to understand these truths, and then to reveal them. . . . The poet who knows that he is creating, divines behind each object—and one only suffices him—symbols, to reveal its archetype; he knows that appearance is only a pretext, a garment which hides it, and beyond which the gaze of the common herd does not penetrate, but which indicates that it is there. The poet contemplates these symbols, piously leaning over them, and then, silently, penetrates into the heart of the matter. And when, visionary, he has perceived the Idea, the harmonious Number of his being, which sustains the imperfect form, he seizes it, then, regardless of the transitory shape which clothed it in time, he knows how to give it its eternal shape, its true form, final and inevitable, heavenly and crystal-clear."

10: 32   . . . to the occult. John Senior examines the relation between Symbolism and the occult in *The Way Down and Out* (Ithaca, N. Y., Cornell University Press, 1959). *Œuvres Completes.* Vol. I, pp. 216-217. This is Enid Starkie's translation in *The Bergsonian Heritage,* ed. Thomas Hanna, Columbia University Press, 1962, pp. 89-90.

11: 10   . . . is literary talk." P 212-213.

11: 15   . . . Plato's world of ideas." U 183.

11: 22   . . . The sacrificial butter." U 183.

11: 25   . . . *into the past.* U 184. My italics.

12: 9   . . . religion of art itself." *Le Cabinet de lectures* (1836). Cited by Joanna Richardson in *Théophile Gautier: His Life and Times* (New York, Coward-McCann, Inc., 1959), p. 288. Vigny held that art is "the modern religion, the modern spiritual belief." Nor is the doctrine confined to French poets. The father-artist in Gerhart Hauptmann's *Michael Kramer* (a favorite of Joyce) says "Art is religion."

12: 18   . . . crawling on the earth." The passage occurs in Gautier's *Histoire de romanticism,* p. 153. Quoted by Shroder in *Icarus: the Image of the Artist in French Romanticism* (Cambridge, Mass., Harvard University Press, 1961), p. 217.

12: 27   . . . paring his fingernails." P 215.

12: 28   . . . in Plato's *Timaeus* . . . Timaeus, 28 *et seq.*

13: 1   . . . see him nowhere." Flaubert, *Correspondence,* Paris, 1926-1930. A translation of the passage is given by Goldberg, p. 231.

13: 5   . . . hammered into life. Ibsen, *When We Dead Awaken,* Act I.

13: 9   . . . that is art—." P 206.

13: 20   . . . an imitator. See *Republic* III 393. Of course, Plato said elsewhere that the poet is "inspired by the divine." *Ion* 533-534.

13: 30   . . . hinder this penetration." *The Demons (Die Dämonen),* trans. Richard and Clara Winston (New York, Alfred A. Knopf, 1961), Vol. II, p. 942.

13: 31   . . . sent into exile. *Republic* III 398.

14: 2   . . . a self-banished man. Daedalus made his wings "in tedious exile now too long detained," but his motive for turning his mind to "unknown arts" was to *escape* from exile and to return to his native land.

14: 14   . . . silence, exile, and cunning." P 247.

14: 18   . . . afar from the life." FW 176.

14: 32   . . . I am different." *Confessions,* p. 1.

15: 11   . . . little in common." *Childe Harold's Pilgrimage,* Canto III, xii.

15: 20   . . . knowledge that predominates." *The World as Will and Idea,* Vol. III, p. 156.

15: 31   . . . in every order." P 161.

16: 1   . . . of his mortal sin. To Stephen Dedalus (as to young James Joyce), Charles Stewart Parnell was the very type of Irish hero, betrayed, turned on, hunted to death by his own people. It is interesting to compare with the remarks made at the *Portrait's* Christmas dinner an observation of Goethe made in 1829 on the tumult in Ireland over Catholic Emancipation—the Irish Catholics, said Goethe, "are like a pack of hounds, which bite one another, but when a stag comes in view, all united immediately to run it down" (*Conversations with Eckermann*). Joyce's Mr. Casey blames the bishops and priests of Ireland who "hounded him into his grave" for turning the people against Parnell. But, as Mr. Conor O'Brien points out in his book on Parnell, the Irish hierarchy held cautiously aloof until Parnell's own party members pressed him to resign. It was Michael Davitt, the old Landleaguer in whose honor Mrs. Riordan kept the maroon velvet-backed hairbrush, who first publically advised Parnell to go. The first ecclesiastic to recommend the Chief's retirement was neither Irish priest or bishop, but the English Cardinal Manning who advised Gladstone to repudiate Parnell. See Conor Cruise O'Brien *Parnell and His Party* (New York, Oxford, Clarendon Press, 1957).

16: 4   . . . yes, proud too!"). Quoted by Richard Ellmann in *Yeats: the Man and the Masks* (New York, The Macmillan Company, 1948), p. 29.

16: 11   . . . into the world." P 251.

16: 20   . . . She wander the loud waters." *Countess Cathleen* in *The Collected Plays of W. B. Yeats* (New York, The Macmillan Company, 1953), p. 30. The lines occur in Scene V.

16: 23   . . . always alone." P 201.

17: 6   . . . and foster brother." P 98.

17: 14   . . . to isolate himself." "The Day of the Rabblement," in *The Critical Writings of James Joyce,* ed. E. Mason and R. Ellmann (New York, The Viking Press, Inc., 1959), p. 69.

17: 18   . . . what the word means?" P 247.

17: 25 . . . alone. Sad too." U 49.

17: 31 . . . drowns his book." U 209.

18: 10 . . . in Flaubert's *Education sentimental*. Flaubert's irony toward his young hero is heavier than Joyce's toward Stephen Dedalus: "He [Moreau] had stopped in the middle of the Pont-Neuf, and, bareheaded, his coat open, he breathed in the air. All at once he felt something imperishable welling up from the depths of his being, an urge of tenderness which made him dizzy, as if waves were moving under his eyes. One o'clock struck from a church tower, slowly like a voice calling him. Then he was seized with one of those tremblings of the spirit which seem to transport one into a higher world. There had come to him an extraordinary talent, the object of which he did not know. He wondered, seriously, if he was to be a great painter, or a great poet; and he decided in favour of painting, for the demands of this profession would bring him closer to Mme. Arnoux. So he had found his vocation! The aim of his existence was now clear, and the future infallible." *Sentimental Education,* trans. Anthony Goldsmith (New York, E. P. Dutton & Co., Inc., 1941), p. 48.

18: 30 . . . his windswept limbs." P 168-169.

19: 31 . . . exile in solitude." Quoted by Meriol Trevor in his *Newman: the Pillar of the Cloud* (London, Macmillan & Co. Ltd., 1962), p. 415.

20: 6 . . . on his violin. Wilfrid Ward, *Newman* (New York, Longmans, Green & Co., 1912), Vol. II, p. 336.

20: 33 . . . the everlasting arms." P 165.

21: 4 . . . only true church." Letter to Harriet Weaver, 1 May 1935. *Letters of James Joyce,* ed. Stuart Gilbert (New York, The Viking Press, Inc., 1957), p. 366.

21: 31 . . . study nearly naked." Letter to Robert Bridges, March 7, 1884, from University College, St. Stephen's Green, Dublin. *The Letters of Gerard Manley Hopkins to Robert Bridges,* ed. C. C. Abbott (New York, Oxford University Press, 1955), p. 190.

22: 5 . . . my life among strangers." *Poems of Gerard Manley Hopkins,* 2d ed., ed. Robert Bridges (London, Oxford University Press, 1930), p. 65. Reprinted by permission of publisher.

22: 10 . . . call it back. . . ." U 49.

22: 13 . . . blots black out . . ." *Poems,* p. 76.

22: 17 . . . original, spare, strange." *Ibid.,* p. 30.

22: 29 . . . upon thy cause." *Ibid.,* p. 68

23: 4 . . . say you disbelieve." P 240.

23: 6 . . . Catholicism is in his bones." cited in Herbert Gorman, *James Joyce: His First Forty Years* (New York, B. W. Huebsch, 1925), p. 75.

23: 8 . . . judgment to come." *Ibid.,* p. 192.

23: 11 . . . such an impress." *Life and the Dream* (Garden City, N. Y., Doubleday & Co., Inc., 1947), p. 381. Mrs. Colum had quoted to Joyce the philosopher Maritain's remark about Baudelaire, "The intellectual structure of his mind was Catholic," whereupon Joyce *"made considerable fun of anyone having a Catholic structure for his mind"* (my italics).

23: 16   . . . of a confessor's manual. Cited by Magalaner and Kain, p. 178, quoting Cecil Maitland in *The New Witness.*

23: 20   . . . and copulate. Joyce, *Letters,* pp. 274-275.

24: 16   . . . disembodied and sword-pierced. This ideal description does not quite match that of the Earwicker's bedroom (FW 559) or that of the Blooms (U 715).

25: 3   . . . draggletail Dublin drab." FW 432.

25: 12   . . . Phoebe Brand's production . . . *James Joyce's A Portrait of the Artist as a Young Man,* adapted from *Stephen Hero* and the *Portrait* by Frederic Ewen, Phoebe Brand, and John Randolph. Presented at New York, the Martinique Theatre, 1962-1963.

25: 23   . . . twenty centuries of authority and veneration." P 243.

26: 9   . . . in the Catholic tradition. The Scholastic philosophy taught to Descartes at La Flèche had been refreshed by influence of the school of Salamanca and Suarez. See André Mattei's *L'homme de Descartes* (Paris, Aubier, 1940), Chap. 1. Young Descartes, whose boyhood health was delicate, was treated indulgently by the Jesuits who allowed him to stay in bed mornings as long as he liked. To the end of his life the philosopher retained the kindliest feelings towards his preceptors.

26: 15   . . . Saint Genevieve in Paris. Ellmann, p. 124.

26: 28   . . . execration greeted *Ulysses.* Empson's remarks are in his *Milton's God* (Norfolk, Conn., New Directions, 1961), pp. 232-234. The offending book is Kenner's *Dublin's Joyce* (Bloomington, Ind., Indiana University Press, 1956), although I cannot find in it the pro-Christianity or pro-Catholicism that annoys Mr. Empson and others so.

26: 31   . . . others he did not." Goldberg, p. 307.

27: 15   . . . cards for reference. James Stephens relates a conversation with Joyce in which the latter told him that his (Stephens') "knowledge of Irish life was non-catholic and so non-existent." James Stephens, *James, Seumas and Jacques,* ed. Lloyd Frankenberg (New York, The Macmillan Company, 1964).

28: 8   . . . a hopeless morass." Reported in *The New York Times,* July 11, 1963.

28: 16   . . . into a biscuit . . ." quoted by Ellmann, p. 418, from a letter from Moore to Edward Marsh, August 3, 1917.

    The behavior of the unfrocked priest in Tennessee Williams' *The Night of the Iguana* is a melodramatic instance of fake blasphemy. A critic has observed that when Shannon flings the crucifix to the ground "we are in the presence of nothing more than that most unpleasant of travesties—blaspheming without travail, without the prior justification of the loss of a deeply held faith." Marion Magid, "The Innocence of Tennessee Williams," *Commentary,* Jan., 1963, p. 40.

28: 15   . . . my father's a bird." U 20.

29: 21   . . . urine, and excrement." Nietzsche cites this catalog in *Genealogy of Morals* ("Guilt and Bad Conscience," p. 7).

29: 24   . . . body without disgust. *Les Fleurs du Mal*, LXXXVIII.

30: 3   . . . ghostly son of God alone. See *Portrait*, 243; U 204-205. An old Catharist prayer runs, "God came down from heaven, and took ghostly shape in Mary." See Zoé Oldenbourg's *Massacre at Montségur* (New York, Pantheon Books, 1961), Appendix C.

30: 25   . . . teachings approach it. See Harry Austryn Wolfson's "Immortality and Resurrection" in *Religious Philosophy* (Cambridge, Mass., Harvard University Press, 1961), pp. 75-76.

31: 14   . . . can understand them." P 36.

31: 23   . . . dreaming of Beauty." *Professor Storitsyn*, Act II.

31: 28   . . . Mann's "colera morbous." FW 211.

31: 31   . . . *A Brilliant Career*. See Ellmann, p. 81.

32: 16   . . . a hidden "underthought." See Eleanor Ruggles, *Gerard Manley Hopkins: a Life* (London, John Lane, 1947), pp. 173-174.

32: 23   . . . of our century, . . . Today—novels, plays, and films come suitably equipped with mythic correspondences. Jules Dassin's film *Phaedra* and John Updike's novel *The Centaur* are obvious examples. Nikos Kazantzakis' *Odysseia* is a giant *sequel* to the Homer epic rather than a parallel, but the story is told again with correspondences in Pérez de Ayala's *Prometeo*, a *"novela poemática"*; one of the characters is a professor of Greek named Marco. *Prometeo* begins with a "rhapsody in the manner of a prologue" in which the history of Marco-Odysseus is told allegorically. Ramón Pérez de Ayala, *Prometeo* (Buenos Aires, Luz de domingo; la caida de los Limones, Editorial Losada, 1939).

33: 4   . . . losing its order. Eliot's " 'Ulysses,' Order, and Myth" first appeared in *The Dial*, Nov., 1923. It has been reprinted by M. Schorer, J. Miles, and G. McKenzie in their anthology *Criticism* (New York, Harcourt Brace & World, Inc. [rev. ed.], 1958), p. 269.

33: 8   "and paradigmatic ear." FW 42, 70, 263.

33: 12   . . . disciple Jolande Jacobi cites . . . J. Jacobi, *The Psychology of C. G. Jung* (New Haven, Yale University Press, 1951). See also John Senior, *The Way Down and Out*, p. 38. For Jung's own statements on archetypes, see his *The Integration of Personality* (New York, Farrar and Rinehart, Inc., 1939), Chap. III, and his *Collected Works* (New York, Pantheon, 1953), Vol. 9, Part 1, "The Archetypes and the Collective Unconscious."

33: 35   . . . Tweedledee, Dr. Freud." Joyce, Letter to Harriet Weaver, June 24, 1921, *Letters*, p. 166.

34: 2   . . . and easily freudened." FW 115.

34: 12   . . . Freud or Jung." Cited by Ellmann, *James Joyce*, p. 706.

34: 19   . . . and here one must." *Peer Gynt*, Act II, Scene vii.

34: 25   . . . and homeless state. Not that Homer's Telemachus is insensitive to the ambiguities of paternity—"My mother says I am Odysseus' son," he says to Athena, "But for myself, I cannot tell. It's a wise child that knows its own father." Odyssey I, 214-216.

34: 31   . . . he any son?" U 205.

35: 5   . . . opposition brings reunion." Joyce, letter to Harriet Weaver, January 1, 1925, *Letters,* pp. 224-225. This is Coleridge on Bruno; see Joyce's review of J. L. McIntyre's *Giordano Bruno* (1903), in Mason and Ellmann's *The Critical Writings of James Joyce,* p. 134.

35: 23   . . . Cursed by God." U 332.

35: 25   . . . like Zero Mostel. Mostel played Bloom in Padraic Colum's adaptation for the stage of the Circe episode in *Ulysses. Ulysses in Nighttown* was produced at the Rooftop Theatre, New York, 1958.

36: 7   . . . on the alert." *Power (Jew Süss,* Munich, 1925) (New York, The Viking Press, 1948), pp. 240-241.

36: 11   . . . solitary mutable man." U 692.

36: 12   . . . "Everyman or Noman . . ." U 712. . . . allround man" U 231. "Noman" is, of course, the Homeric *Outis* (Nobody) the pseudonym by which the resourceful Odysseus outwits Polyphemus.

36: 17   . . . common human lot." *Love and Death in the American Novel* (New York, Criterion Books, 1960), p. 252.

37: 3   . . . in impenetrable darkness." *Pensées* 155.

37: 8   . . . about old Bloom." U 231.

37: 13   . . . has his good points." U 175.

37: 18   . . . overshadow them all." *James Joyce and the Making of Ulysses* (New York, Harrison Smith and Robert Haas, 1934), p. 116.

38: 9   . . . all literary "types" end up. Nathalie Sarraute, *The Age of Suspicion* (New York, George Braziller, 1963), p. 40.

38: 15   . . . repeats an archtetype." *The Eternal Return* (London, Routledge & Kegan Paul, Ltd., 1954), p. 34. So too Jacques Duchesne-Guillemin: "The success of all actions—necessary to the subsistence of the individual and the group—is ensured by their conforming to patterns. The primitive believes these patterns to have really existed, before time began, in the form of mythical events. This seems to be the very core of mythology." *The Hymns of Zarathustra* (London, John Murray, Ltd., 1952), p. 9.

38: 24   . . . abolition of time." *The Eternal Return,* p. 153.

38: 30   . . . Einstein and Whitehead. *Axel's Castle* (New York, Charles Scribner's Sons, 1931), pp. 221-222.

39: 7   . . . time-doctrine very completely." *Time and Western Man,* p. 89.

39: 16   . . . all things away." *The Gates of Horn* (New York, Oxford University Press, 1963), p. 422.

39: 35   . . . they reassemble it?" FW 213.

40: 4   . . . *cannot be abolished.* Bergson, *Creative Evolution* (1907) (New York, The Modern Library, 1944), p. 45. *Oeuvres* (Paris, Presses Universitaires de France, 1959), p. 528. Bergson's arguments against both materialistic determinism and theistic idealism are based on the premise that both these views entail a denial of the reality of time (duration). A. N. Whitehead agrees with Bergson on this point although he substitutes the word "passage" for the Bergsonian *durée.* See his *The Concept of Nature* (1920), (University of Michigan Press, Ann Arbor, 1957), p. 54; and *Science and the Modern World* (New York, The Macmillan Co. 1931), p. 135.

40: 31 . . . and no end." *Jakob Boehme. Ausgewaehlte Schriften, vom Lebendigen Glauben,* ed. Gerhard Stenzel (Guetersloh, Sigbert Mohn Verlag, 1960), p. 205.

41: 1 . . . which to move." *Timaeus,* 33.

41: 12 were human events. . . ." "Concepts of Cyclic and Evolutionary Time" in *The Human Person and the World of Values,* ed. B. V. Schwartz (New York, Fordham University Press, 1960).

41: 19 . . . true to type." *The Decline of the West* (New York, Alfred A. Knopf, Inc., 1926), Vol. 1, p. 4.

41: 24 . . . past 6,000 years." Reported in *The New York Times,* Sept. 29, 1955.

41: 30 . . . our past experience. *Science and the Modern World,* p. 47.

42: 5 . . . Same old dingdong always." U 164.

42: 8 . . . shortest way home." U 370.

42: 15 . . . life is a stream." U 151.

42: 27 . . . coin returned? Never." U 680-681.

43: 9 . . . under the sun." *Three Philosophical Poets,* p. 28.

43: 21 . . . in his coffin. According to Stanislaus Joyce, the ballad "Finnegan's Wake" was one of his (Stan's) vocal specialties in the Joyce family summer days at Bray. See *My Brother's Keeper* (New York, The Viking Press, Inc., 1958), p. 14. The origin of the ballad is obscure. My sheet music copy is titled "Finnigan's Wake," music by Gene Bone and Howard Fenton (Boosey and Hawkes, New York, 1944). The version quoted by Ellmann (*James Joyce,* p. 557) is slightly different. There is a rather tame recording of the song by the Irish tenor Liam Devally in *Songs of the Emerald Isle* (Westminister WF 12035), which also includes "The Croppy Boy," the ballad sung by Ben Dollard in the "Sirens" episode of *Ulysses.*

44: 11 . . . of former humanity. *Human All Too Human* II. Quoted by C. G. Jung in *Psychology of the Unconscious,* (N. Y. Dodd, Mead and Company, 1937), p. 28.

44: 17 . . . trying to awake." U 35.

44: 24 . . . prediction came true." See *The Autobiography of Giambattista Vico,* trans. M. H. Fisch and T. G. Bergsin (Ithaca, N. Y., Cornell University Press, 1944), p. 111.

44: 26 . . . of *Finnegans Wake.* FW 255.

44: 28 . . . appeared in *Ulysses.* FW 452, U 25.

45: 11 . . . end in them." *The New Science of Giambattista Vico,* trans. T. G. Bergin and M. H. Fisch (Ithaca, N. Y., Cornell University Press, 1948), p. 372.

45: 14 . . . decline, and fall." *Ibid.,* p. 57.

45: 23 . . . of all nations." *Ibid.,* p. 57. The Soviet linguist Nikolay Marr put forward a strikingly similar hypothesis in dialectical terms, but was denounced by Stalin for his pains. See G. A.

Wetter, *Dialectical Materialism* (New York, Frederick A. Praeger, Inc., 1958), pp. 196-201.

45: 31 . . . ("O fortunous casualitas!"). The line in the Roman missal reads "O felix culpa, quae talem ac tantum meruit habere Redemptorem." Arthur Lovejoy has written an essay on "Milton and the Paradox of the Fortune Fall," *Essays in the History of Ideas* (New York, G. P. Putnam's Sons, 1960).

46: 21 . . . the seim anew." FW 215.

46: 25 . . . where terms begin." FW 452.

46: 29 . . . drifting down the Liffey. So Joyce explains it to Harriet Weaver. *Letters*, p. 214.

46: 31 . . . by "Denti Alligator." FW 440.

47: 16 . . . in *Ars Poetica. The New Science*, p. 286.

47: 25 . . . day of battle." FW 281. The wildflowers of Quinet—Joyce thought the passage "beautiful"—correspond to the lilts of children (Joyce, *Letters*, p. 295). Edgar Quinet (1803-1877), a close friend of the historian Michelet, was professor at Lyons and at the Collège de France where his liberal and anticlerical views led to his dismissal. He went into exile after 1851, returning to France twenty years later. Quinet is the author of a trilogy of philosophical poems, one of which—*Ahasverus,* is an epic of the Wandering Jew.

48: 6 . . . ever heard dump." Title of section pp. 17-43 in *Three Tales Told of Shem and Shaun: Three Fragments from Work* in *Progress* (Paris, The Black Sun Press, 1929).

48: 13 . . . cyclewheeling history." FW 185-186.

48: 16 . . . that compose it. The *locus classicus* of the *Wake's* self-estimate occurs on p. 120—"and look at this prepronominal *funferal,* engraved and retouched and edgewiped and pudden-padded very like a whale's egg farced with pemmican as were it sentenced to be nuzzled over a full trillion times for ever and a night till his noddle sink or swim by that ideal reader suffering from an ideal insomnia."

48: 29 . . . out by Starloe." FW 382.

48: 31 . . . (It's pure music!"). Joyce's words for his *Wake,* cited by Ellmann, *James Joyce*, p. 716.

49: 6 . . . an alluring enigma." W. H. Gardner, *Gerard Manley Hopkins* (London, Martin Secker & Warburg, Ltd., 1948), Vol. 1, p. 265.

49: 9 . . . into the street." Oliver St. John Gogarty, "Roots in Resentment," a review of *Finnegans Wake* in *The Observer,* May 7, 1939; cited by M. Megalaner and R. M. Kain in *Joyce: the Man, the Work, the Reputation* (New York, New York University Press, 1956), p. 278.

49: 18 . . . a brulobrulo!" FW 117. A. Walton Litz, *The Art of James Joyce* (London, Oxford University Press, 1961), pp. 60-62.

50: 4 . . . (out of patience") FW 108.

50: 9 . . . *your puling fiddle?"* Probably the E flat major quartet, opus 127. See John N. Burk, *The Life and Works of Beethoven* (New York, Random House, Inc., 1943), p. 229.

50: 12	. . . his severe and powerful shoulders . . . Fosco Maraini, *Secret Tibet* (New York, The Viking Press, Inc., 1952), plate 35.
50: 25	. . . of the buckbasket." U 202.
50: 27	. . . the mystery behind." Goethe, *Conversations with Eckermann.* See Chap. III (Thomas Mann), page 151 and note.
51: 3	. . . to explain for." FW 42.
51: 15	. . . raise a Cain." FW 47.
52: 12	. . . adept in magic. Recalling Bertrand Russell's statement in his *History of Western Philosophy* that the first effect of emancipation from the Church was not to make men think rationally but to open their minds to "every sort of antique nonsense," J. S. Atherton points out that it is precisely the philosophers whose work is most full of antique nonsense to whom the emancipated Joyce was attracted. *The Books at the Wake* (New York, The Viking Press, 1960), p. 46.
52: 26	. . . and mummified Pompeiis. *James Joyce* (Norfolk, Conn., New Directions, 1941), pp. 134-135.
52: 28	. . . the Platonic Socrates. *Three Great Irishmen* (London, Victor Gollancz, Ltd., 1952), p. 120.
53: 3	. . . of the particular. Aristotle, *Poetics*, 1451b5.
53: 16	. . . *contained in the universal.*" Cited by Ellmann in *James Joyce*, p. 520.
53: 19	. . . of an allforabit." FW 18-19.
54: 11	. . . all they are worth." Letter to Harriet Weaver, May 21, 1926, *Letters*, p. 241.
55: 11	. . . dearsay you too." FW 558. I have arranged the lines.
55: 19	. . . went is rising." FW 213. Valéry's line is: "Le vent se lève . . . Il faut tenter de vivre!"

II. ANDRÉ GIDE

With the major exception of the *Journals,* most of the references to the French originals of Gide's works are to the *Oeuvres Complets* (OC) (Paris, Gallimard 1932–1939).

References to the French text of the Journals are keyed to the two-volume *Bibliothèque de la Pléiade* edition (BP), (Paris, Gallimard, 1948–1954).

References to the *Journals* in English are to *The Journals of André Gide,* translated by Justin O'Brien (New York, Alfred A. Knopf, Inc., 1949-1955).

Bibliographical information concerning English translations of Gide's novels, dramas, and other separate titles will be found below in the initial reference to the work in question.

59: 30	. . . an income, a prize." Decree and editorial comment published in *L'Osservatore Romano,* Vatican City, June 1, 1952.
59: 33	. . . it *is* the Inquisition. Both Holy Office and Index of Prohibited Books were Counter-Reformation measures initiated in 1542 and 1543 respectively by Alessandro Farnese, Paul III, the Pope who had earlier remarked apropos of Benvenuto Cellini, "An artistic genius is above the laws of morality." The

Index did not receive official status, however, until 1558 under the pontificate of Paul IV. (See Henry Daniel-Rops, *The Catholic Reformation,* New York, E. P. Dutton & Co., Inc., 1962, p. 71, pp. 75-76.) Today Augustin Cardinal Bea, chief of the Vatican's Secretariat for Promoting Christian Unity recommends the abolition of the Index.

60: 5   . . . juries and magistrates." Letter to *The London Times,* June 2, 1952.

60: 10   . . . have been avoided." Cited by Gide in *Journals* III 183; BP I 1070.

60: 23   . . . must be very interesting." Quoted by Thierry Maulnier in *The New York Times Book Review,* Nov. 20, 1952.

60: 28   . . . naturalistic novel. Ellmann, *James Joyce,* p. 752.

61: 9   . . . *The Pastoral Symphony. Ibid.,* p. 708.

61: 13   . . . "deformation" of language. *Ibid.,* p. 544.

61: 24   . . . events being fatal." *Journals* III 166-167; BP I 1051. See also *Journals* IV 50 where Gide puts down his "extraordinary disposition" and "propensity toward happiness" to the "anti-historicity" of his mind. BP II 59.

61: 35   . . . wept for Proserpine." *The Immoralist,* trans. Dorothy Bussy (New York, Alfred A. Knopf, Inc., 1930), p. 61; *L'Immoraliste,* OC IV 54.

62: 4   . . . never read the newspapers." *Journals* I 36. BP I 49.

62: 6   . . . much interest me." *Journals* II 243; BP I 667-668.

62: 9   . . . worth while. *Journals* IV 20; BP II 25.

62: 29   . . . not like the others." *If It Die,* trans. Dorothy Bussy (New York, The Modern Library, Inc., 1935), p. 109; *Si le grain ne meurt,* OC X 173.

62: 32   . . . in his life. Klaus Mann, *André Gide and the Crisis of Modern Thought* (New York, Creative Age Press, 1943), p. 66. In his autobiography Gide says, "This sense of estrangement (which I suffered from particularly when I was with my own people) might very possibly have led me to suicide, if it had not been for the relief I found in describing it ironically in *Paludes." If It Die,* p. 268. OC X 387.

63: 27   . . . novelist at all. Jean Hytier, *André Gide.* trans. Richard Howard (Garden City, N. Y., Doubleday & Co., Inc., 1962), p. 120. (Algiers, Charlot, 1938.)

63: 30   . . . an intellectual pleasure." Hytier, p. 127.

64: 5   . . . some unusual ("novel") event. Of course, what Goethe has in mind is a piece of smaller dimensions (*Novelle*) rather than the big novel (*Roman*). Goethe speaks of his *Wahlverwandschaften* ("Effective Affinities") as a "Novelle." *Conversations with Eckermann* (New York, E. P. Dutton & Co., Inc., 1930), p. 163.

64: 27   . . . was the incarnation. . . ." *Two Legends: Oedipus and Theseus,* trans. John Russell (New York, Vintage Books, 1958), p. 82.

64: 34   . . . in a good light. *The Immoralist,* Preface, p. xi OC IV 7.

65: 2   . . . annex to aesthetics. In one of his "Imaginary Interviews." OC IV 387.

65: 4   . . . aesthetic point of view. *Journals* II 229; BP I 652.
65: 7   . . . to get away!") *Journals* III 106; BP I 983.
65: 18   . . . *horreur du Gide.*" Doctor François Nazier, *L'Anti-Corydon* (*essai sur l'inversion sexuelle*), (Paris, 1924), epigraph. The pun, of course, springs from the French version of the rule: *La Nature a horreur du vide.* ("Nature abhors a vacuum").
65: 20   . . . *La Revue Française.* Cited by Gide in *Journals* II 279; BP I 708.
65: 27   . . . to assure fame. *Journals* IV 34; BP II 41.
65: 28   . . . proscribed his work. See Klaus Mann, *André Gide,* p. 283.
65: 32   . . . love of evil. . . ." Agnes Meyer, *Out of These Roots* (Boston, Little, Brown & Co., 1953), p. 177.
66: 1   . . . is always Gide." *The Correspondence Between Paul Claudel and André Gide* (1899-1926), translated by John Russell (New York, Pantheon Books, Inc., 1952), p. 234.
66: 28   . . . theme of desire. Hytier, p. 21 (18). ("L'œuvre poétique de Gide tourne presque exclusivement autour du thème du désir.")
66: 31   . . . preceded by a sensation. . . ." *Fruits of the Earth* trans. Dorothy Bussy (London, Martin Secker & Warburg, 1949), p. 30. Les Nourritures Terrestres, OC II 76.
67: 2   . . . evidence of truth. *Beyond Good and Evil,* IV, 134.
67: 4   . . . ought to do it." *The Immoralist,* p. 126; OC IV 107.
67: 5   . . . show, why not." William James "The Moral Philosopher and The Moral Life" in *The Will to Believe and Other Essays* (New York, Longmans Green & Co., Inc., 1907), p. 195.
67: 12   . . . divinely natural." *Fruits of the Earth,* p. 111; OC II 166.
67: 17   . . . embrace is joyous." *Ibid.,* p. 153; OC II 211.
67: 24   . . . possession as love." *Ibid.,* p. 31; OC II 78.
67: 28   . . . for later on!" *Journals* III 115-116; BP I 994.
67: 32   . . . of my happiness." *Journals* III 33; BP I 902.
67: 34   . . . fruits of it. *The Renaissance* (London, Macmillan & Co. Ltd., 1925), p. 236.
68: 5   . . . might an ascetic. . . . quenching of it." "New Fruits" in *Fruits of the Earth,* p. 233.
68:6   . . . became André Gide. *The Youth of André Gide* (Chicago, University of Chicago Press, 1963).
68: 11   . . . *volupté qui passe!*" *Fruits,* p. 87; OC II 140.
68: 15   . . . I knew Blidah." Albert Camus, "Rencontres avec André Gide," in *Hommage à André Gide* (Paris, NRF 1951), p. 233.
68: 22   . . . gorged with heat." "Noces à Tipasa," cited by Albert Maquet, *Albert Camus: The Invincible Summer* (New York, George Braziller, 1958), p. 34.
68: 26   . . . as "the cerebrals." "Summer in Algiers" in *The Myth of Sisyphus and Other Essays,* p. 143.
68: 27   . . . Sustentata venus gratissima. *Remedia Amoris* 405.
69: 7   . . . only for Thee." *Journals* I 40; BP I 52. From Lessing's *A Rejoinder.*
69: 12   . . . is not progressive. *Strait is the Gate,* trans. Dorothy Bussy (New York, Alfred A. Knopf, Inc., 1949), p. 204; OC V 221.

69: 20	. . . flesh and frock." *Journals* III 117; BP I 995.
70: 3	for the Absolute. *Le Voyage d'Urien,* OC I 327.
70: 29	. . . of the café." "An Old Man" from *The Complete Poems of Cavafy,* trans. Rae Dalven (New York, Harcourt, Brace, & World, Inc., 1961), p. 7. By permission of the publisher. Original in POIEMATA, (Ikaros, Athens, 1958), p. 11.
70: 32	. . . done obsesses me." *Journals* III 116; BP I 994.
70: 33	. . . yielded to temptation." "New Fruits" in *Fruits of the Earth,* p. 233.
71: 11	. . . *"Go beyond!"* Justin O'Brien identifies the maxim *"Passez outre"* with the late Theseus of 1946 (*Portrait of André Gide,* New York, Alfred A. Knopf, 1953), p. 143. Gide also uses the phrase in *Les Caves du Vatican* in a conversation between Protos and Lafcadio—*"Comprends-tu ce qu'il y a dans ces mots? Passer outre?"* In his *Journal* of 1927, he writes, "It is essential to be able to find happiness beyond." *Journals* II 404; BP I 842.
71: 21	. . . than prudent fixtures. Gide uses Keats's phrase as the epigraph for his *Travels in the Congo* (New York, Alfred A. Knopf, Inc., 1929); BP II 679. See Keats's letter to Fanny Brawne, *The Complete Poetical Works and Letters of John Keats* (Boston Houghton Mifflin Company, 1899), p. 386.
71: 25	. . . up, to leave." *Journals* III 118; BP I 997.
71: 30	. . . 'Detach yourself,' replied Angela." *Marshlands and Prometheus Misbound,* trans. George D. Painter (Norwalk, Conn., New Directions), p. 168; OC III 154.
72: 20	. . . but to be." *Journals* IV 279; BP II 313.
72: 21	. . . individualism to commitment. Simone de Beauvoir, *The Prime of Life* (Cleveland, Ohio, The World Publishing Company, 1962), p. 444.
72: 29	. . . but *lend* yourself." *"Fruits,* p. 69; OC II 119.
73: 4	. . . robbed of it." *Fruits* p. 71; OC II 121.
73: 15	. . . has worn off." *Two Legends: Oedipus and Theseus,* trans. John Russell (Vintage Books, New York, 1958), p. 70.
73: 20	. . . disent toujours: Allons!" "Le Voyage," *Les Fleurs du Mal.*
73: 22	. . . no fun any more." D. H. Lawrence, *Selected Literary Criticism,* ed. Anthony Beal (New York, The Viking Press, Inc., 1956), p. 117.
73: 27	. . . from the grave." *If It Die,* trans. Dorothy Bussy (New York, Modern Library, Inc., 1935) pp. 267-268; *Si le grain ne meurt.* OC X 386.
74: 22	. . . it be salted? See *If It Die,* p. 228, OC X 333.
74: 24	. . . moy est haïssable!" *Pensées,* 155.
74: 27	. . . hate it in himself? *Journals* I 74; BP I 91.
75: 10	. . . and followed them. *Journals* I 33; BP I 44.
75: 24	. . . the other black." Gide, *My Theatre,* trans. Jackson Matthews (New York, Alfred A. Knopf, Inc., 1952), p. 268; OC IV 211.
76: 16	. . . irreplaceable of men." *Fruits of the Earth,* p. 163; OC II

223. I have used Justin O'Brien's translation of the passage; see his *Portrait of André Gide,* p. 128.

76: 20   ... "I know all their names ... *Fruits,* p. 161; OC II 221.

76: 31   ... and perfectly sincere!" *Journals* I 17; BP I 28. "Let us try to understand, in Gide," says Mauriac, "a case of terrible sincerity." *Men I Hold Great* (New York, Philosophical Library, Inc., 1951), p. 117.

77: 3   ... creature of dialogue." *If It Die,* p. 234; OC X 341.

77: 6   ... who bores me." *Journals* I 217; BP I 250.

77: 13   ... of two faiths?" *Journals* III 84; BP I 959.

77: 19   ... threw it away. Albert Guérard believes the concept of the simultaneous impulse to concentration and dissolution of self essential to an understanding of Gide. *André Gide* (Cambridge, Mass., Harvard University Press, 1951), Chap. II.

77: 22   ... of the Gospel." *Journals* III 182; BP I 1069.

78: 15   ... will get through." From Cavafy's poem "Thermopylae" trans. C. M. Bowra in his "Constantine Cavafy and the Greek Past," *The Creative Experiment* (London, Macmillan & Co., Ltd.), p. 34.

78: 31   ... pass over their conduct?" *Joseph in Egypt,* trans. by H. T. Lowe-Porter (New York, Alfred A. Knopf, Inc., 1939), p. 417.

79: 15   ... a leading character ... See *Coleridge's Essays and Lectures on Shakespeare* (New York, E. P. Dutton & Co., Inc., 1939), p. 36.

"That a germ of Michel exists in me goes without saying," said Gide, "... How many buds we bear in us ... that will never blossom save in our books. ... But if intentionally you suppress all of them *but one,* how it grows at once! How it enlarges, immediately monopolizing all the sap! My recipe for creating a fictional hero is very simple: take one of those buds and put it in a pot *all alone;* you soon achieve a wonderful individual. Advice: choose preferably ... the bud that bothers you most. You get rid of it at the same time. This is perhaps what Aristotle called the purging of passions." See Justin O'Brien, *Portrait of André Gide,* pp. 88-90. Original in OC IV 616-617.

80: 13   ... become everything himself." *Journals* II 392; BP I 829.

81: 2   ... it has brought." *The Immoralist,* p. 136; OC IV 115.

81: 31   ... try to suppress." *Ibid.,* pp. 126-127; OC IV 107-108.

82: 3   ... his demonic energies. Michel's primary intention is not to hurt his wife. Marcelline's death is an instance of the kind of evil brought about as a by-product of *energy.* "I believe," Gide writes in 1929, "that often *evil* (a certain evil that is not the result of a *deficiency,* but rather a manifestation of energy) has a greater educative and initiatory value than what you call good." *Journals* III 78; BP I 953.

82: 21   ... masterpiece of luminous cruelty." Charles Du Bos, *Dialogue avec André Gide* (Paris, Editions au Sans Pareil, 1929), p. 104.

83: 1   ... with the weak." *The Immoralist,* p. 181; OC IV 152. Compare this with Gide's note in his *Journal* of 1916: "At lunch as I am telling Em. what new life is given me by anything that upsets my habits, she replies: 'That is because *you* are strong'—and immediately I hear again that knell that rings throughout *The Immoraliste.*" *Journals* II 124; BP I 536.

83: 4 ... "We Immoralists" ... *Beyond Good and Evil,* p. 152; *Ecce Homo,* p. 76, 136, 140, in *The Philosophy of Nietzsche,* Modern Library.

83: 17 ... grimaces of patience." "The Genealogy of Morals," p. 130, in *The Philosophy of Nietzsche.*

83: 27 ... note a resemblance." *Journals* II 307; BP I 739.

83: 33 ... top-heavy with ideas. *Journals* II 420; BP I 859.

84: 1 ... doubleness delighted him. Like Gide's, Nietzsche's mind (as Alfred Baumler said of him) never worked "one-dimensionally"; there were always at least two cross-currents of thought and emotion in him at the same time.

84: 11 ... into a desert." "Evolution of the Theatre" in *My Theatre,* p. 271; OC IV 214.

84: 17 ... managed to be ill." *The Immoralist,* p. 112; OC IV 95.

84: 18 ... brought me to reason." "Ecce Homo" p. 35 in *The Philosophy of Nietzsche,* Modern Library.

84: 32 ... is called virtue." *Philoctetes,* Act IV, Scene ii, *My Theatre;* OC III 58.

85: 9 ... to lie ahead." *Two Legends: Oedipus and Theseus,* p. 53.

85: 15 ... his hero Michel. *Journals* III 262; BP I 1160.

85: 29 ... book of warning." ... kills his wife." Cited by O'Brien, *Portrait of André Gide,* p. 176, both from Yvonne Davet's Introduction to *L'Immoraliste* (Lausanne, La Guilde du Livre, 1951), p. 16.

85: 35 ... admire and envy." *Journals* III 205; BP I 1094-1095.

86: 6 ... put up with it." *Journals* II 112; BP I 990.

86: 8 ... jealous of Christ. *Journals* III 370; BP I 1281.

86: 14 ... teaches us to." *The Counterfeiters,* trans. Dorothy Bussy (New York, Alfred A. Knopf, Inc., 1959), p. 305. This edition includes Justin O'Brien's translation of *The Journal of 'The Counterfeiters';* OC XII 465.

86: 21 ... of personal experience." *André Gide,* p. 109.

87: 7 ... by reading Nietzsche. *Journals* II 420; BP I 858-859.

87: 27 ... much theoretical window-dressing. Mann wrote a review of Guérard's book: Mann, *Gesammelte Werke* (S. Fischer Verlag, Oldenburg, 1960), X 802.

88: 22 ... I am alone." *Strait Is the Gate,* trans. Dorothy Bussy (New York, Random House, Inc., Vintage Books, 1956), p. 226. *La Porte étroite,* OC V 238.

89: 3 ... Gide's *ironic* tales. Hytier, p. 67.

89: 18 ... *unto life eternal.*" John XII 24, 25.

89: 23 ... live in eternity." *Journals* II 175; BP I 594.

90: 2 ... "plunge into the excessive" ... Gide uses the phrase in a letter to Henry Drain. Cited by O'Brien, *Portrait of André Gide* from Yvonne Davet's Introduction to *L'Immoraliste* (Lausanne,

La Guilde du Livre, 1951), p. 16. In his *Journal* of 1912, Gide says, "Whom could I persuade that that book [*La Porte étroite*] is the twin of *L'Immoraliste* and that the two subjects grew up concurrently in my mind, the excess of one finding a secret permission in the excess of the other and together establishing a balance." *Journals* I 318; BP I 365-366.

90: 4   . . . productive of error. Of the critics, Gide remarks in 1914, "But how could I be surprised that they did not immediately see in my *Porte étroite* a critical work." *Journals* II 31; BP I 428-429.

90: 6   . . . in a convent. See *The Correspondence Between Paul Claudel and André Gide*, p. 94, where Claudel is still restrained by politeness.

90: 33   . . . *déplacement* and liberty.") Quoted in full twice in Jean Schlumberger's *Madeleine et André Gide* (Paris, © Editions Gallimard, 1956), pp. 14, 201. The letter was written at a time when Gide's association with Marc Allégret (whom he adopted as his son) was leading to an estrangement between Gide and his wife, an alienation violently worsened by her burning all his letters to her. It is this letter which Schlumberger accuses Gide of suppressing from his (Gide's) memoir of Madeleine Gide, *Et Nunc Manet in Te* (BP II 1121); this memoir is published in English as *Madeleine* (New York, Alfred A. Knopf, Inc., 1952). Here is the letter in my translation by permission of the publisher.

Cuverville, Wednesday, June 1918.

ANDRÉ DEAR,

You are mistaken. I have no doubt of your affection. And even if I had, I would have no cause to complain. My share has been very beautiful. I had the best of your soul, the tenderness of your childhood and of your youth. And I know that, living or dead, I shall have the soul of your old age.

I have always understood as well your need of movement and liberty. How many times in your moments of nervous suffering, the price of your genius, have I been on the point of saying to you, "But leave, go, you are free, there is no cage door to hinder you." (I did not say it for fear of grieving you with too hasty an acquiescence in your departure.)

What causes me anguish—and you know it without need of open avowal—is the road to which you have committed yourself, a road that will lead you and others to destruction. I pity you the more because I love you. It is a terrible temptation that rears itself before you, one armed with every seduction. Resist.

Adieu, au revoir
Your MADELEINE

91: 4   . . . *"extrême milieu"* . . . Hytier, *André Gide* p. 66.
92: 29   . . . without knowing it" . . . *Voyage to the Congo*, p. 27; OC XIII 130.
92: 31   . . . *mot* about Freud. *Journals* II 298; BP I 729.
92: 32   . . . account of intelligence . . . *Journals* I 233; BP I 269.

93: 1   . . . success to fashion." *Journals* II 348; BP I 782.

93: 4   . . . to flattering them." *Voyage to the Congo,* p. 27; OC XIII 130.

93: 10   . . . "Laughter" ("Le Rire"). In English in *Comedy* (Garden City, N. Y., Doubleday and Co., Inc., 1956), p. 61.

93: 16   . . . should never repeat itself." *Comedy,* p. 62. In his *Introduction to Metaphysics,* Bergson states that there is a reality that is external, yet given immediately to the mind, and this reality is *mobility.* Bergson, *Oeuvres,* p. 1420.

93: 22   . . . mobility of life." *Comedy,* p. 85.

94: 24   . . . a moral transformation." *The Two Sources of Religion and Morality,* trans. R. A. Audra and C. Brereton (New York, Garden City, Doubleday & Co., Inc., 1954), p. 100. *Oeuvres* 1060.

95: 6   . . . *Lafcadio's Adventures* . . . Trans. Dorothy Bussy (New York, Garden City, Doubleday & Co., Inc., 1953); first published in the U.S.A. by Alfred A. Knopf under the title *The Vatican Swindle* (1925). OC VII 101.

95: 21   . . . background recall Apollinaire's . . . See Mihailo Pavlovic, "Lafcadio Wluiki et Guillaume Apollinaire," *Mercure de France,* no. 1184, avril, 1962.

96: 18   . . . the least premeditated" . . . *If It Die,* p. 310; OC X 444.

96: 26   . . . God's love is unmotivated. See Anders Nygren, *Agape and Eros* (Philadelphia, The Westminster Press, 1953), p. 76.

96: 27   . . . capable of the gratuitous act." *Marshlands and Prometheus Misbound,* p. 107; OC III 105.

97: 2   . . . really disinterested action." *Philoctetes,* Act II, scene i, in *My Theatre,* p. 141; OC III 31.

97: 33   . . . to love you!" *Lafcadio's Adventures,* p. 249; OC VII 396.

98: 28   . . . mere personal interest. . . ." Cited by O'Brien, *Portrait of André Gide,* p. 192. Gide's claim of no effects without causes had been anticipated by his own Julius who tells Lafcadio that "there is no such thing as inconsequence—in psychology any more than in physics." *Lafcadio's Adventures,* p. 93; OC VII 204.

98: 29   . . . in principle intentional." *Being and Nothingness,* trans. Hazel Barnes (New York, Philosophical Library, Inc., 1956), p. 433.

99: 3   . . . *les jeux sont faits." Ibid.,* p. 451.

99: 13   . . . erasures aren't allowed." *Lafcadio's Adventures,* p. 83; OC VII 191.

99: 21   . . . efface their mark." *Journals* III 123; BP I 1002.

99: 24   . . . any innocent victims. *Being and Nothingness,* p. 554.

99: 28   . . . all the same. Sartre says, "Gide does not know what a situation is, his 'act' is one of pure caprice." See Sartre's "Existentialism Is a Humanism" in *Existentialism from Dostoyevsky to Sartre,* Walter Kaufmann (New York, Meridian Books, 1957), p. 305.

101: 7   . . . If not now, when?" *"Si tu ne fais pas cela, qui le fera? Si tu ne fais pas aussitôt cela. quand sera-ce?"* OC XII 90.

102: 11   . . . exaggeration of an idea." *Journals* I 76; BP I 94.

102: 24	. . . to be worth more . . ." *The Counterfeiters,* trans. Dorothy Bussy (New York, Alfred A. Knopf, Inc., 1959), p. 185; OC XII 291.
102: 33	. . . for good coin." *Ibid.,* p. 307; OC XII 467.
103: 4	. . . drama of our lives." *Ibid.,* p. 189; OC XII 297.
103: 9	. . . is his skin." *Ibid.,* p. 243; OC XII 375.
103: 17	. . . of such misconstructions. For example, *Swann's Way* (Modern Library), p. 80.
104: 8	. . . bored by them." *The Counterfeiters,* p. 173; OC XII 272.
104: 10	. . . honors that have come to it. Shortly before his death, Gide was pleased to hear that a French literary jury, one of whose members was André Maurois, chose *Les Faux-Monnayeurs* as one of the twelve best novels of the twentieth century's first half. In his book *André Gide* (London, Arthur Barker, 1951), George D. Painter puts *The Counterfeiters* "last in any list of the first ten."
104: 16	. . . in receiving it. *Journals* III 114; BP I 992.
104: 23	. . . single novelistic design. *Journals* III 14; BP I 879.
104: 33	. . . precisely that of music." *André Gide: the Ethic of the Artist* (London, Martin Secker & Warburg, Ltd., 1950), p. 192.
105: 4	. . . knows her to be kind" . . . and so on. . . . The names of the amiable citizens of Brunhoff's Celesteville—Philophage, Doulamor, Hatchibombotar, Olur, Tapitor, and so on—recall the names of Urien's companions on his voyage—Cabilor, Odinel, Agloval, Alsafar, Hector, and the rest. Brunhoff's Crustadele, the female Mentor who gives sage advice to the monkey Zephir before he sets out on his perilous journey to the isle of Polomoche and the Gogottes, is faintly reminiscent of Gide's Queen Haiatalnefus (wife of Camaralzaman) in her palace by the sea.
106: 24	. . . object of his love." *The Counterfeiters,* pp. 83-84; OC XII 138.
106: 28	. . . of the author. In *Études,* p. 244, note 1. Cited by Linette F. Brugmans, *The Correspondence of André Gide and Edmund Gosse* (New York, New York University Press, 1959), p. 63 n.
107: 7	. . . of your sons." Letter to Suzanne Allégret, 23 Jan. 1923, *Journals* II 322; BP I 754.
109: 2	. . . travel first class" . . . *If It Die,* p. 148; OC X 226.
109: 3	. . . abdication of reason." *Journals* II 421; BP I 860.
109: 7	. . . of this, however" . . . *Journals* III 45; BP I 916.
109: 8	. . . combat the church." *Journals* III 231; BP I 1125.
109: 11	. . . of a gangrene." *Journals* II 381; BP I 817.
109: 17	. . . the slightest flame" . . . *Journals* III 292; BP I 1195.
109: 19	. . . it is the priest." *Journals* III 172; BP I 1058.
109: 23	. . . very beautiful bearing. . . ." *Journals* III 336; BP I 1244.
109: 24	. . . his vaguest concepts. "New Fruits" in *Fruits of the Earth,* p. 212.
110: 3	. . . arrive at God. . . ." *Journals* IV 113; BP II 122-123.
110: 19	. . . still-born child. *Journals* IV 298-302; BP II 334-339.

111: 2   . . . of an old man." *Journals* II 404; BP I 842. Contrast this with his remark on serenity in *Journals* IV 53; BP II 62.

111: 5   . . . near to death." Theseus in *Two Legends,* p. 109.

111: 13   . . . this is false." *Journals* III 57; BP I 929.

111: 24   . . . to do, seems impious." *Journals* IV 69; BP II 80.

111: 25   . . . Anexoria. *So Be It* or *The Chips Are Down* trans. Justin O'Brien (New York, Alfred A. Knopf, Inc., 1959), p. 35. *Ainsi Soit-Il ou Les Jeux Sont Faits,* BP II 1164.

112: 5   . . . destined to disappear." *Ibid.*, pp. 165-166; BP II 1243.

112: 26   . . . as the desert. At Cuverville in the summer of 1905, **Gide** wrote in his diary: "Avancée solennelle du soir. J'erre comme un forcené parmi cette paix aussi aride pour moi que le désert." *Journals* I 144; BP I 170.

III THOMAS MANN

Titles of Mann's works in English refer to editions published in New York by Alfred A. Knopf, Inc. Except where otherwise noted, the English translations are by Mrs. H. T. Lowe-Porter. References to the German originals are keyed to Mann's *Gesammelte Werke* (Oldenburg, S. Fischer Verlag, 1960).

     Epigraph (1) From author's conversation with Thomas Mann, Princeton, January 27, 1941.

     Epigraph (2) Sigrid Undset, *Return to the Future* (New York, Alfred A. Knopf, Inc. 1942), pp. 236-237.

115: 5   . . . current will do." My translation from *Les Caves du Vatican,* OC VII 375: "*Savez-vous ce qu'il faut pour de l'honnête homme un gredin? Il suffit d'un dépaysement . . .*"

115: 19   . . . and suburban citizen." *The Magic Mountain* (1924), 1953, p. 4; *Werke* III 12.

116: 8   . . . sympathies, enchantments, temptations." Letter cited by Berthold Bierman in *The Stature of Thomas Mann.* ed. Charles Neider (New York, New Directions, 1947), p. 248. Compare Mann, *A Sketch of My Life,* pp. 43-44, *Werke* XI 125-126.

116: 27   . . . and avoid discussion . . . In his preface to Stendhal's *Chartreuse de Parme,* Balzac contrasts the "literature of ideas" (Stendhal) with the "literature of imagery" (Hugo).

116: 29   . . . for the movies. Mann comments on the motion picture possibilities of the Davos novel in his essay "On the Film" (in *Past Masters,* 1933). In 1946 Mann sold the motion picture rights of *The Magic Mountain* to the late Alexander Korda. A film project was sketched, including planned shots of corpse-carrying bobsleds against a background of Alpine scenery. It was rumored that Gregory Peck was considered for the role of Hans Castorp.

117: 23   . . . become sports hotels. "The Making of the Magic Mountain," *Atlantic Monthly,* January, 1953. This article is now appended to the 1953 Knopf edition of *The Magic Mountain,* q.v., p. 721.

117: 29   . . . health of the guest. For example, the hotel Schweizerhof where this author lodged during a visit to Davos at the close of World War II.

118: 9   . . . on his lung. At least so says an eminent tuberculosis specialist with whom I discussed the matter. A. E. Ellis's novel *The Rack* (Boston, Little, Brown & Co., 1959)—a sort of poor man's *Magic Mountain* set in the Haute Savoie where young tubercular students from English universities (veterans of World War II) are sent for repair—makes clear that surgical concepts and even techniques of the time did not change radically from those of Hans Castorp's day. Claude Faux's *Les Jeunes Chiens* (*The Young Dogs*) (Paris, René Julliard, 1959) is a dreary sanatarium novel with a similar setting. In 1945, Mann underwent an operation for the removal of an abscess (nontubercular) on his lung; he describes this vividly in Chapter XIII of his *The Story of a Novel* (1949), 1961.

118: 11   . . . development of genius. See, for example, Lewis J. Moorman, M.D., *Tuberculosis and Genius* (Chicago, University of Chicago Press, 1940). On the other hand, the late Merrill Moore, psychiatrist and poet, wrote me that that if the alleged connection between disease and genius seems true, there may be several alternate explanations. "For example (1) genius is more articulate, so we hear more of its problems and ailments; (2) If one assumes that geniuses are writers, painters, and composers, then one refers to a sedentary people whose careers may have been chosen partly on account of physical disabilities." (Letter from Merrill Moore, Aug. 17, 1940).

118: 23   . . . perfectly healthy human being" . . . *The Magic Mountain,* p. 16; *Werke* III 29-30.

118: 24   . . . the *sick* animal" . . . *Genealogy of Morals* II 13.

118: 26   . . . necessary to individualization." *Aphorisms.*

119: 6   . . . your bodily frame." *The Scarlet Letter* (Boston, Houghton Mifflin Company, n.d.), pp. 166-167.

119: 12   . . . surplus of life." *Ecce Homo,* p. 12, in *The Philosophy of Nietzsche* (Modern Library).

121: 17   . . . artistic being that I am." Ernest Newman, *The Life of Richard Wagner* (New York, Alfred A. Knopf, Inc., 1946), Vol. II, p. 158.

121: 3   . . . and organic part. . . ." *The Magic Mountain,* p. 32; *Werke,* III 50.

121: 10   . . . ultimately fall ill." Letter to Rohde, *Selected Letters,* ed. Oscar Levy (London, 1924), p. 114.

121: 17   . . . to the Joseph novels." "The Making of The Magic Mountain" in *The Magic Mountain,* p. 720.

122: 8   . . . *the successful writer.* "At Lübeck," runs Dr. Joseph Goebbels's diary for 5 December, 1925, ". . . I sense the old Hanse spirit and think of *Buddenbrooks.* . . . Town Hall: War Chamber, Senate Chamber. Those carvings! Work that took a lifetime. I always think of Thomas Mann. . . ." *The Early Goebbels Diaries,* ed. Helmut Heiber (New York, Praeger, 1962), p. 52.

122: 17   . . . naked before God. Fritz Kaufmann makes much of Protestant "inwardness" and its relation to Mann's work. *Thomas Mann: The World as Will and Representation* (Boston, Beacon Press, 1957), pp. 4-5. The title of Kaufmann's study shows the importance of the relation he finds between Schopenhauer and Mann.

123: 5   . . . potently, and gladly!" *Buddenbrooks* (1901), 1955, pp. 526-527; *Werke* I 656-657.

123: 12   . . . such rapturous concentration . . . Compare Gide in his autobiography, "I plunged into *The World as Will and Idea* with unspeakable rapture." *If It Die,* p. 200; OC X 296.

123: 13   . . . edition of 1844. See *The World as Will and Idea,* trans. R. B. Haldane and J. Kemp (London, Routledge & Kegan Paul, Ltd. [1883] 1948), Vol. III, p. 249.

124: 15   . . . Ixion stands still." *Ibid.,* I 254.

124: 29   . . . all clear to me!" Ernest Newman, *The Life of Richard Wagner,* Vol. II, p. 435. Newman discusses the question of Schopenhauer's influence on Wagner on p. 431. On that subject, Denis De Rougemont said: "Whatever Nietzsche and Wagner himself may have thought, it seems to me that this [Schopenhauer's] influence is greatly exaggerated. A composer of Wagner's caliber does not put 'Ideas' to music." *Love in the Western World* (New York, Pantheon Books, Inc., 1956), p. 231.

125: 7   . . . all typical rakes. *A Survey of Contemporary Composers,* 2d ed. (London, Oxford University Press, 1929), p. 154. The theme of redemption through the love of a woman (or even a little girl) is prominent in Graham Greene's novels.

125: 19   . . . fire—against Germans. Mann relates the incident of the opera glasses in his *Reflections of a Non-Political Man* (*Betrachtungen eines Unpolitischen*), *Werke* XII 130. (The *Reflections* has not been translated into English.)

125: 27   . . . *such a knight."* *The Birth of Tragedy,* p. 308, in *The Philosophy of Nietzsche* (Modern Library).

125: 35   . . . is for deliverance." From Mann's eulogy of the writer Friedrich Huch, cited by F. D. Hirschback, *The Arrow and the Lyre* (The Hague, Martinus Nijhoff, 1955), pp. 53-54; *Werke* X 412.

126: 8   . . . that Hamlet teaches" . . . *The Birth of Tragedy,* p. 206 in *The Philosophy of Nietzsche* (Modern Library).

126: 13   . . . without being born to it." "Tonio Kröger" (1903) in *Stories of Three Decades,* 1936, p. 106; *Werke* VIII 300. In his 1915 *Reflections,* Mann said that the German people (*Volk*) are "called to action but not born to it." *Werke* XII 148.

126: 17   . . . of his differentness. In his Fontane essay of 1910, Mann quotes the older novelist in a Tonio mood: "I take back everything I said (while I could still dance) in favour of lyric poetry, and against all good-looking, laughing, well-washed youthful victors over young girls' hearts. The bookworm, be he ever so decent and clever, is really only pleasing to himself and a small handful of others. The world passes him by and beckons to life and beauty." "The Old Fontane" in *Essays of Three Decades,* 1947; *Werke* IX 18-19.

Even Mauriac's heroes occasionally muse like Tonio: "I chilled people, just by the look of me. "The more I realised it, the stiffer I got. I never knew how to dress myself, how to choose a tie, or how to knot it. I was never able to let myself go, or laugh, or play the fool. It was unimaginable that I should join any gang of bright young people; I belonged to the race of those whose presence spoils everything." *The Vipers' Tangle* (Garden City, N. Y., Doubleday & Co., Inc., 1957), p. 22. *Oeuvres Complètes* (Paris, Grasset, 1950) III 359.

126: 18   . . . else—and failing." Quoted by Jean Cocteau in his speech of acceptance to the French Academy, Oct., 1955.

126: 23   . . . conceal a break." *Beyond Good and Evil*, p. 66; in *The Philosophy of Nietzsche* (Modern Library).

126: 30   . . . or "Artist's Melancholy." Erwin Panofsky, *Albrecht Dürer* (Princeton, N. J., Princeton University Press, 1955), Vol. I, p. 162.

127: 3   . . . tell them apart." *Ecce Homo*, p. 40; in *The Philosophy of Nietzsche*.

127: 17   . . . lovely and commonplace." *Stories of Three Decades*, p. 132; *Werke* VIII 338. Thus Tonio joins Joyce's Stephen and Gide's Michel in gazing into a world of shadowy figures unborn. Stephen: "I desire to press in my arms the loveliness which has not yet come into the world." Michel: O great new God! grant me the knowledge of other newer races, unimagined types of beauty."

127: 18   . . . the burgher element . . . See *A Sketch of My Life*, p. 7; see also the passage in *Reflections* beginning "*Ich bin Städter, Bürger, ein Kind und Urenkelkind deutsch-bürgerlicher Kultur.*" *Werke* XII 115.

128: 1   . . . a mimic and a jester . . . In his Chekhov essay (one of his last two pieces of writing, read to the Zürich Authors' Society in the spring of 1955) Mann identifies as the primitive origin of all art, "the inclination to ape," the jester's desire and talent to entertain." In *Last Essays*, 1959, p. 182. "Chekhov" is translated by Tania and James Stern.

128: 7   . . . error quite natural . . . Mann returns to the double theme of the swindler as artist-type in his last work of fiction, the 1954 sequel to the 1911 fragment *Felix Krull*.

128: 9   . . . seer in him . . . "Romanticism," says André Malraux, "has always tended to read into the artist the magician and the man possessed." *Voices of Silence* (Garden City, N. Y., Doubleday and Co.), p. 590

128: 18   . . . of his *objectivity*. *The World as Will and Idea*, III 154-155.

128: 27   . . . festivities next door." "Disorder and Early Sorrow," in *Stories of Three Decades*, p. 516; "Unordnung und Frühes Leid" in *Werke* VIII 640.

129: 7   . . . like a respectable being" . . . *Stories of Three Decades*, p. 102; *Werke* VIII 294.

129: 15   . . . a German type. Yet to his fellow German writer Hermann Kesten, Mann seemed "utterly German in his external appearance." *The Stature of Thomas Mann*, p. 25.

129: 17   . . . actor Clifton Webb. Mary McLeod Brennan on visit to the Manns at Princeton, N. J., March, 1941.

130: 3   . . . matter of one's work." "Frederick the Great and the Grand Coalition" in *Three Essays*, 1932, pp. 159-160. *Werke* X 90. The same lines appear in *Royal Highness*, p. 102.

131: 8   . . . over unto Death." Mann quotes the whole sonnet in his Platen essay (1930), *Essays of Three Decades*, p. 260; *Werke* IX 269.

132: 24   . . . calm and bright." The translation of George's Maximin poem is taken from E. K. Bennett's *Stefan George* (London, Bowes & Bowes Publishers Ltd.; Yale University Press, 1954).

133: 2   . . . their beginning here." *The Complete Poems of Cavafy*, p. 109. By permission of the publisher.

133: 9   . . . *die and rise.* This is a free translation of Goethe's *"Stirb und werde"*—more literally "werde" means here "become," "develop," "evolve organically."

133: 26   . . . nodded benign approval. Hugh Thomas describes Casares Quirogo, premier of Republican Spain, speaking in the Cortes just before the outbreak of the military revolt in Spain—his eyes "marked by a strange ironic optimism, only explicable as a symptom of the tuberculosis from which he was already suffering. How rightly did Thomas Mann contend in *The Magic Mountain* that this disease expresses the predicament of the liberal civilisation of which Casares was the Spanish representative!" *The Spanish Civil War* (New York, Harper & Brothers, 1961), p. 4.

134: 27   . . . had no meaning. *Decline of the West* (New York, Alfred A. Knopf, Inc., 1926), Vol. II, p. 273.

135: 1   . . . lonely poet-hero. See Arnold Hauser, *The Social History of Art* (New York, Alfred A. Knopf, Inc., 1951), on the theme of romantic homelessness (Vol. I, p. 664) and the Byronic hero (Vol. II, pp. 700-701), the latter a description that fits perfectly Hesse's Steppenwolf, Harry Haller.

135: 8   . . . dramatists, and novelists. Hans Rosenhaupt's *Der Deutsche Dichter um die Jahrhundertwende und seine Abgelöstheit von Gesellschaft* (Bern-Leipzig, Paul Haupt, 1939) studies the theme of social alienation in a number of German-writing poets, novelists, and dramatists—Rilke, George, Hofmannsthal, Mann, Hauptmann—from 1890.

135: 16   . . . to rescue himself." *Wilhelm Meister*, Book I, chap. 9.

135: 32   . . . soul is infinite." *Three Philosophical Poets*, pp. 131-132.

136: 27   Erich Heller makes a similar point in *The Ironic German*, p. 74.

137: 29   . . . my eternal desire." *The Magic Mountain*, pp. 341-342. (I have translated from the French) ; *Werke* III 475-476.

137: 33   . . . life that brings corruption." *The Desert of Love*, trans. Gerard Hopkins (New York, Pellegrini & Cudahy, 1951), p. 176. OC II 136.

138: 6   . . . but its passion." *Love in the Western World*, p. 45.

138: 19   . . . all the impulses." *Notes from the Underground* VIII (Constance Garner trans.).

140: 9   *"Syllabus of Errors"* . . . prop. no. 80. See E. E. Y. Hales, *Pio Nono* (New York, P. J. Kenedy & Sons), p. 258.

140: 31   . . . Verlaine drunk was *tremendous." Journals* I 175. ("Verlaine ivre était *formidable."* EP I 203.)

141: 11   . . . this fabulous monster. Mann, Letter to Gerhart Hauptmann, April 11, 1925; Mann, *Briefe 1889-1936*, p. 234. See *Encounter,* Dec., 1962, p. 7.

141: 26   . . . to you, Frau Fischer." *The Turning Point* (New York, L. B. Fischer, 1942), p. 234, reprinted by permission of A. A. Wyn, Inc., New York. For a totally different and coherent Hauptmann, see Arthur and Barbara Gelb's account of an in interview in which Hauptmann expressed his opinion on Eugene O'Neill: *O'Neill* (New York, Harper & Brothers, 1962), p. 757.

142: 18   . . . of the Olympians." *The Birth of Tragedy,* p. 181, in *The Philosophy of Nietzsche* (Modern Library).

142: 31   . . . always creates life." *Doctor Zhivago* (New York, Pantheon, 1958), p. 90.

143: 22   . . . hours barely existed. *Cities of the Plain* (New York, Modern Library, 1927), I 313; *Sodom et Gomorrhe* in *À la recherche du temps perdu* (Paris, Bibliothéque de la Pleiade, 1954), vol. II, p. 285.

144: 11   . . . passage one to another." *Science and the Modern World* (New York, The Macmillan Co., 1931), p. 135.

144: 29   . . . for it unconsciously." These lines from Bergson's *Essai sur les Données Immédiates de la Conscience* ("Time and Free Will") form the epigraph to the chapter on Bergson in Richard Thieberger's *Der Begriff der Zeit bei Thomas Mann* (Baden-Baden, Verlag für Kunst und Wissenschaft, 1952).

145: 7   . . . not a second!" *The Magic Mountain,* p. 66; *Werke* III 95.

146: 24   . . . category of time. Proust, *Cities of the Plain* II 175; p. 178; *À la recherche du temps perdu,* Pléiade II, 981, 983.

146: 27   . . . long or short." Qualen of Mann's early story "The Wardrobe" (1899) had no watch, disliked calendars, tried not to be aware of the hour or of the day of the week.

147: 19   . . . nails from growing." *The Magic Mountain,* p. 544; *Werke* III 753.

147: 31   . . . that damn book." *Time* magazine, Sept. 3, 1951, p. 74.

148: 22   . . . knowing All-soul . . ." *The Magic Mountain,* p. 654; *Werke* III 908-909.

149: 8   . . . an endless present." *Buddenbrooks,* p. 527; *Werke* I 658-659.

150: 17   . . . at any time." "The Making of the Magic Mountain," *The Magic Mountain,* p. 720.

150: 33   . . . "fanatical" (*fanatisch* . . .) "Fanatical" was one of Adolf Hitler's favorite words. See Helmut Heiber, *Adolf Hitler* (London, Oswald Wolff, Ltd., 1961), p. 108.

151: 8   . . . root-pierced grave." *The Magic Mountain,* p. 540; *Werke* III 746-747.

151: 13   . . . the mystery behind." "Bunter Bilder dem Volk, dahinter für die Wissenden das Geheimnis," is Mann's paraphrase of

Goethe's remark to Eckermann, "Wenn es nur so ist, dass die Menge der Zuschauer Freude an der *Erscheinung* hat; dem Eingeweihten wird zugleich der höhere Sinn nicht entgehen. . . ." ("Let the crowd take pleasure in the spectacle; the higher import will not escape the initiated. . . ."). *The Beloved Returns,* 1940, p. 309; *Werke* II 640; Eckermann, *Gespräche mit Goethe* (Basel, Verlag Birkhauser, 1945), I 209.

152: 19 . . . nothing but masterpieces?" Mann quotes this in "Goethe's Career as a Man of Letters" in *Essays of Three Decades,* p. 54.

153: 8 . . . filling-in of details. *A Sketch of My Life,* p. 58; *Werke* XI 136.

153: 11 . . . the chief butler." *Journals* I, p. 105, EP I 126.

153: 24 . . . story in passing . . . See *The Autobiography of Goethe* ("Poetry and Truth") (London, 1874), VIII 300-302.

153: 32 . . . *Elan* thrown in. *Joseph and His Brothers,* 1934, p. 38 *et seq.; Werke* IV 39 *et seq.*

154: 25 . . . he is Gilgamesh . . . *Joseph in Egypt,* 1938, p. 508; *Werke* V 1133.

154: 28 . . . and lose all." *Ibid.,* p. 547; *Werke* V 1169.

156: 1 . . . forth much fruit." *Young Joseph,* 1935, p. 262; *Werke* IV 621.

157: 11 . . . to us for years." *Letters of Sigmund Freud,* ed. E. L. Freud; trans. Tania and James Stern (New York, Basic Books, Inc., 1960), p. 393.

157: 15 . . . of the Freudian school." "Freud and the Future" in *Essays of Three Decades,* p. 418; *Werke* IX 488.

157: 23 . . . to Freud's doctrine . . . In his essay "Freud and Literature," Lionel Trilling finds Mann at fault for exaggerating the anti-rationalist side of Freud, for making it "seem that the 'Apollonian,' the rationalistic side of psychoanalysis is, while certainly important and wholly admirable, somehow secondary and even accidental. He gives us a Freud who is committed to the 'night side' of human life." Yet Trilling (as Mann does) points out the anticipation of Freud by Schopenhauer and Nietzsche (he invokes the *Zeitgeist* here as his category of explanation) and—like Mann too—claims psychoanalysis as one of the culminations of the "Romanticist" literature of the nineteenth century. *The Liberal Imagination* (Garden City, N. Y., Doubleday & Co., Inc., 1957), p. 38.

158: 8 . . . and to ourselves." *Joseph the Provider,* 1948, p. 255; *Werke* V 1505-1506.

158: 12 . . . to these fools occur." *Faust,* Part II, Act I, scene in the Imperial Palace.

159: 6 . . . Egypt to conquer? Freud, *Letters,* p. 432.

159: 11 . . . *and historical will.*" "Freud and the Future," *Essays of Three Decades,* p. 419 (my italics); *Werke* IX 488-489. Compare Mann's remarks of 1941 to the University of California (Berkeley) chapter of Phi Beta Kappa with which, approving the motto of the fraternity ("Philosophy the Guide of Life") and deploring the absolutism of the German mind, he praises the "healthy pragmatism of the Anglo-Saxon tradition that would insist that mind be in the service of practical life." Mann goes on to say with charming seriousness that had Nietzsche come as a refugee to the United States, he doubtless would been made an honorary member of Phi Beta Kappa. *Order of the Day,* 1942, p. 257.

159: 18   . . . God and his Word. *Doctor Faustus,* 1948, p. 81; *Werke* VI 110. To Mann's philologist Zeitblom, Philosophy is the queen of the sciences—"like that of the organ among instruments: she afforded a survey; she combined them intellectually, she ordered and redefined the issue of all the fields of research into a universal picture, an overriding and decisive synthesis comprehending the meaning of life, a scrutinizing determination of man's place in the cosmos."

159: 20   . . . time and death. "What I Believe" in *Order of the Day,* p. 163.

159: 23   . . . would say so." *Reflections of a Nonpolitical Man, Werke* XII 534.

159: 24   . . . created for man. Erika Mann, *The Last Year of Thomas Mann* (New York, Farrar, Straus & Cudahy, Inc., 1958), p. 81.

159: 30   . . . and William James. Fritz Kaufmann makes the same point in his *Thomas Mann: The World as Will and Representation,* pp. 18-19.

159: 35   . . . give up the ghost." Quoted by Mann in "Freud and the Future," *Essays of Three Decades,* p. 420; *Werke* IX 490.

160: 8   . . . *Totem and Taboo* . . . F. D. Hirschbach, *The Arrow and the Lyre,* p. 79.

160: 24   . . . mother by violence. *Joseph and His Brothers,* p. 87; *Werke* IV 86.

161: 2   . . . the begetting night—" *Joseph in Egypt,* pp. 544-545; *Werke* V 1175.

161: 6   . . . Joseph is "late" . . . *Ibid.,* p. 196; *Werke* IV 835.

161: 12   . . . some uncommon truth" *Ibid.,* p. 214; *Werke* IV 852.

161: 16   . . . take his place. *Ibid.,* p. 352; *Werke* IV 987.

162: 11   . . . of this world? . . ." *Joseph the Provider,* p. 513; *Werke* V 1739.

162: 21   . . . not an ordinary one. *Joseph in Egypt,* p. 403; *Werke* V 1035.

162: 30   . . . the gentle hills." *Joseph the Provider,* p. 586; *Werke* V 1803.

163: 10   . . . before killing him. The relevant Mann parergon here is his essay "Nietzsche's Philosophy in the Light of Recent History," trans. Richard and Clara Winston in *Last Essays,* p. 141 *et seq.* Mann supports Dr Möbius' account of Nietzsche's illness as a case history of syphilis, remind his readers how in 1865 the twenty-one-year-old philologist told his friend Paul Deussen of his infection in Cologne at a house to which he was led by a guide whom Mann says he has always envisioned as a devil's emissary. Compare *Doctor Faustus,* 1948, p. 141.

163: 13   . . . possessed by a demon. Apropos of Wolf's "brain disease," his English biographer says, "What one hears in private of some of the details of his life, interesting as it is to the moral pathologist, is not yet a matter for the public ear." Ernest Newman, *Hugo Wolf* (London, Mathuen & Co., Ltd., 1907). Like Mann's Leverkühn, Wolf was terrified of the prospect of artistic sterility and constantly complained of it.

163: 28   . . . unparalleled, final collapse." *Doctor Faustus*, p. 175; *Werke* VI 233.

164: 19   . . . of our birth." *The Stature of Thomas Mann*, p. 89.

165: 14   . . . this general condition. George Lukacs, *Thomas Mann* (Berlin, Aufbau-Verlag, 1949), p. 85.

165: 21   . . . poétes maudits. *Primal Vision: Selected Writings of Gottfried Benn* (New York, New Directions, 1960), p. 188.

165: 33   . . . go to Hitler." "Germany's Guilt and Mission," *Decision*, July, 1941.

166: 13   . . . piping, whinnying" . . . *Doctor Faustus*, p. 378; *Werke* VI 502.

166: 30   . . . always *Tristan*." Klaus Mann, *The Turning Point*, p. 8.

167: 2   . . . suffering, and enthusiastic." J. H. Meisel in *The Stature of Thomas Mann*, p. 95.

167: 10   . . . of the sea." Letter to the Editor, *Common Sense* Jan., 1940, p. 13.

167: 21   . . . the square hole. . . ." "A Brother" in *Order of the Day*, p. 156.

168: 12   . . . is the *Volk*. "Preface" to *Reflections of a Nonpolitical Man*; *Werke* XII 30.

168: 13   . . . his burgher forebears." In his wartime *Reflections*, Mann distinguished between the Bürger and the Bourgeois. The former is cosmopolitan and humane. The latter is the national-international Rhetorbourgeois, enemy of true humanity and the true Germany. "It is no accident," says Mann in the *Reflections*, "that when I search for an image of the Bürger, it is a face from medieval Nürnberg that appears before my eyes" (*Werke* 102 *et seq.*) Mrs Karl Lotze pointed out to me that in *The Magic Mountain* the old grandfather of Hans Castorp is the last representative of the Bürger class, while James Tienappel is already a bourgeois; only the English suit he is wearing reminds us of his cosmopolitan heritage.

168: 27   . . . strength shine forth. *Neue Rundschau* Berlin, November, 1914. Mann requotes three of these Schiller lines in his *Reflections*, *Werke* XII 166. Romain Rolland denounced Mann's *Neue Rundschau* article as "monstrous."

168: 31   . . . not a virtue. According to Martin Flinker, Mann's insights into the political in the *Reflections* rose from convictions that he never wholly abandoned. Mann never became a convert to any specific form of political ideology. It was Mann's old disgust with "politics," says Flinker, that made him abandon his U.S. residence shortly before his death. Thomas Mann's *Politische Betrachtungen im Lichte der Heutigen Zeit* ('s-Gravenhage, Mouton & Co., 1959).

169: 2   . . . the Seven Sleepers . . . Compare Goethe in *Dichtung und*

Wahrheit ("Poetry and Truth") on his attitude toward the events of 1789: "In our little circle, we took no notice of news and newspapers; our object was to know Man; as for men, we left them to do as they chose."

169: 6   ... all, teaching all. Goethe *Essays of Three Decades,* pp. 173-174; *Werke* IX 171.

169: 14   ... his brother Thomas. On the *"Brüderkrieg,"* see Hermann Weigand, *Thomas Mann's Novel "Der Zauberberg"* (New York, D. Appleton-Century Co., 1933), p. 172, and Kurt Sontheimer, *Thomas Mann und die Deutschen* (Munich, Nymphenburger Verlagshandlung, 1961), pp. 25-30.

170: 2   ... help solve it . . ." Reported by *The Daily Worker,* New York, Sept. 11, 1948.

170: 6   ... only a success story" . . . *The Black Swan,* p. 41; *Werke* VIII 897. "I have returned to Europe," Mann declared in 1953, "I have changed the basis of my life at seventy-eight years which is—at this time of life—not easy. And I will admit that, as in the case of 1933, the political influenced my decision. An unhappy world constellation has brought changes in the atmosphere of this favoured country risen to such enormous power, changes which can be experienced as depressing and giving rise to concern. Coercion to conformity, called loyalty, spying after opinions, distrust, education for denunciation, withholding of passports for renowned but ill-favored scientists, cruel banishment of the unorthodox into the economic desert, this all is unfortunately everyday practice. In short, freedom suffers from its defence, and some fear it is at the point of being destroyed."

Comprendre. 1953.

170: 18   ... to have no effect." Stefan George in answer to Hofmannsthal's request that he help to persuade literary leaders in England and Germany to sign a peace petition. E. K. Bennett, *Stefan George,* p. 19.

170: 34   ... go to sleep.' " "Theodor Storm" in *Essays of Three Decades,* p. 285; *Werke* IX 266.

171: 3   ... novelist with delight. *The Story of a Novel,* p. 129; *Werke* XI 230-231.

... period of translation." Letter to this author, Dec. 12, 1948. Printed by permission of author.

171: 24   ... and beloved pieces" . . . Erika Mann, *The Last Year of Thomas Mann,* p. 114.

172: 21   ... their poetic value." Letter to Heinrich Mann, Jan. 3, 1919, trans. Ralph Mannheim, *Encounter,* Dec., 1962, p. 3. *Briefe 1889-1936,* p. 154.

172: 22   ... lovelier, worthier life." "Chekhov" in *Last Essays,* p. 203.

Index